P9-DEL-097

TAKING THE FEAR OUT OF CHANGING

DENNIS E. O'GRADY, Psy.D.

TAKING THE FEAR OUT OF CHANGING

Guidelines for getting through tough life transitions

NEW INSIGHTS PRESS

DAYTON, OHIO

Additional copies of this book may be ordered through bookstores or by sending $14.95 plus $3.00 for postage and handling to:

New Insights Press
P.O. Box 214
Bellbrook, OH 45305-9998
1-513-298-0505

Copyright © 1992 by Dennis E. O'Grady

All rights reserved. No part of this book may be reproduced, by any means, without permission in writing from the publisher, except by a reviewer who wishes to quote brief excerpts. For information contact New Insights Press, P.O. Box 214, Bellbrook, OH 45305-9998

This publication is designed to provide accurate and authoritative information in regard to the subject matter covered. It is sold with the understanding that the publisher is not engaged in rendering psychological, medical or other professional services. If expert assistance or counseling is needed, the services of a competent professional should be sought.

Publisher's Cataloging-in-Publication Data

O'Grady, Dennis E., 1951-
    Taking the fear out of changing : guidelines for
    getting through tough life transitions / Dennis E.
    O'Grady. – Bellbrook, Ohio: New Insights Press.
       p.   cm.
    ISBN 0-9628476-0-7
    1. Change (Psychology). 2. Self-help techniques.
    3. Self-actualization.   I. Title.

BF637.C4038   1992
158.1 – dc20   91-68577

Manufactured in the United States of America

23456789 ML 9876543

I dedicate this book to
Kerry, Erin and Sydney.
My love for you,
Is the world to me.

ACKNOWLEDGMENTS

The acknowledgments page is a formal way to share my thanks with those people who most influenced this work.

My very warm thanks are extended to —

William Cornell, M.A., Certified Transactional Analyst Teacher and Trainer, Psychotherapist, The Learning Place, Pittsburgh, Pennsylvania. His encouragement and guidance of this project and many others has always been impeccable.

Ruth Collins, Office Manager, New Insights Psychological Services, Dayton, Ohio. Her loyalty and sheer hard work permitted me to focus creatively on this book.

James Rafferty, Ph.D., Assistant Professor, Wright State University School of Medicine and Psychiatry, Dayton, Ohio. His insight into couples' issues is as irreplaceable as is his irrepressible Irish warmth.

John Mould, Ed.D., Retired, Miami University Student Counseling Services, Oxford, Ohio, from whom I've modeled much of my professional identity.

Eric Berne, M.D., beloved father of Transactional Analysis theory, deceased, who made psychology come alive for me through his pithy writings.

Special thanks go to my clients who continually amaze and astound me with their wisdom — and their ability to use it against terrible odds. (You know who I'm talking about.)

Loving thanks to my beautiful wife Kerry who could have endlessly griped about the weekends this book took away from our new family — but didn't.

> May God grace you when —
> You try, but fail
> You lose hope
> You find a way to get back up again . . .
> And may God bless you when you succeed.

FOREWORD

I first came to know Dr. O'Grady when he was a student studying for the Doctor of Psychology degree in the School of Professional Psychology at Wright State University. I was pleasantly surprised and pleased when he first showed me the manuscript for this book and asked me to write a foreword.

Professors like to see how their former students have put the teachers' ideas into practice and, if the book is good, to claim that they had spotted the students' special talents right away. In this instance, I can take no such credit. Dr. O'Grady clearly has gone beyond whatever basics of change that he may have learned from me, and I cannot say that I had ever predicted that he would do so in such fine fashion. But, reflecting on his student days, what he achieves in this book is not very surprising. As a student, Dr. O'Grady always seemed able to maintain a positive "can do" attitude and possessed a keen interest in the practical utility of what he was learning. His interests lay in how to make psychological knowledge "user friendly" for the ordinary person. Now, drawing on what he learned from his professors and on a decade of clinical work as a psychotherapist, he has produced a notable compendium of practical applications of psychological knowledge.

Written for the lay person, *Taking the Fear Out of Changing* is not just another instance of the "how to" books which seem to litter the landscape. Of course, it *is* a "how to" book, but all resemblance to the others ends there. This is a book written to stimulate the thinking, the feelings and the actions of readers in such a way as to help them with the difficult process of change.

What other author tells you in the first chapter that you should not read his book from cover to cover? Instead, you are encouraged to read the sections that appeal to you and to accept only those lessons that make sense to your own situation. Each chapter is crafted to stand alone without being dependent on information presented earlier. The reader is led to use his or her own intuition about where and how to begin and to learn to trust the inner wisdom that is in each of us.

Each chapter begins with a quiz to help readers assess their personal attitudes toward the topic, and then proceeds with practical pointers and provocative questions. Each chapter includes a section on how to apply the lessons learned to a current, close relationship. Following a summary, the chapters close with a "counterpoint" section in which the author anticipates arguments that the reader may have and attempts to engage in an active dialogue that forces further thinking about the topic.

Taking the Fear Out of Changing is likely to be of practical utility to a very wide audience: busy executives or managers interested in improving their interpersonal skills, married people who want to improve relationships with their partners, parents interested in learning to deal differently with their children, psychotherapy patients who wish to supplement the hard work of therapy and many, many others.

For several years, Dr. O'Grady has been offering sound, practical advice on a variety of psychological topics to thousands of newspaper, magazine and industrial publication readers. A talented teacher and lecturer, he gradually has honed his advice through interactions with live audiences. The writings and the lecture material are based on his clinical work in over a decade of practice. Thus, what he has to say comes from his study and treatment of people who are in a change crises and his discovery of what has worked for them. Given his background, experience and interests, Dr. O'Grady is especially well-qualified to write this book. I wish I could say that he learned it all from me.

This a practical, useful and different book. Dr. O'Grady has succeeded, and succeeded admirably, in producing a text that is both instructive and empowering for all those who want to change but are afraid to try — which is almost all of us.

— Ronald E. Fox, Ph.D.
President-Elect of the American Psychological Association

CONTENTS

TAKING THE FEAR OUT OF CHANGING

INTRODUCTION:

YOU CAN TOO CHANGE!

Words spoken without heart,
Never to heaven go.

THE SUREST ROUTE TO HAPPINESS IS TO GROW AND CHANGE

A shy workshop participant confessed to following me around town to hear me speak on self-esteem, success and change. She admitted that she was using the material and feeling much happier and more relaxed with her life, even though external situations hadn't really changed that much for her.

After my workshop on "Choosing Loving Relationships," the "retiring" septuagenarian boldly approached me and, giving me a big hug, said:

"Dennis, I love you!" She blurted this out, blushing red, taken aback by her boldness.

Then suddenly she sounded steamed, "And you had just better tell your wife I said so!"

She continued, lovingly, "And tell her to take care of that baby of yours that's on the way."

Pausing, she concluded, with a warm and strong look, "And while you're at it, tell Kerry I love her too."

Moved by the imperious yet loving manner of my admirer, I responded, "I love you too, and I'll tell Kerry the moment I get home."

I kept my promise and shared the lady's heartfelt wishes with my wife as soon as I returned home that evening. I was reminded how important it can be to know something about an author's life; how such knowledge can help us feel more attuned to the integrity of his work.

TO THE READER
WITH BEST WISHES FOR SUCCESS

For the past ten years my practice has specialized in self-esteem counseling and relationship improvement. I've studied how people change unexpectedly against great odds, and how people "can't" seem to change despite their most diligent efforts.

My psychotherapy clients have taught me a great deal. In large part, I am passing along a compilation of their best advice on how to make great changes. This book is a step-by-step discussion of the principles that have helped my clients change the most rapidly.

My own feelings about becoming a first-time father to my daughter Erin, and the creation of this work are running equally deep. My own personal changes over the past few years have given me firsthand knowledge about how change can totally go against the book.

What can you expect from me? My job is to show you from the heart how to:

1. **Remove negative emotions.**
2. **Understand difficult relationships.**
3. **Take positive action when fear is devouring you.**
4. **Keep your self-esteem up.**
5. **Give yourself loads of change permissions.**
6. **Change your life into whatever you want it to be.**

Being genuine seems urgently important to me now more than ever. The result is a book that has not had to make any compromises, and I hope that you will let it help you change.

The final decision to change or not must and should be yours.

HOW TO USE THIS BOOK MOST SUCCESSFULLY

What's the best way for you to get the most out of this book while spending the least amount of your valuable time reading it? Easy.

DON'T READ THIS BOOK FROM COVER TO COVER. I mean it! I've carefully designed this book for busy people. Read only what appeals to you.

You won't miss out on anything if you start at the end of this book with a discussion on self-esteem, or in the middle of the text to learn about setting goals for success. Either way, you will get good results.

A bold claim: if you allow yourself to read only what interests you, and then put this book down, you are going to bump up against the principles that will help you change. So whatever you do, skim this book — don't make it a laborious project.

I'm certain you will come across topics in these pages you've already mastered. So skip along! I've purposely designed this book to be simple, yet thorough and complete. Don't presume that you need to digest all of the information to be found in these pages.

I think you have in your hands an unusual book that can help you change. Steal my advice and run with it! Use the information to get unstuck and reclaim your right to take charge of your success. Teach your family to do the same.

I will also be encouraging you to stop looking in the rearview mirror of life at what you didn't get, or at who you aren't any longer, and to get on with your life.

Wipe the slate clean. Whatever failures you have had in the past do not need to be with you one day longer. You can change your life for the better today.

What Lasting Positive Change Means

If change means greater independence, why do you struggle so with it? Are you afraid of being too happy and successful? You bet! Success means learning to be who you are and feeling worthwhile to boot.

In spite of your favorite change-excuses that include criticisms of yourself as too lazy, too busy or too ignorant to change, I've rarely found this to be the case with either my psychotherapy clients or members of change-seminar audiences.

I've been pleasantly surprised to find out that past failures do not in any significant way predict future failure. Then why is change so difficult? I believe we adults have grown numb to the tremendous rewards that accompany change.

What rewards? I believe that genuine change means you acquire five key benefits:

1. CHANGE MEANS BECOMING WHO YOU REALLY ARE!

The Fear: As a child, you learned quite painfully that "change" meant giving in and giving up your higher self to parental demands.

The Challenge: Change should bring high self-esteem, satisfaction, relationship intimacy and meaningful success to your life.

Change doesn't mean denial, but expression of your personality.

To Build High Self-Esteem: "Being successful means being me."

2. CHANGE MEANS TURNING NEGATIVE EMOTIONS INTO HIGH SELF-ESTEEM!

The Fear: Do you have to feel miserable in order to change? No. In fact the reverse is true. The happier you are, the quicker you can change, provided you stay open and refuse to say "Hold it right there. Stop the presses. Don't change a single thing. I'm happy right now, so I better not change anything."

The Challenge: The fear of change causes self-criticism, goallessness, pleasing too much, complaining instead of changing, negative strokes and disasters of all kinds. Therefore, changing will help you rid yourself of resentment, better tolerate controlling people and learn how to prepare in advance to cope with future successes and frustrations.

To Build High Self-Esteem: "It's okay to feel worthwhile."

3. CHANGE MEANS CHOOSING TO BE SUCCESSFUL AND HAPPY!

The Fear: The fear of change means altering who you really are or what you really feel and taking frustrations "on-the-chin-with-a-grin" in order to be a good girl or boy. You must learn to own up to your strengths and goals and fears of happiness or be controlled by them.

The Challenge: Being free to change is at the root of every victory. Resisting changes, or disrupting productive changes because of fear or frustration, is at the foundation of every life crisis and relationship tragedy.

To Build High Self-Esteem: "I choose to use my strengths."

4. CHANGE MEANS GROWING FROM ROMANTIC RELATIONSHIPS!

The Fear: There are more than a thousand ways to lose a lover. The fear of conflict reduces good communication skills. Good relationships encourage change.

The Challenge. To grow and change when you don't really need to as a couple. Staying ahead of the change race will help steady your self-esteem when you stumble over power plays, unfair fights and unconstructive conflicts that create negative feelings.

To Build High Self-Esteem: "The less I blame, the more I change."

5. CHANGE MEANS LETTING GO OF FEAR TO FEEL MORE ALIVE!

The Fear. The fear of the unknown, the fear of failure, the fear of commitment, the fear of disapproval and even the fear of success get in the way of changing. You are not a bad or weak person. You are being consumed by the overriding fear of change.

The Challenge. In exchange for giving up your fears and reinforcing small steps towards success, you will be paid more than an equal amount of self-esteem.

To Build High Self-Esteem: "I take positive action in spite of my fears."

As a psychotherapist, I know how hard it is to stop seeing change as an enemy. But I have also witnessed, time and time again, the marvelous prizes my clients have won by finally getting up enough courage to change.

Traveling into unknown change regions is uncomfortable and scary. You stand to become more who you are and to be richly rewarded for your daring. As these change fears are spelled out, my intent will always be to give you more hope and results than self-help hype.

God created us to be "awe-filled," not awful people, or people who feel awful. God stacked the deck in our favor by granting us the ability to change regardless of our age, income level, education or personal history. Sometimes we tend to forget this.

MINDPLAY:

DEDICATION TO THE ONE YOU LOVE

I want you to dedicate this book to those changes you most desire now. You will appreciate your thoughtfulness later when you achieve your goals. Enjoy looking back from time to time on what and who motivated you to learn better ways to handle yourself in all of your significant relationships. That is the destination for which you are setting sail. Make your dedication to the one you love.

➤ I DEDICATE THIS BOOK TO:

➤ HE/SHE IS SPECIAL TO ME BECAUSE:

➤ AND WHAT I/WE MOST WANT TO CHANGE IS:

Are you up to becoming a change-expert? "Sure, why not," you say? All right. Let's begin!

BECOMING YOUR OWN CHANGE-EXPERT

Whether fed up right now or feeling fine, you have some things to learn about making positive changes and accepting successful results. Begin by inviting change into your mental home as a welcome companion.

A disclaimer: There will be no hocus-pocus, pretty promises or shallow reassurances that you should be "hunky-dory" when, in fact, reality right now may be a real downer for you. I'll be teaching you how to stop tolerating loads of frustrations and encouraging you to unload piles of old rejections and resentments.

To start, claim the following as your basic change-rights:

I Can Change!

Even if you don't want to change, or have failed before, you can change today! I will be showing you how to initiate change by making use of fun quizzes, mindplays, inspirational exercises, practical communication tips and chapter counterpoints. I want you to feel more loved and less lonely each moment.

It's Never Too Late To Change!

Easy for me to say, I know. But there is hope to spare for you and yours, no matter how tense the current situation may be. I will be showing you how to communicate better, use your own inner wisdom for outer miracles and be a more loving person or partner. Or it may be the time for you to find the person of your dreams.

You Can Grow And Change!

By observing and studying psychotherapy clients over the past ten years, I've discovered that the flame of growth can never be completely extinguished. Until the day we die, we humans are blessed with repeated opportunities to change and choose the life we wish to live.

So why wait a day longer to embrace what you most want to have in your life? Start believing, "I can TOO grow and change!"

Even if patterns of failure have been haunting you for what seems an eternity, start telling yourself, "I can grow and change even though I've failed a thousand times before." Of course, I know that you require more than sugary pep talks in order to make lasting, dramatic changes.

Are you ready for the hard work of change? Are you ready for the serendipity of setting your mind to the "I can TOO grow and change!" frequency? Fantastic.

COUNTERPOINT:

"MUST I TAKE YOUR ADVICE?"

Must you buy my philosophy lock, stock and barrel? No way! Please don't, for that would go against the values of change you will learn in this book.

★ *Are the practical tips easy to apply?* No, not at all. Use the practical tips as you best see fit. I don't want to create a rigid, "you've-got-to-change-or-ELSE" state of mind.

★ *Does this book promote or motivate change?* You will judge that. I can only say that these insights have helped countless people from all walks of life, who have desired to improve their self-confidence, better understand a difficult relationship or get a tired body or spirit back into shape.

★ *What if I'm already successful?* Does the work help people like me? Yes. These principles have guided high-achievers to maximize the permission to be successful, and to learn to tolerate the extreme joy (and sometimes panic) of having what they most want.

★ *How about addictions?* Clients use this information as part of their recovery to free themselves to change compulsive habits and as a guide for learning the communication skills of intimacy.

★ *Should I focus on just one of my problems?* Yes. Your chances for success will be increased. But you can use the tools you find in this book again and again in a wide variety of situations.

★ *Will changing my attitude reduce my stress?* Yes, and give you a sense of humor regarding frustrating people too. The good news of which this book speaks is that these change and communication strategies work equally well in business, marital and parent-child relationships.

★ *What if I've been unable to change up until now?* So what? Usually the reason for the resistance is self-criticism which I will show you how to overcome. The great news: You already know a lot about change. I want to reawaken your "change-able-ness."

★ *BUT I really don't like to take psychological advice.* Do you mind? Absolutely not. Your changes and decisions are your own to make. Most personally: When you're not sure how to do what this book suggests, do what is right for you and be yourself. Use your own good advice to change.

★ *Do you use this stuff?* The permissions and practical pointers you will find in this work are what I pour over when I find myself trapped in "CAN'TISM." And yes, I do try my best to take my own good advice.

Remember, above all, read what applies to YOU in these pages and skip the rest. Change is a custom-tailored affair. And don't forget that changing is meant to be fun, not laborious. May God activate the principles of change in your life, and give you the hope you need to be the person you were always meant to be.

DEO
June, 1992.
Dayton, Ohio.

1

BECOMING A CHANGE-EXPERT

We've given each other some hard lessons lately,
But we ain't learnin'.
We're the same, sad story, that's a fact —
One step up and two steps back.

Bruce Springsteen, "One Step Up,"
from the album *Tunnel Of Love*, copyright 1987.

BEING OPEN TO CHANGE LEADS TO SUCCESS

Change means learning. It means the ability to learn lessons as quickly as you can, before your self-esteem sinks, your loving relationships turn to war or your heartfelt aspirations for success burn so low you can't recover.

Haven't you experienced the phenomenon of taking one step forward in your change goals, only to find yourself taking two steps back and feeling more discouraged and disappointed than before? Of course.

You have had to learn some hard lessons to be where you are today. Hard lessons are an inescapable part of the human condition. How you experience them is another story — the story of change.

And haven't you unmercifully criticized yourself for blowing a good chance to bring about something fine in your professional or family life? Probably so. You are prone to taking many of your inner talents for granted, and over-focusing on your weaknesses when your self-esteem is low.

"One step up and two steps back." How's a person to keep going?

It's no wonder that keeping a positive attitude toward change is difficult. Maybe we need to take care of first things first: changing your attitude about change into a change-expert's belief system that emphasizes success over fear.

Are you staying ahead, or lagging behind, in these fast-changing times? If you are successful, then you have a great deal to lose. If you aren't successful, then you have a great deal to gain.

Either way, being open to change is the only sure-fire way to guarantee your success.

THE SUCCESS QUIZ

Each quick quiz has been designed to help you get a handle on the concepts being discussed. Answer these items to determine if your attitudes about change are going to guarantee your success, or result in your eventual failure.

[Please note: Each item number corresponds with the same number chapter in this book, and can be used as a useful guide to your reading]

TRUE	FALSE	
❑	❑	1. Successful people know that the hardest thing to change is a hardening of their attitudes.
❑	❑	2. All failures stem from two sets of innocent sounding but deadly words — "I CAN'T" and "YES, BUT.."
❑	❑	3. Winners analyze how they might undermine their own hard-earned successes.
❑	❑	4. A big cause of failure is the failure to set big enough goals.
❑	❑	5. Unexpected pain can result from huge setbacks or successes.
❑	❑	6. My choices and options are all open to me now.
❑	❑	7. Change-experts grab hold of good advice and run far and fast with it.
❑	❑	8. Complaining is a good habit.
❑	❑	9. Giving positive strokes to myself is as important as giving positive strokes to others.
❑	❑	10. I often struggle with how to balance pleasing myself with pleasing others.
❑	❑	11. The fear of failure is really an excuse that most of us use to be unassertive.
❑	❑	12. High self-esteem results from making small positive changes in spite of fear.

ANSWERS AND DISCUSSION

1. *True.* Change-experts must stay abreast of changes and welcome them to remain successful. Nothing kills off change faster than staid attitudes that resist change.

2. *True.* Believing "I CAN'T" fuels negative emotions. Stress results from resisting needed changes and creates more negative emotions. Negative emotions act to abort new changes from taking hold.

3. *True.* The only people who have not experienced the fear of success are those people who have not yet attained it. Winners analyze how they might sabotage their successes.

4. *True.* Success means living your potentials to the fullest with the help of important goals. The fear of commitment makes most of us stop short of setting big goals.

5. *True.* Success does not magically bestow happiness. In fact, success forces you to let go of old painful childhood beliefs which said you weren't lovable or worthwhile. Success is not as easy to digest as many would care to think.

6. *True.* Your choices only seem fixed or frozen in time. You can re-choose the same decision or make a new choice at any time. This means you are free to make your life whatever you want it to be.

7. *True.* The fear of disapproval distracts many of us from taking our own good advice. Change-experts do not reject fabulous advice to prove that they aren't being pressured or controlled by others. Experts will even use advice that an advice-giver refuses to use.

8. *True.* Complaining is a good habit when it creates a sense of belonging and attachment. Sadly though, complaining can be used as a substitute for taking charge of our lives and venturing into the unknown.

9. *True.* Stroke yourself if you want to change fast! Of course, self-criticism is easier than self-stroking. Self-criticism is a sly way that beginning successes are not adequately reinforced in order to maintain them. Stroking others is easiest but still occurs too infrequently.

10. *True.* Equally pleasing self and others is best. The quickest way to ruin a romantic relationship is to stop it from changing. Constructive conflict helps couples balance the art of self-pleasuring with partner-pleasuring. Equality between partners is always best.

11. *True.* The fear of failure is one of the five major excuses people use to avoid taking small positive actions in spite of fear. Success means getting back up again after a failure. Assertiveness is developed by contradicting fears in order to conquer them.

12. *True.* There is no security like being really good at what you do. Self-worth, self-control and positive self-image are the three hallmarks of high self-esteem. Confidence comes from conquering the fear of change.

YOUR SCORE?

10-12 Correct: **CHANGE-EXPERT.** You aren't afraid to embrace change and learn everything you can from the experience.

4-9 Correct: **CHANGE-RESISTER.** You resist making needed changes which limits your success and increases your stress level.

0-3 Correct: **CHANGE-PHOBIC.** Fear is in charge of your life and you must learn quickly how to venture into the unknown to learn and grow.

Begin to feel successful about change!

Use negative feelings as a call to reexamine the quality of your self-esteem, loving relationships and your career aspirations. Start right now to use frustration to guide and support you in your change efforts.

Change means putting your identity in full public view for possible critical review. By doing so, you will be striving for a level of success and reaching for a sense of happiness that few people ever savor.

Being who you are means you stop using "shoulds" that shut down your chances for change and make you feel like a victim stuck in "I CAN'T" disability thinking (see Chapter 2).

Self-criticism is deadly to your self-esteem. The permissions you find in these pages can help you fight back against "shouldistic" thinking.

Shoulds cause negative feelings which affect you invisibly, much like unseen radiation poisoning affects your healthy body. Slowly, but surely, you are weakened without ever having seen the real cause.

MINDPLAY:
WHY SHOULD YOU HAVE TO CHANGE?

I've designed the "mindplays" as a form of self-therapy. The "interplays" allow me to talk more with you about your responses. I would now like to focus your attention on how self-criticism shuts down your capabilities.

The statements below are subtle hypnotic commands NOT to change. Are any of these anti-change messages hitting you where it hurts most? Are you saying them to anyone else?

Check any of these self-critical messages you might have been exposed to recently:

- ❑ I should change
- ❑ I should stop procrastinating
- ❑ I shouldn't be feeling this way
- ❑ I'm not doing well enough
- ❑ I'm too weak
- ❑ I'm too confused and wishy-washy
- ❑ It's all my fault
- ❑ I should have known better
- ❑ It should be easier
- ❑ I should be content with what I've got
- ❑ I should be more understanding
- ❑ I should feel more worthwhile
- ❑ I should know what to do
- ❑ I should be happy
- ❑ I should stop feeling so sorry for myself
- ❑ I should grow up and act more mature

- ❑ I should have more willpower
- ❑ I should be different
- ❑ I should be more forgiving
- ❑ I should be better
- ❑ I've got to be perfect
- ❑ I've got to be in control
- ❑ I've got to be the strong one
- ❑ I've got to have security
- ❑ I've got to win
- ❑ I've got to hurry past my fears
- ❑ I should just accept that life is frustrating
- ❑ I shouldn't complain
- ❑ (Other self-criticisms that stall out changes)

INTER PLAY:

"Should" messages flow around you every day to discourage you from changing what frustrates you the most. Self-criticism is the number one change resistance.

You Are More Capable Than Your Self-Criticisms: These messages make you lose hope in your abilities to change in order to welcome what you most want into your life. You are much more capable than these lies think you are.

Don't Let "Shouldism" Shut Down Change Before You Even Begin: You will resist taking good advice when you feel change is forced on you. Changing becomes a drag, and self-criticisms take over. You should only change what you want to.

You Can Change When You Feel Free to Fail: Should you pull off a complete change the very first time you attempt something new? Definitely not! Choose your own changes.

You Have a Right to Be Happy AND Successful: The purpose of success is to learn to be yourself in the face of pressure to be like everybody else. Some people are happy, and some people are successful. You deserve to have both happiness and success in your life.

How do most change-experts think about life so that they keep grounded and sane? How do they keep a positive attitude toward change to keep stress from sapping their precious psychological energy?

THE TEN KEY ATTITUDES OF CHANGE-EXPERTS

Have you ever felt forced to change, and found that this slowed you in making the change?

You can choose to change or refuse to change. As a potential change-expert, you can choose to change anything you wish to and refuse to change what isn't in your best interests to change. Change-experts feel, think and take action.

How can you know when to keep trying to change or to quit? Knowing when to flow with change, when to resist it and how to plan for it in advance, are the keys to becoming a change-able person.

Let's spell out the ten top attitudes that permit change-experts to take positive action in spite of fear to achieve high self-esteem:

1. EXPERTS CHALLENGE THEIR FEARS OF CHANGE.

Hopeful News: The rewards for change are huge. Learning key skills can help you cope more effectively and happily with stressful life transitions.

Change Attitudes: Look inside for attitudes to change, and strengths to claim, instead of avoiding change for fear of being overwhelmed.

Take Action: Identify and express your strengths, and keep stroking them when you succeed. Don't transform your strengths into weaknesses.

For High Self-Esteem: "I claim the right to nurture my unique talents and strengths."

2. EXPERTS BELIEVE CHANGE LEADS TO HIGH SELF-ESTEEM.

Hopeful News: Change just has a bad name because you have been reared to believe you must change to make others happy. Permissions give encouraging messages instead of punitive ones.

Change Attitudes: Parental pressure: "You had better change — OR ELSE! — you won't be tolerated by us." Parental permission: "Go after what you most want."

Take Action: Listen to free advice and deftly use it to succeed. As an expert you must seek out advice and use your own good advice without saying, "Yes, BUT.."

For High Self-Esteem: "I claim the right to use good advice to grow."

3. EXPERTS KNOW THAT CHANGE MEANS CHOICE.

Hopeful News: You stand to gain the most from good choices. Getting control over negative emotions will provide you with a better perspective and fresh options.

Change Attitudes: Your choices are your own to make. Don't let yourself be a victim to others' choices. Finding the person or career of your dreams can only occur when you decide to take the necessary steps to get what you want.

Take Action: Resentment and anger is best reduced by making new choices. Accept that a sense of independence stems from experiencing choice and making changes.

For High Self-Esteem: "I claim the right to make new choices that are good for me."

4. EXPERTS PLEASE SELF AND OTHERS ABOUT EQUALLY.

Hopeful News: Change requires you to stretch beyond the security of the status quo, risk fear of the unknown and keep changing in spite of "change-back" pressures to please others at your own expense.

Change Attitudes: Pleasers' self-esteem is connected with how much social approval they receive. High self-esteemers have a strong need to please the inner self and loved ones about equally.

Take Action: Don't wait any longer to assert your needs, and attack your insecurities. You don't need to sacrifice your happiness in exchange for approval. Fun, happiness and pleasure are your birthrights. They need to be realized each day of your life.

For High Self-Esteem: "I claim the right to start pleasing myself more."

5. EXPERTS MAKE A COMMITMENT TO THEIR OWN GOALS.

Hopeful News: High quality work and romantic relationships result from setting goals. Change requires you to deal assertively with your needs and aspirations.

Change Attitudes: Be equally ambitious at work and home. Treat your romantic relationship as a separate entity that needs nurturing, romance and intense sexuality, without giving up your need for individuality.

Take Action: Set big goals in motion. Review your goals when you feel frustrated. Depend on a close inner circle of advisors to guide you. Use negative emotions to fuel higher self-esteem.

For High Self-Esteem: "I claim the right to improve my self-worth by setting goals."

6. EXPERTS TAKE POSITIVE ACTION IN SPITE OF FEAR.

Hopeful News: You can take positive action in spite of feeling afraid. Experts exert control over frightening events and unpleasant environments.

Change Attitudes: Choose to be around people who value you. Learn to prefer positive strokes and avoid people who say you are worthless. Make equal effort a prerequisite to a relationship. Make the tough decision to move on when your self-esteem is being played with.

Take Action: Use no-fault practice to face down your fears. Challenge excessive self-criticism, and brainstorm for a change. Experiment with no expectations of success. Treat fear as you would a respected teacher.

For High Self-Esteem: "I claim the right to love myself even when others react in disapproving ways."

7. EXPERTS DON'T BLAME OR COMPLAIN BUT CHANGE.

Hopeful News: The more pain you feel, the greater your potential for happiness. Pain is an indication that you are either blocking out necessary changes or embarking on new ones.

Change Attitudes: Tame the bad habit of complaining by learning to change what you complain about. The purpose of pain is to force you to think more clearly about unmet needs. Analyze yourself first — and blame others never.

Take Action: Decline to be a passive patsy of complaining. Give up trying to control others through complaining. Find out what is at the root of your frustrations. Stick to your limits so you won't feel bad later on down the line.

For High Self-Esteem: "I claim the right to use all of my feelings constructively — including anger."

8. EXPERTS AIM TO LEARN SOMETHING NEW FROM EVERY FRUSTRATING SITUATION.

Hopeful News: You can stay ahead of avoidable frustrations by having game plans for success built into your life. Experts limit the impact of frustrations on their self-esteem by learning something new from every difficult person or situation.

Change Attitudes: Assume that you are largely competent and capable, and that you don't have to live in an energy depleting situation. Assume that the past cannot dictate your future, and that your self-worth is sizable.

Take Action: Frustrations are a signal that changes are long overdue, and adjustments are needed to make living more meaningful, genuine and satisfying.

For High Self-Esteem: "I claim the right to live my own life free of resentment."

9. EXPERTS ARE QUICK TO REINFORCE SMALL POSITIVE CHANGES.

Hopeful News: The paradox of change is that the more you are changing, the less you may feel like you are making any progress. The result is that you can quit too soon due to frustration. At this point, you need support to keep up the momentum.

Change Attitudes: Be the first one to spot small positive changes. Begin making small changes, even when you are really depressed, and keep changing even when you are successful. Accept more reassurances from yourself.

Take Action: Stick to your goals like glue. Predict setbacks and unexpected pain and prepare for them. Avoid getting bent out of shape by stupid mistakes, and defuse stealthy guilt bombs.

For High Self-Esteem: "I claim the right to reinforce myself for small positive changes."

10. EXPERTS KEEP CHANGING EVEN WHEN EVERYTHING IS GOING WELL.

Hopeful News: You already have much of what it takes to change what you desire. Keeping an open attitude to change guarantees your success.

Change Attitudes: You can achieve your goals with adequate information, practice and hope. You can change today and be different. You can transfer old skills to new areas to move forward.

Take Action: Work to improve your self-esteem on a daily basis. Require yourself to take positive actions in spite of fear. Don't settle for second best. Claim the right to have your changes noticed and stroked by loved ones.

For High Self-Esteem: "I claim the right to change myself even when everything is going well.

Why are you so prone to picking out your faults, languishing in your guilt and stubbornly resisting change when it's just what you wish to order up for yourself? Typically, you have a bad case of hardening of the attitudes.

Worse yet, maybe you think there is something wrong with you if you don't change. Or maybe you just don't know the way. Any negative attitude will keep you from changing and claiming your right to be happy and successful.

MINDPLAY:

WHAT IF I WERE A NO-LIMIT PERSON?

The goal of this "What If Anything Were Possible" exercise is to think about your life from the vantage point of having all change options open to you again.

If there weren't any constrictions imposed on you such as the reality of time, money, education, self-esteem, current vocation or other factors, what NEW CHOICES might you make today?

No matter what your current trials and tribulations are, I want you to begin brainstorming again. The best answers come from inside yourself. So take time to rev up your mind and start searching for the answers to your dreams and goals.

How would you be living if you were a No-Limit person?

➤ IF I HAD HIGH SELF-ESTEEM I WOULD:

➤ IF I TRULY LOVED MYSELF I WOULD:

➤ IF I RESPECTED MY INNER WISHES I WOULD:

➤ IF I KNEW MY TIME ON THIS PLANET WERE RUNNING OUT I WOULD:

➤ IF I REALLY LET MYSELF GET EXCITED I WOULD:

➤ IF I STOPPED USING MY FAVORITE ALIBIS I WOULD:

➤ IF I HAD EXPERIENCED A PERFECT CHILDHOOD I WOULD:

➤ IF I THREW OUT MY OLD RESENTMENTS I WOULD:

➤ IF I DIDN'T SETTLE FOR SECOND BEST I WOULD:

➤ IF I FELT DESTINED TO HAPPINESS AND SUCCESS I WOULD:

➤ IF I REALLY THOUGHT ABOUT MY LIFE I WOULD:

➤ IF I COULD START ALL OVER AGAIN I WOULD:

➤ IF I FELT TOTALLY SECURE WITH MYSELF I WOULD:

➤ IF I DID MORE OF WHAT I LOVED TO DO I WOULD:

➤ IF I REALLY BELIEVED I COULD DO ANYTHING I WOULD:

INTER PLAY:

Is there a pattern to your responses? For example, are you holding yourself back from an important goal due to the fear of failure? Begin opening up your attitude to change.

Think Your Way Past Anger To Greater Success: Use frustration to focus your mind on finding answers to your problem. Consider what actions you would take if you were guaranteed to be successful.

Of Course You Will Trip And Fall Sometimes: A new behavior you want to do may be easy for others to do, but taxing on your entire being. Do not require yourself to get your changes right on the very first try.

Get Back To The Basics of What You Most Want To Do: For instance, "If I did more of what I love to do, I would change my job from mechanical engineering to sales." "Teaching Sunday School really makes me happy." Begin setting your goals and checking them twice for authenticity.

You Are More ABLE Than YOU Realize: Of course, when you are frustrated from falling flat on your face, you are going to feel incapable of change. Being angry at yourself for a lack of competence is bound to make it easy to give up or lose hope. When you lose hope — keep going.

Beware of self-imposed limits that strip you of the confidence to be able to do something new; whether physical, mental, financial or religious rationalizations are used to imprison you.

SUCCESS MEANS GETTING BACK UP AGAIN

Unfortunately, change is rarely a straightforward process. There are failures, roadblocks and difficult people who specialize in keeping you the same.

Getting back up again after you have been knocked down is what success is all about. Success means longing, hope and eventual attainment of mastery. Success means striving to be a winner.

My psychotherapy clients have told me over and over how maddeningly difficult it is for them to change. It is AS IF deliberate changes were somehow incredibly selfish, invitations to pain-filled living or terribly sinful!

What my clients tell me is this: "It's just so confusing! If I knew how to change the situation, I certainly would be the first one to do so!" Many of us are unaware of the universal fear of change, feel unable to change or else we get stuck in the complicated stages of change without ever knowing it.

The truth: You don't have sufficient experience or haven't been taught effective change strategies that are guaranteed to work across a wide variety of situations. In fact, you have been taught to resist both comfortable and uncomfortable changes alike. Change heralds both happiness and unexpected pain.

Accepting what you want from life isn't as easy as you might presume. My job is to teach you the necessary skills to become a change-expert, should you want to. I am going to give you an array of tips that can be used again and again throughout the many transitions of your life.

CHANGING NEGATIVE ATTITUDES

Changing old ways of thinking isn't easy, but it is necessary for building your self-esteem. "Bad" attitudes are lies told about your good character that interfere with the bigger challenge of self-acceptance.

Giving up before you begin, or quitting soon after you start, results from the rigid belief system that you are a static human being who can't transform into a different person. You are capable of change until the day you take your last breath. But why should you wait that long?

The two words most responsible for the maintenance of rigid attitudes are: "I CAN'T..." For example, "I can't change" is a belief that makes you feel like a victim, and dooms your efforts to achieve change.

Sticking to goals occurs when you determinedly declare: "I CAN TOO DO IT!" Replacing victim beliefs with this type of coping statement encourages new behaviors during the trying times of breaking difficult mental and physical habits.

Do you ever feel like giving up on tough new change projects? Do you ever succumb to the temptation of being self-critical? If so, find out which of these coping statements CAN help you out the most:

1. I CAN CHANGE TODAY.

To Achieve Self-Control: Keeping an open attitude to change forces you to make the best use of your time by living in the present. Go ahead and change despite your current age, life situation or length of time you have been practicing the negative attitude.

Work Daily On Your Self-Esteem: Experts believe it's never too late to change.

2. I CAN BE DIFFERENT.

To Achieve Self-Control: Interrupting bad mental habits means you cast off easy methods of anxiety-reduction, and throw away your security blankets. Change requires the courage to live in harmony with disruptive emotions.

Work Daily On Your Self-Esteem: Experts know that negative thinking is not a helpful way to deal with anger.

3. I CAN SEE MYSELF ACHIEVING THE GOAL.

To Achieve Self-Control: Use the power of imagination to visualize yourself moving toward your goal. Developing a positive attitude requires you to be alert to the hidden costs of staying the same.

Work Daily On Your Self-Esteem: Experts visualize a bright future of accomplishment in advance of the reality.

4. I CAN GET OVER ANY HURT.

To Achieve Self-Control: Risking success and real intimacy can bring out unresolved grief issues locked away deep in your mind. Take time to heal forgotten wounds, and assimilate the best traits of the lost person into your personality.

Work Daily On Your Self-Esteem: Experts do not let negative attitudes be an indirect expression of unresolved grief.

5. I CAN COPE WITH THE STRESS OF THE UNKNOWN.

To Achieve Self-Control: Switching from a bad situation to a good one turns on all of your body's senses, creative energies and self-actualization drives in unpredictable and profound ways.

Work Daily On Your Self-Esteem: Experts attempt to redefine anxiety as "the excitement of being fully alive."

6. I CAN HAVE WHAT I DESIRE.

To Achieve Self-Control: Peace of mind, grudge-free living and self-pride come from the hard work of having your dreams come true. High self-esteemers struggle with accepting the best of life's rewards.

Work Daily On Your Self-Esteem: Experts deal honestly with self-defeating guilt feelings.

7. I CAN FINISH WHAT I START.

To Achieve Self-Control: Procrastination applies to the reluctance to begin a change project, the ambivalence of continuing it or the resistance to follow-through on hard won wins.

Work Daily On Your Self-Esteem: Experts finish strong by taking lots of little steps in the right direction.

8. I CAN ASK FOR HELP WHEN I'M OVERWHELMED.

To Achieve Self-Control: Low self-esteem states happen every day to high self-esteemers. People who undergo dramatic change often feel like scared and vulnerable children again.

Work Daily On Your Self-Esteem: Experts know when hope is low; asking for help must take a high priority.

9. I CAN LEARN FROM MY MISTAKES.

To Achieve Self-Control: It is crucial for those of us who have been abused, or who have abused our own bodies, minds or relationships to forgive ourselves. Choose to learn something new from old failures to avoid repeating them.

Work Daily On Your Self-Esteem: Experts do not accept failure as the final decree.

10. I CAN LET MY BEST TRAITS COME OUT.

To Achieve Self-Control: Negative attitudes keep great talents hidden from view, and feelings of being bad and worthless running strong. Challenge yourself to be on friendly terms with your secret strengths, and use them as allies to master difficult tasks.

Work Daily On Your Self-Esteem: Experts keep stroking their strengths to succeed.

No, changing a negative attitude is not easy. But you can still get your changes right despite previous attempts that might have failed.

YOU CAN TOO CHOOSE new changes right now! And watch closely how your self-acceptance grows as you master negative emotions.

Permissions are another forceful way to fight frustrations. No, high self-esteem won't make your frustrations magically disappear, and it requires much more than just thinking positive messages. But they can give you hope when hope is hard to come by.

❦ SELF-ESTEEM PERMISSIONS ❦

Use these self-esteem themes to help fight against your current frustrations and the frustrating people in your life who are beating down your self-esteem. Make them your new companions.

Each permission is exactly opposite to each of the ten unspoken failure beliefs that are more in control of you than you think. Self-defeating beliefs are negative messages learned in childhood that determine much of your behavior as an adult. For example, "You can't think clearly when you're feeling angry," is a common unspoken negative belief.

Select one permission for yourself to say during the upcoming week. Pick out one that just seems natural or feels right. Remember, you will change more quickly when you work on your self-esteem. Here are the allies of change:

I Can Do It!

Declares your intention to do the difficult and learn from your failures, instead of accepting them as the final word.

I Am Open To My Feelings!

Declares your intention to use emotion and intuition on par with rationality.

I Think Clearly!

Declares your intention to think accurately about your problems and strengths, instead of avoiding them.

I Can Be Me!

Declares your intention to be an individual of merit and worth.

I Am Worthwhile!

Declares your intention to love yourself, even when those you value respond in rejecting ways.

I Am Open To Success!

Declares your intention to set goals and attain them without guilt.

I AM AT MY BEST!

Declares your intention to be at your best even when you are stressed.

I AM FULLY ALIVE!

Declares your intention to live again, instead of just getting by.

I CHOOSE TO FEEL CLOSE TO OTHERS!

Declares your intention to disclose personal thoughts, and be emotionally available for intimacy, free of power plays.

I ENJOY LIFE!

Declares your intention to enjoy life as it unfolds mysteriously around you.

I FIT IN JUST AS I AM!

Declares your intention to embrace the masculine and feminine in us all.

I EXPLORE MY GIFTS!

Declares your intention to discover what is special about your talents or strengths that you could contribute to the world to make it a better place.

A guarantee: These permissions are central to your change-success.

Do not underestimate their power to improve your life.

Some options: Type or write out the permissions, use them as a book marker or say them out loud while you are driving.

Only you can fight the battle to reclaim your self-esteem.

Being disappointed about change is normal. But what do change-experts do to pick themselves up again? They read anything inspirational!

♦ THE WINNER'S CREDO ♦

When you are convinced that you won't ever be able to accomplish your goals, read down the "Winner's Credo" to help keep yourself on the winning track.

♦ Winners say, "Yes," while Losers say, "Yes, but."

♦ Winners reveal love, while Losers conceal love.

♦ Winners say, "I did," while Losers say, "I didn't."

♦ Winners appreciate, while Losers denigrate.

♦ Winners say, "Now," while Losers say, "Later."

♦ Winners persist, while Losers quit.

♦ Winners say, "I love you," while Losers say, "You must love me."

♦ Winners give things away, while Losers hoard everything.

♦ Winners say, "I'm sorry," while Losers say, "You should be ashamed."

♦ Winners accept others, while Losers judge others.

♦ Winners say, "I'll do my share," while Losers say, "Do something for me."

♦ Winners dare to be out front, while Losers lag behind.

♦ Winners say, "I'm responsible," while Losers say, "It's not my fault."

♦ Winners make something work, while Losers tell you why it won't work.

♦ Winners say, "I'll try," while Losers say, "I won't."

♦ Winners listen to criticisms, while Losers block them out.

♦ Winners say, "I owe you," while Losers say, "You owe me."

♦ Winners laugh at themselves, while Losers laugh behind backs.

♦ Winners say, "I can," while Losers say, "I can't."

♦ Winners protect nature, while Losers destroy nature.

♦ Winners say, "Maybe," while Losers say, "No way."

♦ Winners have a few close friends, while Losers make a million acquaintances.

♦ Winners say, "Thank you," while Losers say, "You don't appreciate me."

♦ Winners are open, while Losers put up walls.

♦ Winners say, "I could," while Losers say, "I should."

♦ Winners reciprocate, while Losers intimidate.

♦ Winners say, "I want," while Losers say, "I don't need anything from you."

♦ Winners pray thankfully, while Losers pray regretfully.

Make this one life you have to live worth every precious moment you can squeeze from it. Be a winner every second of every day by using fail-safe beliefs.

THE SUCCESS MEDITATION

This success meditation is particularly helpful when you are feeling a bit lost, lonely or like a loser who has been run over by forces or disappointments beyond your control.

It carries a hopeful message about the permission to succeed in your own special way. I love to read this success meditation to people eager to climb the ladder of success, or to those whose hurts have forced them to give up prematurely.

Put yourself in a relaxed frame of mind. Imagine a nurturing parent reading these positive value messages to you. Listen as the words describe what being a successful person steeped in self-esteem means.

SUCCESS MEANS: Self-respect. Standing up for important values. Putting people first. Placing more stock in feelings than reasons. Being genuine in the face of any temptation to be phony.
Success means being a real person.

SUCCESS MEANS: Taking time. Taking time to think about your needs. Taking time to be a creative problem-solver. Accepting reassurances when you are hurting. Being open to learning new things.
Success means being as brave as you can be in the face of discouragements.

SUCCESS MEANS: Falling flat on your face and getting up again. Trying something different, even when you feel you can't. Talking openly instead of pushing your point down a closed throat. Communicating rather than just talking.
Success means telling the whole truth.

SUCCESS MEANS: Giving more than is required to get a good grade. Keeping your promises. Playing the business game in straight ways. Setting your goals carefully. Adding your own

special, personal flair to whatever you do.
Success means being assertive.

SUCCESS MEANS: Taking the hard road instead of the fast track. Helping yourself to heaps of helpful feedback. Receiving support when you are suffering from a serious setback. Spearheading your own sincere causes.
Success means making all of your wishes come true.

SUCCESS MEANS: Complimenting anyone and everyone with whom you come into contact. Nurturing yourself by being the most positive person you can be. Solving problems, instead of passing them on to the next gal or guy. Turning down easy money that is bound to make you feel guilty.
Success means nurturing what is right and good.

SUCCESS MEANS: Crying when you are hurt. Eating when you are hungry. Loving the people who love you back. Avoiding those people who find you boring or who hate your guts.
Success means respecting your needs for positive strokes.

SUCCESS MEANS: Laughing loud belly-laughs and being able to laugh at yourself. Telling the type of joke that puts everyone in a good light. Really loving your time on this planet.
Success means loving the mystery and serendipity of it all.

SUCCESS MEANS: Always remembering your roots. Putting people and quality relationships ahead of fame and fortune. Diving down deep into the wellsprings of your strengths.
Success means being the best person you are capable of being.

SUCCESS MEANS: Always reaching towards the stars. Accepting help from angels. Staying away from devils. It means loving your parents and forgiving them the error of their ways, as they forgive yours. Coming to know your weaknesses and not repeating them for all eternity.

Success means the freedom to learn.

SUCCESS MEANS: Being thankful for all you have. Being thankful for all you've been taught. Learning to change big weaknesses into mighty assets. Always taking the time to thank God, when you have lost the habit.

Success means highlighting the good times.

SUCCESS MEANS: Respecting the little guy and the big shot equally. Doing the right thing even when it hurts or may prove to be the wrong move for your career.

Success means being proud to be a person whose handshake is more binding than a legal document.

SUCCESS MEANS: Keeping hope when hope is slim. Valuing all the hard work that it took to get where you are. Enjoying your travels as you speed along toward your destination.

Success means choosing hopefulness instead of despair.

Success comes from being who you truly are. You must allow yourself the permission to feel deserving, so you can feast upon the high rewards that are yours for changing and growing.

Lasting success comes from two sources:

✔ Valuing growing and changing on a daily basis.

✔ Standing up for your right to be who you really are.

Success means interacting with the world in realistic and moral ways to achieve your goals. It means being in control of what you say to yourself. It means learning whatever you need to know to get ahead.

WINNING IN ROMANTIC RELATIONSHIPS THROUGH CHANGE

Each chapter in this book contains information about how to be a relationship expert. Only by changing can you win in your romantic relationships. The fear of change is responsible for relationship stagnation.

Romantic relationships lose the pizzazz of intimacy due to the fear of change. Unfortunately, relationships that perpetuate negative feelings stall out the individual changes that each partner needs to make.

The fear of change is responsible for many rejections, resentments and revenge paybacks. Couples who fear change are doomed to remain swamped by those three negative feelings. Since hurt feelings escalate quickly and are hard to stop, couples who don't change can't navigate stress well.

Are you feeling distant from your lover? Change is the way to closeness, while non-change is certain to lead to greater distance and disappointment.

There are many ways to make sure you and your lover do not become frozen figures in a non-change frame.

1. SPEAK YOUR MIND.

Learn From Love: Keeping secrets from a partner reduces your chances for emotional closeness. Only through self-disclosure can you really be known for who you are.

Change Negative Attitudes: "I refuse to remain a victim."

2. DON'T LET THE FEAR OF REJECTION RUN YOUR LOVE LIFE.

Learn From Love: Rejection often occurs in good relationships. Wise couples use rejections as a signal to change and grow.

Change Negative Attitudes: "I let go of the need to control others."

3. COLLECT RESENTMENTS SLOWLY BUT DROP THEM QUICKLY.

Learn From Love: Resentments reduce nurturing and our ability to choose change. All negative feelings shut down creative change.

Change Negative Attitudes: "I learn something new from every frustrating situation."

4. LET YOURSELF BE LOVED.

Learn From Love: The opposite of self-esteem is anger. When you learn from frustration and conflict, loving feelings will increase proportionately.

Change Negative Attitudes: "I please myself and others about equally."

5. MAKE POSITIVE PAYBACKS COMMONPLACE.

Learn From Love: Positive strokes fuel change, and result from learning the change skills you need to be a successful couple. Catch your lover in the act of doing something good — and never let them forget it!

Change Negative Attitudes: "I am positive to a point and then I set limits."

6. NEVER GIVE UP YOUR IDENTITY TO BE LOVED.

Learn From Love: A healthy balance of togetherness and separate outside interests creates the strongest union. Pleasing too much always results in eventual distance or power plays.

Change Negative Attitudes: "I depend upon a close inner circle of advisors."

7. PLAN CHANGES WHEN EVERYTHING IS GOING OKAY.

Learn From Love: Romance must be planned into every single relationship on a regular basis especially during times of success or strife. Keep thinking about novel ways to improve your relationship.

Change Negative Attitudes: "I make my emotional attachments matter."

8. USE CREATIVE METHODS TO SOLVE PROBLEMS.

Learn From Love: Most couples must create new roles to suit their needs, and not rely on their parents' ways. Brainstorming works best to create new rules and roles.

Change Negative Attitudes: "I turn negative emotions into high self-esteem."

9. FOLLOW THE GOLDEN RULE OF GOOD RELATIONSHIPS.

Learn From Love: The golden rule is change yourself first, change your relationship second and never believe for a second that you can change your partner without his or her consent.

Change Negative Attitudes: "I operate from my strengths and correct my weaknesses."

Good relationships value change to stay vibrant. Don't stifle yourself from feeling really happy.

The more able you are to change yourself, the more often your relationship will be forced to change to keep up with your growing self-esteem.

PERMIT YOURSELF TO USE NEW CHANGE ATTITUDES

Are you really serious about wanting to change? You are? Feel free to change by adopting these new change attitudes:

- ✔ **REFUSE TO REMAIN A VICTIM.**
- ✔ **LET GO OF THE NEED TO CONTROL OTHERS.**
- ✔ **LEARN SOMETHING NEW FROM EVERY FRUSTRATING SITUATION.**

✔ **AIM TO PLEASE YOURSELF AND OTHERS ABOUT EQUALLY.**

✔ **BE POSITIVE TO A POINT AND THEN SET LIMITS.**

✔ **DEPEND UPON A CLOSE INNER CIRCLE OF ADVISORS.**

✔ **MAKE YOUR EMOTIONAL ATTACHMENTS MATTER.**

✔ **TURN NEGATIVE EMOTIONS INTO HIGH SELF-ESTEEM.**

✔ **OPERATE FROM YOUR STRENGTHS – CORRECT YOUR WEAKNESSES.**

✔ **DON'T BLAME OR COMPLAIN – CHANGE.**

Refuse to remain a victim of your own fears.

COUNTERPOINT:

"YOU CAN'T REALLY TEACH OLD DOGS NEW TRICKS, RIGHT?"

Entirely wrong! It's not age, but attitude, that causes change.

Clients of all ages have told me: "I'm just too old to change. It's too late for me to change." Nonsense! We can become more wise and change-able as we age.

What are some youthful tips for breaking free of antiquated thinking to renew your selfhood no matter how old you are? Here are a few of my favorites:

★ *Beware of cozy self-limiting thinking.* "I CAN'T change" excuses will keep you slowed down, self-critical and unable to give yourself comfort when you're hurting.

★ *Your traumas and failures can make you great.* You are guaranteed to grow and change when you try to learn something new from every single frustration. Changing makes you feel young.

★ *Don't take the easy road of old behavior that adds to stockpiles of ancient guilt.* New choices can be made every second of every minute and every hour in each new 24-hour day. Say good-bye to guilt by changing.

★ *Play healthy tricks on your mind to keep it young at heart.* When you feel like you are resisting change, say to yourself in a loud voice, "I refuse to change. I REFUSE to change." Get mad about denying yourself the pleasures of change.

★ *Feel free to change something about yourself that other people have been bugging you about for eons.* Strange but true: Loved ones may be nonplused or ignore you for awhile after you have changed. Why? Change brings new successes, and new successes can bring fear of the unknown.

★ *Don't confuse analyzing your childhood with true change.* Talking about problems doesn't necessarily mean resolving them. Knowing "why" you do something is much different from changing "what" you are doing. No matter what, be realistic, even when it hurts.

Do you want to be a change-expert? "Absolutely!" you say? Fantastic.

Learn to trust yourself again to learn and grow unimpeded. Even though change takes hard work, changing also is the best way to consistently bring you and yours many pleasures.

Even if you are feeling stuck, beaten or helpless to alter life's circumstances that are driving you up a wall and back down again, — HAVE HOPE — and keep going forward.

In Chapter 2, I will show you how to keep going on the spectacular road of success that you are now setting out to travel.

2

WHY CAN'T
YOU CHANGE?

"I think I can, I think I can.
I know I can, I know I can!"

Watty Piper, *The Little Engine That Could*,
Putnam Publishing Group, 1988.

LEARN FROM FRUSTRATION

Negative emotions are normal. But whether you are stuck in one place or you are changing rapidly, negative emotions should not be allowed to have sole authority over your self-worth.

Every life transition has its slowdown, pass-through checkpoints — those negative emotions that you must conquer to keep going forward and growing. Keep taking small positive steps down the road of self-change!

The fear of change comes out most forcefully in "I can't..."

thinking. In fact, self-criticism (see Chapter 3) is the major form of resistance created by CAN'TISM. As you will be learning, five specific fears stem from the fear of change to negatively impact your self-esteem.

Self-worth develops by learning how to handle your fears, frustrations and depressive thoughts much better. Self-esteem is earned daily in many large and small ways by getting unstuck from victim thinking.

Don't be soft on frustration or fear. Instead, why don't you just go and give yourself the permission to change by using strategic self-change thinking. Keep reminding yourself, "I CAN TOO CHANGE!"

THE SELF-WORTH QUIZ

Find out how well you are coping with stress by answering the following questions.

TRUE	FALSE	
❑	❑	1. Fighting against negative emotions is the best way to conquer them.
❑	❑	2. People should feel guilty if they mistreat others.
❑	❑	3. I'm unwilling to show affection or have sex with my partner after an argument.
❑	❑	4. Self-worth requires giving up all of my excuses.
❑	❑	5. People who apologize profusely for their mistakes have great self-worth.
❑	❑	6. I am often critical of myself even when I haven't done anything wrong.

TRUE	FALSE	
❑	❑	7. Rejection is painful because my personal strengths have been diminished.
❑	❑	8. Holding on to grudges is normal.
❑	❑	9. Telling people what you really think of them may hurt them.
❑	❑	10. Self-actualized people rarely feel bad.
❑	❑	11. Every negative feeling has something important to teach me.
❑	❑	12. Change means saying good-bye to people or places that constantly frustrate me.

ANSWERS AND DISCUSSION

How would people who work for self-worth answer this quiz?

1. *False.* A negative emotion can be defined as any emotion that makes you feel out of control, since you can't choose when to be rid of it. Suppressing negative emotions makes them persist. Accepting and dealing with them is harder to do, but better.

2. *True.* Displeasers who should feel guilty about harming others don't, while pleasers don't often speak up assertively because they worry about hurting others.

3. *False.* Affection and sexuality must continue —particularly during times of strife. Don't back away from romantic activities and establish a precedent of avoidance when times are tough. Strive to separate bad moods from giving good strokes.

4. *True.* Self-worth requires you to stop waiting for the perfect time, person or situation to arise in order to go ahead and change. Instead, foster the belief that your life is largely under your own control.

5. *False.* People who over-apologize for preventable errors are playing the victim game. In fact, saying "I'm sorry" is a ploy used to dump unresolved anger in your lap. Learning from mistakes instead of repeating them develops lasting self-worth.

6. *True.* Improving your self-esteem means blaming yourself less while also behaving better to win acceptance. When you become trapped in self-criticism, reclaim your identity by assuming that failures don't have to be permanent states.

7. *True.* Barbed rejections shame your secret strengths. Self-worth requires you to respond assertively to unfair rejections. Rejectors manipulate your feelings by spurning your strengths.

8. *True.* Resentment is normal. It comes from losing a sense of control over a person or a situation that depletes your self-worth. Accumulated resent-

ment makes you believe that your choices are limited and angry paybacks are justified.

9. *True-or-False.* True, when your motivation is to prove that you are right and they are wrong. False, when the purpose of the communication is to create more intimacy by using anger responsibly.

10. *False.* High self-esteemers are committed to learning something worthwhile from every painful experience. They use anger as a healing force to change everyday frustrations into positive energy for growth.

11. *True.* The ability to act competently despite feelings of inadequacy is a learned skill. The mission of negative emotions is to teach you how to love change as a way to love yourself more.

12. *True.* Being open to change is the best way to protect your self-worth. Many negative feelings are reinforced in unchanging work situations or relationships. A decision should be made to improve or jettison these frustrations.

Did you know that trying too hard to change negative emotions can actually intensify them? Learning from your negative feelings is the best way to master them.

Self-worth is the payoff you receive for taming your anger and changing. Treat yourself with respect and dignity. Self-worth is the declaration to learn from life instead of resisting it.

TRAVELING THE ROAD OF SELF-CHANGE

It's time to start to put a little extra punch and power back into your personality. You will need to get up some steam as you head up steep change hills. But don't you give up! It's time to start thinking differently about your capabilities.

It's time to go for a few tiny changes. Begin by taking just a couple of small steps to start believing in yourself again.

Forget waiting for magic and miracles. Don't expect to see the results just yet. Begin by changing your attitude. Remember, there is no magical prescription that I (or anyone else, for that matter) can write for you to build your confidence.

But give yourself a break – CUT YOURSELF SOME SLACK – when you're feeling low and unable to change. Give yourself some extra empathy when you feel all alone. (All right. You've got me. Easier said than done, I know.) And then forge ahead.

You've probably forgotten, like we all do when we are jailed by fear, that feeling like a victim is absolutely energy consuming. Depression is energy consuming. Resentment is energy consuming. You probably suppose you should be able to rise up against all odds! You aren't alone.

FIGHTING "CAN'TISM"

Norman Vincent Peale, the Godfather of Positive Thinking (and a farmboy from Ohio) summarizes his philosophy in this way:

"Believing is everything. Don't say, 'I can't.' Say instead, 'I CAN! I WILL!'"

"I CAN'T..." is an incredibly bullheaded statement, made by an uppity belief system that needs to be put in its place. It implies absolutism, rigidity, certainty, ultimate predictive truth, finality and change impossibility.

Beliefs aren't God, although they may sound Godlike. CAN'TISM beliefs are stubborn ways by which your self-will is undercut by a pessimist-agent working undercover pulling dirty tricks in your brain.

The words, "I can't..." are words spoken in sadness, frustration, broken-heartedness or futility by all of us. The words create the same effects in every human being. That's why the words hurt us so.

When you think of *CAN'TISM:*

✔ Think of self-criticism

✔ Think of runaway fear

✔ Think of stubborn frustrations

✔ Think of difficult people

✔ Think of unyielding stress

✔ Think of nagging self-doubts

✔ Think of ruined self-worth

The two words, "I can't..." get stuck in an angry throat and hide from the light of day. CAN'TISM is a deceptive and depressive way of thinking that hides your weaknesses from the healing forces of insight, love, freedom and feeling worthwhile.

CAN'TISM kills off more new ideas before they can get planted in fertile soil than all other beliefs put together. The C-word is an assassin that kills, maims, tortures and destroys with sadistic glee the sweet labors of love.

It is a killer you must face down. It is the bounty hunter that gets paid big bucks for bringing in your hide -- Dead or Alive.

MINDPLAY:

HOW AM I KILLING OFF
MY CHANCES WITH CAN'TISM?

Take a few moments and list some life possibilities and choices you chose to kill off with the words "I CAN'T..."

➤ Because of CAN'TISM I don't aggressively pursue:

➤ CAN'TISM encourages these self-criticisms:

➤ CAN'TISM contributes to my negative feelings by:

➤ Doors I close in my life due to CAN'TISM are:

➤ CAN'TISM impacts my loving relationships by:

➤ My stress level is raised by CAN'TISM in these ways:

➤ CAN'TISM stops me from trying these new ideas:

INTER PLAY:

Self-change means you accept the responsibility to assert your right to be happy by making new choices. Self-change also means beginning again after you have failed miserably.

You CAN Win at Self-Esteem: Why can't you have the confidence you desire? You can live a resentment-free life.

You CAN Win at Self-Control: Why can't you control what you say to yourself? You can treat your mind to lots of respect and positive strokes.

You CAN Win with the Opposite Sex: Why can't you have friends of the opposite sex without anything sexual going on? Men and women need to learn from one another.

You CAN Win at Your Work: Why can't you contribute something really great to the world? You must hone the special talents you have to give to the world.

You CAN Overcome Stress: Why can't you beat stress? Five quick ways to conquer stress are: 1.) Change of attitude, 2.) Laugh, 3.) Change of scenery, 4.) Time management, and; 5.) Positive strokes for balancing multiple roles. These are all guaranteed ways to clamp down on runaway stress.

Let's find out where your self-esteem might be getting stuck in CAN'TISM.

There are eight ways to get stuck in "I can't..." victim thinking. Determine which dastardly belief is used to undercut your abilities.

GETTING UNSTUCK FROM VICTIM THINKING

The universal fear of change fuels all negative thinking including "I can't..." thinking. CAN'TISM rationalizes away the fear of change by saying, "I'm not capable." Said more truthfully: "The fear of change is in charge of my life and won't dare be challenged by me."

Consider the following list of VICTIM MOTTOES fueled by CAN'TISM. Contrast them with the subsequent list of SUCCESS MOTTOES. False beliefs feel true and real enough, but they are based in fear, which makes you think you cannot change when in fact you can.

Knowing what not to think is not enough. You must interrupt the beliefs and replace them with a multitude of self-change beliefs and permissions that high self-esteemers use.

Each victim motto corresponds with a more powerful, successful and self-accepting way of thinking. This is a proven psychological technique called: "Fighting fire with fire."

Here then are the eight core CAN'TISM BELIEFS. Check the victim mottoes that may be desecrating your self-esteem.

THE VICTIM MOTTOES

1. _____ I CAN'T CHANGE

2. _____ I CAN'T GO IT ALONE

3. _____ I CAN'T SEE THINGS BEING ANY DIFFERENT

4. _____ I CAN'T HAVE IT ANYWAY

5. _____ I CAN'T STICK TO IT

6. _____ I CAN'T ASK FOR WHAT I WANT

7. _____ I CAN'T RISK FAILURE

8. _____ I CAN'T TAKE IT ANYMORE

Start to get mad at the lies told about your capabilities and chances for change. Get upset at self-limiting and depressive beliefs that invite failure. Get mad enough to challenge slick self-criticisms.

Rank-order your top three spirit-killers. But try to conquer them one at a time. Okay...Okay. I know it's never easy to fight against something you can't see. But the successful battle for your own mind must start and finish in your own head.

Don't be surprised if you find different beliefs popping their ugly heads up at different times when you are stuck. Negative beliefs hate to lose. Devious, deceitful and full of devilry to the end, such beliefs go for your jugular when controlling your mind fails.

Don't fret. I'm going to give you a great many tips on how to defeat self-criticism. For now though: START THINKING WHEN YOU ARE FEELING FRUSTRATED. Start thinking that you can change and be in control of what you think and feel.

Let yourself brainstorm novel and creative ways to cure yourself of outdated victim thinking. You can think clearly even when you are mad, scared or sad. Coming up with beliefs that encourage you to think, feel and act at your best will help you succeed.

You certainly don't need to be your own worst opponent by using victim thinking.

Each positive saying corresponds to the victim motto you may have checked off above. Then each success motto corresponds with the same numbered self-change strategy. Use the permissions that match your self-putdowns.

Challenge being a victim by saying the statements to yourself before, during and after you are feeling stuck and doubting your competencies.

THE SUCCESS MOTTOES

1. _____ I CAN CHANGE
   I WILL CHANGE!

2. _____ I CAN GO IT ALONE
   I WILL GO IT ALONE!

3. ——— **I CAN SEE THINGS BEING DIFFERENT**
       I WILL BE DIFFERENT!

4. ——— **I CAN HAVE IT**
       I WILL WORK HARD TO HAVE IT!

5. ——— **I CAN STICK TO IT**
       I WILL STAY WITH GOOD CHANGES!

6. ——— **I CAN ASK FOR WHAT I WANT**
       I WILL ASK!

7. ——— **I CAN RISK FAILURE**
       I WILL RISK SUCCESS!

8. ——— **I CAN TAKE FEELING GOOD**
       I WILL ACCEPT FEELING HAPPY!

Don't just take my word for it. I realize that success takes a great deal of intellectual work and working through. But any good habit can be started by breaking the back of "I CAN'T."

You must learn to take positive action in spite of fears that tell you to hold back. I am going to give you some examples of success beliefs that high self-esteemers use each day to feel good.

Thinking positive thoughts, though, is not enough. You need to regularly use change permissions, remove negative feelings, take positive actions and learn from your failures.

Change-experts don't wait to receive a diploma before feeling they are allowed to make dramatic changes. Instead, they take positive action without delay, and assume the inner self will feel more capable as the change journey unfolds.

You can learn what you need to learn as you travel along. But you must begin moving in some direction by using success beliefs!

Don't be soft on CAN'TISM any longer. Start tomorrow off on a new foot. Here are some ways to turn your fears into greater self-worth.

SELF-CHANGE STRATEGIES

Begin making some new assumptions about change. Assume first that the fear of change should not be in control of your life. There are eight success beliefs people who choose to work daily on their self-esteem use to take charge of their lives.

Each of the eight "I can't..." mottoes is represented in the upbeat, change-categories below in the same order of appearance. I've also repeated the previous success motto that applies to each self-change strategy.

Begin making some new assumptions about your skills, traits and abilities. Don't give me a hard time about this. You must put these assumptions in your brain in a very active way. You get the idea. Be forceful, bold and downright stubborn in good ways about good beliefs.

Self-change means you accept the responsibility to assert your right to make new choices and to benefit from them. What you are unhappy about can be changed when you give yourself the luxury to pursue new options. Purge victim thinking by confronting the self-defeating assumptions that are used to discredit your capabilities.

Remember: Fight back! You don't have to be stuck in a bad job, marriage or mental attitude even when your victim beliefs spout off otherwise. Self-victimization can only occur when you assume the self is incompetent, inadequate or impaired beyond repair. Victim thinking sounds rational, but it is always distorted and prejudiced, yet oddly comfortable.

Challenge false beliefs that victimize you, and adopt new success beliefs to raise your self-esteem. Do you want to be successful and feel strong surges of self-worth? Then you must challenge CAN'TISM.

One of the key differences between low and high self-esteem is the beliefs that go round and round in your mind.

SELF-CHANGE BELIEF #1:

ASSUME THAT THE INNER SELF IS LARGELY COMPETENT AND CAPABLE.

Use the Success Motto: I CAN CHANGE!

Taking the time to develop competencies contradicts the "I can't change" victim motto. You can learn new skills from experts who already have acquired them.

Challenge False Beliefs: The Presumption of Incompetency means you aren't held responsible for the quality of your life. You alone are responsible for taking good care of yourself.

Defeat the Victim Motto: The "I can't change" victim motto programs you to believe you are limited in your ability to acquire valuable resources to redress painful situations. Giving up before you start is the result.

To Add to Your Self-Worth: You have a great many more secret strengths and abilities than you give yourself credit for. If you were told when you were a child that you were a quick learner, how different might your life have been?

Believe in Your Success: "I am a competent and lovable adult who makes good choices to change."

SELF-CHANGE BELIEF #2:

ASSUME THAT YOU DON'T HAVE TO LIVE IN AN ENERGY-DEPLETING SITUATION.

Use the Success Motto: I CAN GO IT ALONE!

Planning your life and writing down your goals develops the maturity to contradict the "I can't go it alone" motto. Building a strong identity is your birthright.

Challenge False Beliefs: The Presumption of Immaturity means you aren't held accountable for the choices you do and don't make. Learn how to make good choices and receive good consequences from them.

Defeat the Victim Motto: The "I can't go it alone" victim motto programs you to believe you don't have the independent nerve to leave people who disapprove of you. Trying too hard to please frustrating people is the result.

To Add to Your Self-Worth: Self-respect is built on the permission to alter bad situations that do not fulfill your adult needs. Are you really so frightened that you can't cope with life on your own terms?

Believe in Your Success: "I correct weaknesses instead of protecting them."

SELF-CHANGE BELIEF #3:

ASSUME THAT THE PAST CANNOT DICTATE YOUR FUTURE.

Use the Success Motto: I CAN SEE THINGS BEING DIFFERENT!
The past is part of the wonderful fabric of your life, and you must let go of the past to go forward. Looking forward to a good future contradicts the "I can't see it being any different" motto.

Challenge False Beliefs: The Presumption of Future Hardship means you aren't required to assert your will and try to influence your destiny. Start assuming that efforts planted today will yield handsome crops in the future.

Defeat the Victim Motto: The "I can't see it being any different" victim motto programs you to believe you don't have free choices occurring each and every new day, when in fact you do. The result is procrastination and negative feelings that steamroll over your self-esteem.

To Add to Your Self-Worth: Superior brainpower means you have the ability to respond in totally different ways than you did a moment ago. What decisions would you make if your future were guaranteed to be a resounding success?

Believe in Your Success: "I stand up to being rejected."

SELF-CHANGE BELIEF #4:

ASSUME THAT YOUR SELF-WORTH IS SIZABLE.

Use the Success Motto: I CAN HAVE IT!

Taking good advice and accepting positive strokes will always help keep your attitude open to change. You can have more than you need by working hard for it and contradicting the "I can't have it anyway" motto.

Challenge False Beliefs: The Presumption of Inadequacy means you don't have to take yourself seriously and think about what you want to do with your life. What activities add meaning to your life? Reach out to new information, people and events when you are feeling worth little.

Defeat the Victim Motto: The "I can't have it anyway" victim motto programs you to believe that your value is so negligible that you can't ever have what you want. The result is that you don't strive for, nor feel deserving of, achieving the success that builds high self-esteem.

To Add to Your Self-Worth: Exhibit and focus on the magnificent traits you have inside. What might you feel compelled to contribute if you felt worthy?

Believe in Your Success: "My mistakes don't make or break me."

SELF-CHANGE BELIEF #5:

ASSUME THAT YOUR MENTAL AND PHYSICAL HEALTH IS UNDER YOUR CONTROL.

Use the Success Motto: I CAN STICK TO IT!

Pleasing yourself and others about equally leads to satisfaction and happiness through equality. Putting your physical and psychological health under your conscious control repudiates the "I can't stick to it" motto.

Challenge False Beliefs: The Presumption of Insufficient Willpower means you don't have to assertively address frustrations and remove the frustrating habits or people that bother you the most. Assume that skill and willpower is built up like a muscle from practice – practice – practice.

Defeat the Victim Motto: The "I can't stick to it" victim motto programs you to believe that you are unable to persevere with wise thinking, eating, communication, exercise and sleeping habits. The result is pleasing yourself too little, and indirectly taking out anger on your own body or mind.

To Add to Your Self-Worth: Peace of mind, freedom from guilt and worry-free living are the prizes that result from taking charge of your urges. Do you separate good anger from bad actions? Do you know that anger is an emotion and not a behavior? Become friends with your anger.

Believe in Your Success: "I can be caring even when I'm angry."

SELF-CHANGE BELIEF #6:

ASSUME THAT FEELING DEPRESSED ISN'T NORMAL.

Use the Success Motto: I CAN ASK FOR WHAT I WANT!

Since happiness is normal for high self-esteemers, you must claim your right to it in order to contradict beliefs that claim you should live with frustrations and without what you want. Sometimes, happiness comes from asking straight for what you want.

Challenge False Beliefs: The Presumption of Incurability means you will tolerate more resentment, pain and frustration than you need to. Treat your mind, body and spirit to the caring respect they deserve.

Defeat the Victim Motto: The "I can't ask for what I want" victim motto programs you to accept feeling blue for too long as if it were a normal state. The result is boredom and negative feelings and too few or no positive strokes.

To Add to Your Self-Worth: Accept that happiness is normal and not a fleeting ghost. Are you too lethargic when it comes to asking for physical strokes, exercising and self-nurturing?

Believe in Your Success: "I take care of my own pain."

SELF-CHANGE BELIEF #7:

ASSUME THAT FAILURES ARE NEVER PERMANENT STATES.

Use the Success Motto: I CAN RISK FAILURE!

Reassuring yourself that you can handle whatever crises might arise from venturing into the unknown contradicts the "I can't risk failure" motto.

Challenge False Beliefs: The Presumption of Ineptitude means that you can't step outside of your normal comfort zones. Use fun ways to deal with the anxiety that accompanies exploring the unknown.

Defeat the Victim Motto: The "I can't risk failure" victim motto programs you to believe that trial-and-error experimentation should not be required to perfect a new skill. You need to feel free to make plenty of mistakes and learn quickly from them.

To Add to Your Self-Worth: Failure is never a permanent state if you do not allow yourself to wallow in it for very long. Do you equate failure with disapproval, rejection or with moving toward success and self-esteem?

Believe in Your Success: "Failure is an overrated event."

SELF-CHANGE BELIEF #8:

ASSUME THAT LOYALTY BREEDS INTIMACY NOT CONTEMPT.

Use the Success Motto: I CAN TAKE FEELING GOOD!

Making a decision to make all of your attachments and relationships matter contradicts the "I can't take it anymore" motto.

Challenge False Beliefs: The Presumption of Isolation means you don't spend enough time setting goals, adding romance and building teamwork into your love life. Learn to be yourself instead of acting out shallow relationship roles.

Defeat the Victim Motto: The "I can't take it anymore" victim motto programs you to believe that nonconstructive conflict, power plays and inability to change are normal in love relationships. You have the right to benefit from intimacy, and to learn and grow from conflict.

To Add to Your Self-Worth: A sense of belonging in the world, enjoying your body and turning negative emotions into high self-esteem is a natural state you deserve. Are you consistently open, close and giving with lovers and friends?

Believe in Your Success: "I take risks even when I'm afraid."

Self-change means you accept the responsibility to fight off victim-thinking and challenge life to deliver the very best of everything it has for you.

Having a winning relationship with your inner self, with loved ones, and with life requires that you learn to snatch your self-esteem back from the jaws of depression and frustration.

Resentment results from victim beliefs and restricts your choices, which victimizes you further. Shortly I will be giving you some fail-safe tips to reduce the resentment and stress that is keeping you stuck in one place going nowhere.

REMEMBER THE BASIC STRATEGY OF SELF-CHANGE

New beliefs
Permit new choices
Adding new successes
And renewed hope
In being who you really ARE.

RECLAIMING SELF-ESTEEM FROM FRUSTRATION

Self-esteem is inversely related to your favorite depressive beliefs. Raise one, and the other is bound to take a big fall. All victim beliefs lead down a road to a town called Resentment.

Soon you may agree with me that your very own cherished change-objections just might be the biggest lines of all time. Your favorite negative self-beliefs will also be exposed as hypes or self-delusions that you allow to control your mental life.

Don't worry; you are in good company, since most of us "nice-caring-self-critical" people do the very same depressing thing. We all lie to ourselves and don't spell out our strengths often enough. Then we act in self-defeating ways that fit the belief and have depressing proof of our incapabilities.

Unfortunately, you are an expert at self-betrayal and pay the physical and psychological price for that denial. You need to drop self-criticism, unrealistic expectations, fears and facades and face yourself and reality squarely to claim your right to be happy.

I believe that you can achieve exactly what you set out to achieve and I will argue the case for productive and dramatic change. You really can have it all! (Or much of what you want when you are willing to go ahead and grow.) You'll be learning how.

For now, though, be ULTRA-NEGATIVE! Let's discover what negative attitudes fuel frustration and are standing in the way of your ultimate happiness.

MINDPLAY:

THE MOST DEPRESSING THINGS
I THINK ABOUT MYSELF?

You will notice that each concept is stated twice in a different format. Try to give two different answers. I'm doing this because victim thinking usually runs quite deep.

Let yourself delve into your depression. You won't end up getting lost in the emotions. I'll be helping you use your answers to come up with self-change strategies later. Begin brainstorming what negative victim beliefs are kicking you in the rear end. Be open and creative with your answers.

1. I CAN'T CHANGE BECAUSE:

_____

_____

_____

➤ CAN'T CHANGE _____

2. I'M SLOW TO CHANGE BECAUSE:

_____

_____

_____

➤ BECAUSE _____

3. WHAT'S HOLDING ME BACK IS:

_____

_____

_____

➤ IT'S _____

4. I'D CHANGE 'IF IT WEREN'T FOR':

_____

_____

_____

➤ DUE TO _____

5. BUT I'D HATE TO HAVE TO GIVE UP:

_____

_____

_____

   ➤ I WON'T GIVE UP _____

6. THESE HANG-UPS ALWAYS GET IN MY WAY:

_____

_____

_____

   ➤ MY HANG-UPS _____

INTER PLAY:

Do you assume you are doomed before you even begin focusing on your changes? Have you been knocked down by failures to the point of being unwilling to get up again?

You Aren't Bad but Victim Beliefs Are: Victim beliefs are responsible for keeping you down for the count. You aren't bad but victim beliefs are!

Has a Fast One Been Pulled On You: Have you noticed the trick I've pulled on you? Read the underscored words in this mindplay and form them into a sentence. Did you catch the hidden message?

CAN'T CHANGE
BECAUSE I WON'T GIVE UP MY HANG-UPS!

Don't get mad at me. It's the same trick you play on yourself — daily. If your inner reality is: "I can't change due to my hang-ups," you will order up outside reality to match this negative belief to a tee.

Your subconscious mind won't revolt against such a message. It won't challenge such a warped conclusion by saying, "That's exactly what and why I need to change! Every person who has ever changed did so in spite of their hang-ups!"

Alibis, excuses or rationalizations — we all use them to maintain the status quo and to avoid the uncertainty and overwhelming fear of change. Can you give up always needing to be right when it means traveling down the wrong road? The wrong road is called the fear of change and always leads to a town called Resentment.

MASTERING RESENTMENT TO CHANGE AND GROW

Lack of change results in resentment toward yourself, loved ones and colleagues at work.

Resentment results when someone or something has more control over your life than you do — including victim beliefs. Paradoxically, resentment works to make you more dependent on the person or thing you resent. The solution is to respond more independently by changing.

Choice and intimacy are most negatively impacted by resentment.

The purpose of romantic relationships is to exchange strengths, not to collect resentments. Equality between the sexes develops when one partner is allowed to do what the other partner is able to do. Equality is a necessary prerequisite for harmony.

Resentment can be defined as the healthy anger that arises when you don't receive near equal payments of interest and attention back from a person you deem to be important to your self-esteem. Resentment is incurred when the balance sheet of giving and receiving is out of whack.

How does resentment affect you? Unrecognized resentment robs you of the right to make good choices to move forward with your life. It also makes you procrastinate in making choices important to your self-esteem.

Resentment reinforces your fears and makes you too frightened to try the new. Resentments have a long shelf life and can stay active for years without losing their potency. Resentments are stockpiled until a breaking point is reached, and unexpected action taken.

The usual cure for resentment is to make new choices that benefit you. You must also add back into your loving relationship what has been taken out of it due to resentment. The assertive use of anger (see Chapter 6) helps on both these fronts.

HOW TO TELL IF YOU ARE FEELING RESENTFUL

Here are some indicators to tell if resentment is ruling you.

1. **Your complaints don't bring desired changes.**

2. **You feel consumed by depression or anxiety.**

3. **Dreams and goals have been sacrificed.**

4. **You're giving much more than is your fair share.**

5. **Key choices have been restricted.**

6. **Trying to communicate results in misunderstanding.**

7. **Distancing, loneliness and isolationism occurs.**

8. **There seems to be no solution to a standard problem.**

9. **You feel frightened and vulnerable.**

10. **A sense of helplessness and betrayal exists.**

11. **It seems impossible to stop being so upset.**

Complaining is a common way that resentments are expressed.

Complaints which stem from resentment are wearing and difficult to listen to. Your skin may crawl when you hear someone talk about their resentments.

Worse still, resentment will rob you and yours of passionate romance.

EFFECTS OF STOCKPILED RESENTMENTS ON ROMANCE

The effects of resentment are severe on you and your lover.

1. **Goodwill and mutual effort evaporates.**

2. **Problems get escalated instead of resolved.**

3. **Conflicts replace confidence.**

4. **Sexuality declines.**

5. **Caring is questioned.**

6. **Your worst fears come to life.**

7. **A spontaneous sense of play is lost.**

8. **Closeness feels like hard work.**

9. **Grudge matches take precedence over goal-setting.**

Resentment is dissipated when you and your partner feel free to make choices that improve both your self-esteem and add to intimacy.

How can you set up an atmosphere of change? Since resentment can occur in any relationship, you must release the resentments as quickly and efficiently as you can. Reducing resentment always adds to self-worth.

RUGGED TIPS TO REDUCE RESENTMENT

The purpose of reducing resentments is to make you feel better. And when you feel better you will feel more in control of your life, and be more willing to go out and try new changes free of the fear of failure.

Here are some quick-hit, resentment-freeing tips:

1. STOP PURSUING SOMEONE WHO DOESN'T WANT YOU.

Reduce Resentments: Equal interest is essential for self-esteeming relationships. Don't let someone run you around the mulberry bush making promises to change but not following through.

Be a Change-Expert: Make good choices to change.

Choose Self-Worth: "I deserve to be loved for who I am."

2. CLAIM ENTITLEMENT TO A BLAME-FREE EXISTENCE.

Reduce Resentments: Stop nitpicking yourself. Are you absolutely responsible for every problem? Some events are simply beyond your control.

Be a Change-Expert: You don't have to do things right the very first time.

Choose Self-Worth: "I don't need to punish myself in order to grow."

3. USE GOALS TO GUIDE YOU.

Reduce Resentments: Go back to your original goals when you are feeling put down. Have a mission to add excitement and direction to your life.

Be a Change-Expert: Excel just to make you happy.

Choose Self-Worth: "I search for a purpose to my life."

4. FORCE YOURSELF TO BECOME LESS DEPENDENT ON THE RESENTED PERSON.

Reduce Resentments: Stop trying to force your antagonist to change. Go ahead and change yourself first. Make yourself matter.

Be a Change-Expert: Your choices affect you the most.

Choose Self-Worth: "I go on with my life when people disapprove of me."

5. REARRANGE YOUR DAY TO FREE UP VALUABLE TIME FOR YOURSELF.

Reduce Resentments: What are you putting off that makes you feel good? What happened to those activities that put a smile on your lips? Make sure that you spend some time with yourself.

Be a Change-Expert: Correct weaknesses instead of protecting them.

Choose Self-Worth: "Time for me keeps me healthy."

6. WORRY LESS ABOUT WHAT OTHERS WILL THINK OF YOU.

Reduce Resentments: Try not to dwell on the negative comments angry people have said about you. Dwell on the accolades instead. Displeasers will try to convince you that everyone is siding with them against you.

Be a Change-Expert: You can stand being rejected.

Choose Self-Worth: "I trust myself to know what is best for me."

7. HAVE MANY SOURCES OF POSITIVE STROKES.

Reduce Resentments: Depending on just one person to meet all of your emotional needs is asking for trouble. Expand your circles of support. Resentment is a loud call to become more independent.

Be a Change-Expert: Risks must be taken to change and grow.

Choose Self-Worth: "I choose to be around people who enjoy me."

8. USE ANGER ASSERTIVELY.

Reduce Resentments: State your opinions openly. Try something new for the heck of it. Think out problems from crazy angles. Speak up to someone who intimidates you.

Be a Change-Expert: Feel angry but behave assertively.

Choose Self-Worth: "I think clearly when I'm angry."

9. BE GOOD TO YOURSELF IN SMALL WAYS.

Reduce Resentments: Learn to enjoy the smaller things in life and be silly again. Read a fun novel, cross-stitch, talk with somebody you normally wouldn't.

Be a Change-Expert: You have the right to be selfish sometimes.

Choose Self-Worth: "My needs are important."

10. BE AWARE OF INVISIBLE LOSSES THAT ARE CUTTING YOU DOWN.

Reduce Resentments: Your unresolved grief is affecting you more than you think. If you are having trouble changing, look for a loss that is weighing you down and mourn it.

Be a Change-Expert: Take care of your own pain.

Choose Self-Worth: "I do not avoid happiness by refusing to mourn."

11. APPRECIATE THAT BEING OLDER IS BETTER.

Reduce Resentments: Your age is a blessing and can help you have what your want. High self-esteem is appealing at every age.

Be a Change-Expert: Take pride in your own good advice.

Choose Self-Worth: "It's never too late to grow and change."

12. BE SELF-EMPATHETIC IF YOU ARE NATURALLY INCLINED TO BE SENSITIVE.

Reduce Resentments: By trying to please others, sensitive people can fail to be who they are. Be different than others even when you are criticized for it. Your job is not to be a psychologist to everyone without pay.

Be a Change-Expert: Trust yourself to learn and grow.

Choose Self-Worth: "Being different is not only acceptable--it's preferable!"

13. PERFORM THE RESENTMENT RITUAL.

Reduce Resentments: Schedule a weekly meeting time to air resentments with your lover. Find new ways to let grudges go. Figure out what loving behavior will even the score.

Be a Change-Expert: Release resentments to change.

Choose Self-Worth: "I find ways to give my lover positive paybacks!"

Being unable to change is a result of stockpiled resentment. Resentment restricts your choices and makes you feel stuck.

MINDPLAY:
THE MANY THINGS I GIVE UP JUST TO BE RIGHT?

Successful people don't mind being wrong. They learn from their mistakes and grow from them. Being narrow-minded means being failure-minded.

What are you giving up due to justifying your resentments? Mark a few of the prices you pay for being "right."

- ❏ Being myself
- ❏ Success
- ❏ Feeling important
- ❏ Thinking clearly
- ❏ Being open to all of my feelings
- ❏ Feeling close to others
- ❏ Enjoying life
- ❏ Fitting in just as I am
- ❏ Self-worth

- ❑ Peace of mind
- ❑ Great sex
- ❑ Starting over again
- ❑ Moving
- ❑ Power
- ❑ Sensitivity
- ❑ Learning
- ❑ Friendship
- ❑ Sleep
- ❑ Happiness
- ❑ Money
- ❑ Getting help
- ❑ Strengths
- ❑ Physical health
- ❑ Working things out
- ❑ A job promotion
- ❑ Self-improvement
- ❑ Trusting the opposite sex
- ❑ Goals
- ❑ Marriage
- ❑ Great ideas
- ❑ Moving on
- ❑ Good communication
- ❑ Learning from a dispute
- ❑ Confidence
- ❑ Fun with my kids
- ❑ Good advice
- ❑ (so many others...)

INTER PLAY:

Resentment keeps you trapped in trying to prove you are right instead of trying to change and lead a life that is right for you.

The Need to Be Right Will Always Make You Wrong: If you need to be right, then other people must be wrong. If others must be wrong, then you cannot afford to listen to them.

All Forms of Blame Slow Down Change: The compulsive need to be right and blame others for your problems is a core reason that certain frustrations seem impossible to change. When blame stops, change starts.

Self-Criticism Is the Major Resistance to Change: Being stuck in your own negative opinions will always make you lose sight of your own good ideas. When you open up your mind, change starts.

Taking Advice and Accepting Help Are Strengths of Winners: The more you need to be right about your problems, the less you will seek out and accept help. When you seek out help, change starts.

Old Negative Self-Opinions Die Hard: Being successful means you must drop old childhood beliefs that you are inferior or worthless. When you let go of old self-opinions, change starts.

Must you be right even when it comes to living a restricted life due to your resentments? It's time to put your hang-ups in their place, and stop altering your life to accommodate their demands.

Stress results when you aren't changing fast enough to keep up with your needs. Stress also results from undergoing rapid change. Either way, be sure to take care of yourself when you are under stress!

NINE EASY WAYS TO UNLOAD STRESS

The stress-relax rule is: The more control that you perceive you have over stressful situations the greater your ability will be to relax. My job is to give you some methods to do just that.

Take charge of your stress. Purposefully try to make yourself feel like a capable, take-charge-type-of-person who will never quit trying to feel better — EVER. Maybe your victim thinking will get the hint and take a hike. Also, learn to flow with the stresses you can't control.

You need to become an expert at reducing the impact of stress on your self-esteem. Your task, then, is to make little decisions and try out small behaviors that will pack a big wallop of self-control when you are feeling blown apart by stress.

Here are nine ways to be at your best when you are under stress:

1. NEVER BETRAY YOUR ULTIMATE VALUES.

Reduce Stress: Honesty remains the best policy for taking the punch out of stress. Be true to yourself. Be true to others who deserve your loyalty.

Respect Your Values: Stress is created when your behavior doesn't match the values you cherish. Keep your word during power plays, avoid paybacks and play politics sparingly.

Build High Self-Esteem: Being genuine will help you sidestep many avoidable problems.

2. GET GROUNDED IN YOUR PRIMARY GOALS AGAIN.

Reduce Stress: Stress will make you feel frenzied, harried and beside yourself.

Set Your Goals: You need to review your goals to become psychologically rooted again when stress tries to blow you away.

Build High Self-Esteem: Make sure you have your long-term big goals in writing. Keep them in your daily planner, and refer to them when difficult people try to bug you.

3. BREAK NORMAL ROUTINES.

Reduce Stress: Create brief mental rest stops during the day.

Use Time Wisely: For example, close your office door and read the newspaper, write a thank you note to someone who has helped you or take a brisk walk around your building.

Build High Self-Esteem: Solo decisions that grant a fresh perspective will give you a renewed sense of being in charge.

4. REFUSE TO BE ULTRA-RESPONSIBLE.

Reduce Stress: When you are stressed out, go easy on trying to be as helpful as you normally would be.

Make Good Choices: Hold back your energy a little to conserve it. Stick to basic priorities. To avoid storing up resentments, stop rescuing others from their own problems.

Build High Self-Esteem: Be sure you take your needs into account, even though you may not always be able to get your needs met.

5. PUMP UP YOUR MIND WITH PERMISSIONS.

Reduce Stress: Use coping statements when you aren't sure what else can be done to manage stress and massage hurt feelings. Permit yourself some kindness when you are feeling self-critical.

Choose Your Own Changes: Forcefully say to yourself: "I have more control than I give myself credit for." "I can handle this." "I really cope well." "I'll manage just like I always do."

Build High Self-Esteem: Treat yourself to kindness by using coping statements. Try to enjoy life even when it stinks.

6. CUT YOURSELF SOME MENTAL SLACK.

Reduce Stress: Stop and mentally go inside yourself and check out your feelings when you are running on fast-forward. Slow down your fear reactions to study them.

Accept Positive Strokes: Take a deep breath, and ask yourself: "Am I feeling frightened, angry, lonely or what right now?" Listen to the answer, then give yourself what you need instead of stuffing feelings.

Build High Self-Esteem: Let yourself be a kid again. A

competent adult like you still requires a whopping dose of positive strokes.

7. ASK FOR MORE HELP.

Reduce Stress: There are plenty of times when it's best to swallow your pride and accept gifts of help from people who love you.

Take Good Advice: Supporters don't automatically know what you have been thinking about or how much stress you are under.

Build High Self-Esteem: Tell everyone invested in you how they can be a bigger source of help right now. People who care will gladly get behind you to lend a hand. Inform your partner when you would prefer an understanding ear to advice.

8. CREATE A SAFE HAVEN AT HOME.

Reduce Stress: Home is the place where you should be approved of as a unique person, no matter what you have or have not accomplished during the day.

Stop Criticizing: Create a mental getaway from the intense focus that work requires. Use disagreements to promote couple goal setting. Don't be afraid of conflict when it will add positive, stress-removing changes in your lifestyle.

Build High Self-Esteem: Since guilt adds to stress, avoid taking out unfair frustrations on family members.

9. BE MORE DEMANDING OF SELF-PLEASURE.

Reduce Stress: Laughter and play are surefire ways to stop stress dead in its tracks. Play with pets, watch funny home videos or lounge in a bubble bath to feel more alive.

Respect Your Values: Make a point to be the first one to be giving, but also take some private time to rejuvenate your batteries and enjoy being with yourself.

Build High Self-Esteem: It is crucial to be selfish enough to take decent care of your needs.

Unload some of the weight of stress from your shoulders. Avoid unloading it on other people. You deserve to capitalize on all life offers, and that includes a relaxing, fun-filled, stress-reduced life.

ARE YOU PRESUMED GUILTY UNTIL PROVEN INNOCENT?

Pre>sump>tion (pri-zump'shen): 1. Behavior or language that is boldly arrogant or offensive; effrontery. 2. The act of presuming or accepting as true. 3. Acceptance or belief based on reasonable evidence; assumption or supposition.

Have you become too comfortable with any of these strange masochistic beliefs that stem from self-criticism?

The Presumption of Incompetency.

The Presumption of Immaturity.

The Presumption of Future Hardship.

The Presumption of Inadequacy.

The Presumption of Insufficient Willpower.

The Presumption of Incurability.

The Presumption of Ineptitude.

The Presumption of Isolation.

INTER PLAY:

Self-change means making some new assumptions about your inner capabilities. Are you being too hard on yourself, so self-critical that you are slowing down good changes by resisting them?

Are you a raving Megalomaniac? Predicting that you are going to fail in advance of sustaining new changes is a form of mental grandiosity that creates inaction.

Have you become your own Hanging Judge? Assuming the worst about yourself is an outrageously self-punitive and hostile action.

Are you utterly convinced that you are somehow bad or inferior? Trying anything new to unleash your strengths will be seen as a waste of time when you are busy worshiping your weaknesses.

Have you given up trying to find new answers? Do you use biased evidence to prove you have fatal flaws in your character, abilities or self-worth? Do these judgments cast your life in cement? You can find the answers you need to feel better. Just keep looking!

Are you a die hard, doom-and-gloom thinker? Do you fatalistically conclude: "Why should I even try to make my life better?"

Self-criticism is the major way most people resist making needed changes. Start becoming aware of the amount of angry and discouraging comments that you direct at yourself.

Even though you may have failed many times before to accomplish your goals, the past can remain the past and you can go on into a brighter future.

The following ten key permissions to keep choosing change and the chapter counterpoint tell you why.

PERMIT YOURSELF TO KEEP CHOOSING CHANGE

Ten key change permissions keep you open-minded about your change potentials instead of resisting them.

✔ **MAKE GOOD CHOICES TO CHANGE.**

✔ **CORRECT WEAKNESSES INSTEAD OF PROTECTING THEM.**

✔ **STAND UP TO BEING REJECTED.**

✔ **FEEL ANGRY BUT BEHAVE ASSERTIVELY.**

✔ **EXPECT TO DO THINGS IMPERFECTLY.**

✔ **TAKE CARE OF YOUR OWN PAIN FIRST.**

✔ **EXCEL JUST TO MAKE YOURSELF HAPPY.**

✔ **ASSERT YOUR RIGHT TO BE SELFISH SOMETIMES.**

✔ **TAKE PRIDE IN YOUR OWN GOOD ADVICE.**

✔ **TRUST YOURSELF TO LEARN AND GROW.**

Keep these permissions handy to refresh your spirits when you are winded from the change race.

COUNTERPOINT:

"HOW CAN I HOPE TO SUCCEED WHEN I'VE FAILED SO MANY TIMES BEFORE?"

Don't give your previous failures the power to predict your future. Make you own way in life!

The only real failure is the failure to try. Here are some ways to counteract depressive thinking.

★ *Act like a scientist studying the self.* Your inner wisdom must be dignified. Ask yourself, "Aren't I supposed to wait until the scientific proof is in before jumping to conclusions?"

★ *Avoid jumping to conclusions.* You may be lacking crucial information necessary to succeed. Ask yourself, "What have people done to master this issue before me?" "How can I do more of what they do?"

★ *Vocalize your right to be innocent until proven guilty.* Feeling bad isn't a good reason to punish yourself by forestalling changes. Ask yourself, "How can I change even when I'm feeling bad?"

★ *Don't use previous failures as proof positive for remaining passive.* Previous failures only prove that you haven't found the solution yet. Ask yourself, "Do I avoid my fear of the unknown by focusing on my failures?"

★ *Act out the internal Judge role.* Establish what is fair punishment for your heinous crimes. Ask yourself, "What sentence would be sufficient for my wrongdoing?"

★ *Never accept reasonable sounding (but wrong) excuses that you cannot change.* All rationalizations disable your self-esteem and shut off your real capabilities. Ask yourself, "How might I be quite ABLE to change?"

★ *Claim your right to be an animal with a highly-developed brain.* Your creative problem-solving capacities are incredible. You are not a rat in a maze without free choice. Ask yourself, "What do I need to learn to succeed?"

★ *Challenge cozy self-prejudices.* Self-criticisms are fancy lies. Challenge yourself, "How have my negative attitudes become self-fulfilling prophecies?" "Am I complaining about my life more than changing it?"

In the next chapter, I'm going to teach you how to stop cozying up to your resistances. I'll be telling you how to ease up on self-criticism binges, and how to use the fear of change to your advantage.

3

REASONS ADULTS RESIST CHANGE

Do get mad,
And do get even ...
Get mad and get even by changing.

A positive twist to the revenge theme:
"I don't get mad, I just get even."
A popular saying.

ALL FORMS OF BLAME IMPEDE CHANGE

All forms of blame slow down and impede change. Self-blame is the socially sanctioned way you have been taught to rigidly resist taking realistic risks on your own behalf to be successful.

Self-criticism feeds the mind huge doses of negative strokes. Since you have been trained to be a self-criticizer, you can learn better ways to talk to yourself. Most adults have learned to be excessive self-criticizers.

Self-criticism was originally intended to keep you attuned to the needs of the group and to better yourself. Now, however, criticism is used across the board to riddle your best strengths, diminish your self-esteem and undermine your hard-won successes.

How frustrated have you been with yourself lately? Do you like the person who gazes back at you in the bathroom mirror? Losing control and feeling resentful fuels self-criticisms and reduces your self-esteem.

THE SELF-CRITICISM QUIZ

Answer the following questions to find out if you are on good terms with yourself, or whether you are busy feeding yourself too many self-criticisms.

YES   NO

❑   ❑   1. Self-criticism keeps me doing the very same things I despised having done in the first place.

❑   ❑   2. The most damaging form of self-criticism is "shouldistic" thinking.

❑   ❑   3. Failure to reinforce yourself for small wins inadvertently reinforces self-criticism.

❑   ❑   4. Being a compulsive pleaser is a misguided way to eliminate criticism.

❑   ❑   5. Self-criticism fosters procrastination.

❑   ❑   6. Guilt is a good type of self-criticism.

❑   ❑   7. Unfair criticism from a lover may stem from high anxiety.

YES	NO	
☐	☐	8. Kids quickly learn to give themselves positive strokes versus negative pokes.
☐	☐	9. Advice-giving is frequently a way to control, manipulate or criticize.
☐	☐	10. Criticizing co-workers or loved ones helps strengthen their self-esteem.
☐	☐	11. Complaining about weaknesses of the opposite sex is an indirect way to reduce self-criticism.
☐	☐	12. A common form of self-blame is made plain by a lack of confidence in our own brains.

ANSWERS AND DISCUSSION

1. *Yes.* Self-criticism unmotivates you by discouraging any new actions that may give a healthy refill to your low self-esteem.

2. *Yes.* Believing that you "should" be different than you are can keep you stuck in the rut of bad habits spinning your wheels interminably.

3. *Yes.* Baby steps must be taken to reach big goals. Immediate self-reinforcement following small successes is required to maintain change momentum and reduce self-criticisms.

4. *Yes.* Fear of disapproval makes you please too much. Pleasing too much to receive positive strokes lowers self-esteem and independent thinking.

5. *Yes.*   Self-criticism and procrastination are a two-way street. Self-criticism makes you afraid to venture into the unknown. Failure to make good decisions or stick with them fosters self-criticism too.

6. *No.*   Not usually. Guilt usually causes self-flagellation which leads to stagnation. The guilt of hurting someone else, which may be unavoidable when you change, keeps you running away from being who you are.

7. *Yes.*   Blaming is a symptom of high anxiety. Typically, your lover is venting the poisonous negative thoughts and emotions that have been trapped inside for too long.

8. *No.*   Children look to parents for a healthy role model of self-stroking. Many parents don't provide one.

9. *Yes.*   Tasty advice stays on the vine when you think an advisor is trying to control your behavior. Or you may stop listening to great advice because you fault yourself for not coming up with the ideas first.

10. *No.*   Critical barbs feel rejecting and stick in our minds long after the incident is forgotten. Accurate, timely and specific negative feedback does foster growth. Few of us know how to give such helpful feedback.

11. *Yes.*   Criticizing the opposite sex is one way to temporarily displace self-criticism. It is a way of

blaming a group of people for a wrongdoing, and reassuring ourselves that we cannot be controlled by them.

12.   *Yes.*   The brightest people I know judge themselves too "dumb" to understand how change works. Viewing yourself as a good "thinker" keeps you seeking creative solutions to difficult problems.

Self-criticism is the result of fearing change. The less you change, the more often you will use yourself as a convenient target of criticism.

Fears stem from the universal fear of change. There are frustrations inherent in every change stage, including coping productively with the fear of success. Fears are like stepping-stones across a wide river that you must master one at a time to stay dry.

Ironically, self-criticism will cause you to close your eyes when you are trying to cross the river, which will make it impossible for you to see what lies ahead of you. You can't move forward and blame yourself at the same time for tripping up and getting wet.

The more you self-criticize, the more you are resisting positive changes. (Beware of criticizing yourself for being self-critical though). In reverse, the more you change the more you will force yourself to put an end to the bad habit of self-criticism.

Self-blame is a wicked thing. I want to tell you how the sultry crooning of self-criticism can beguile you to fight against changes that would prove good for you.

Yes, I know. Everyone is a self-critic. But negative thoughts just unravel your self-esteem and prevent you from changing. Today is a good day to put a halt to damaging your self-esteem via self-criticism.

PUTTING A HALT TO SELF-CRITICISM

Within you lives a fork-tongued, smooth-talking salesman. All gussied up in a pin-stripped suit, he lurks behind every thought just waiting to latch onto a loose mental thread of weakened character so he can unravel your self-esteem — big-time.

What he is promising to sell you is a better character, something any self-respecting person can't afford to live without (or so we are told). What he is really selling you is that you're no good the way you are.

If you happen to stumble on the rugged road of life, he is right there commanding you to stay down, to save your energy rather than go on. He sells you on the idea of playing it safe if you know what's good for you. "Have no fear," he croons. "I will take care of everything. All you are required to do is take it easy and sign on the dotted line."

This honey-lipped, inner-enemy feeds on fear, insecurity and false hope. He tells you to steer clear of trying new things because you will screw them up. He reminds you of your second-class status in life, with a low growling, "Who do you think you are, anyway?"

This authoritative sounding demon-voice is as stifling as stale air. It chokes out your growth urges by hypnotizing you into focusing only on your weaknesses, and fooling you into forgetting about your strengths.

This little voice is barely audible, but it drones on nonstop about one kind of dread or another. "Trust me," this salesman coos beguilingly, "for I'm only trying to help you." He helps you, all right — to stay stuck, going nowhere full tilt most of your life. Self-criticism is the real name of the salesman, the enemy alien who lives within you.

Self-criticism unmotivates you by discouraging any new actions that may give a healthy refill to your low self-esteem. Plus, it keeps you doing the very same things you despise having done in the first place.

We mortals seem to think we have to take a hefty dose of criticism every day. Our reasoning runs like this: "How can I become a better person with a stronger character if I don't take a critical look at myself now and again?" But negative self-analysis most always backfires by focusing the limelight on what you don't do well and pushing into the shadows what you are capable of doing better.

Displeasers are those "looking out for number one," sly charismatic people who are the users in the world but feel guiltless. They alone are the weak people who could benefit from walloping self-criticism. Not you, and not me. But it never crosses displeasers minds that they might be in the wrong or that they have a character flaw that needs correcting.

Displeasers who should criticize themselves don't, and pleasers who should eat lightly of self-blame gorge themselves on it.

Many of us are criticism-bingers. When we make a mistake or suffer a set back we put our self-esteem up against the wall, blindfold the spunky child-self who says we're great and let the inner enemy take aim and fire away.

Sooner or later all good people get fed up with stuffing themselves full of all sorts of put-downs. When we are bloated and ready to burst at our seams, we dump the whole mess on some passerby, usually someone we love. Verbal self-abusers turn the same criticisms used on their own psyche to other people.

Many people use self-criticism as a defensive shield against hearing others. They beat you to the knockout punch by quickly spilling out the guts of their failures, in effect saying, "Hey, lay off buddy, I've already said 'Gotcha' to myself." But trying to admit all your faults before someone else has a chance to point them out not only keeps you distant in relationships, but traps you in an internal septic tank with no way out.

CHALLENGING SELF-CRITICAL SHOULDS THAT SHUT DOWN CHANGE

"Shoulds" shut down changes of every kind. They are a form of self-harassment that is logical sounding but emotionally damaging.

What are some of the common "shouldistic" self-criticisms that zap your self-esteem? Here are some typical anti-change criticisms:

I'M TOO WEAK.

Feel Free to Change: The walls of self-control were never built in one day. If you think you're too dependent to quit a job or an unhealthy relationship, think again.

Use Your Strengths: Usually people are trying to learn some basic values or life lessons by staying in bad situations. Stop putting your inner strength to the test all the time.

Claim Self-Acceptance: You must be really strong if you are going to tolerate such massive amounts of self-criticism and still survive.

Feel All Your Feelings: "I learn from all of my feelings."

I SHOULDN'T BE FEELING THIS WAY.

Feel Free to Change: Nothing makes you lose contact with life's excitement faster than being told your feelings are all wrong.

Use Your Strengths: All feelings ebb and flow and are okay and need to be accepted. Negative emotions are escalated by undue criticism.

Claim Self-Acceptance: Instead of critical self-talk, give yourself a little empathy and understanding.

Feel All Your Feelings: "I demand to be fully alive."

THIS SHOULD BE EASIER.

Feel Free to Change: What a mouthful. To assume that the things that were meant to be must come easily is pure hokum.

Use Your Strengths: Most successful people have been rejected time and again. Nurture your dreams.

Claim Self-Acceptance: Grit and persistence is necessary to overcome the self-doubts that plague you and keep you in the security of mediocre roles. Nurture yourself.

Feel All Your Feelings: "I do the difficult."

I SHOULD BE CONTENT WITH WHAT I'VE GOT.

Feel Free to Change: Why should you be feeling satisfied when you are feeling frustrated and discontented? You can't and shouldn't.

Use Your Strengths: Don't pressure yourself to feel happy when you are feeling frustrated. It will only add to your frustrations.

Claim Self-Acceptance: Use your discontent to fuel new goals. Challenge yourself to be thankful for what you've got, and still reach outward for more happiness.

Feel All Your Feelings: "I choose to pursue my goals even when I'm feeling bad."

I'M NOT DOING WELL ENOUGH.

Feel Free to Change: Maybe you could have done more or done it better, but you did what you could at the time.

Use Your Strengths: Nothing is wrong with a healthy self-reminder that you may wish to spend your time or talents more productively.

Claim Self-Acceptance: Poking viciously at yourself rarely helps if it makes you so tired you lie down and quit. Start correcting little things you have control over.

Feel All Your Feelings: "I explore my unique talents and gifts."

I'M TOO CONFUSED AND WISHY-WASHY.

Feel Free to Change: People who think they are stupid are some of the brightest and most conscientious folks around.

Use Your Strengths: Don't weigh out your decisions so carefully on the scales of justice that you never decide. You will never have enough facts.

Claim Self-Acceptance: Don't delay taking risks today. Follow your hunches and head toward the finish line. Act smart, especially when you are feeling dumb.

Feel All Your Feelings: "I intend to be at my best."

IT'S ALL MY FAULT.

Feel Free to Change: Little kids believe they cause the sun to rise, birds to die and their parents to love and want them or reject them.

Use Your Strengths: All events are not causally related to your actions. Learn to let criticisms roll off your back.

Claim Self-Acceptance: Learn to judge better which painful events are random in your life, and which events you have some responsibility to correct.

Feel All Your Feelings: "I feel free to be who I am even when I'm disapproved of."

I SHOULD HAVE KNOWN BETTER.

Feel Free to Change: So okay, you think everybody has a crystal ball, right? Many painful events cannot be predicted.

Use Your Strengths: There is no way for you to predict what will happen with a new relationship or a new job opportunity or anything else that will happen in the future.

Claim Self-Acceptance: Start paying closer attention to the patterns in your behavior that do sabotage your success.

Feel All Your Feelings: "I am important and worthwhile no matter what you think of me."

I SHOULD BE MORE UNDERSTANDING.

Feel Free to Change: Why should you be more understanding when you are hurting inside?

Use Your Strengths: Sometimes it makes sense to instead feel sorry for yourself for awhile. Or, use anger in a helpful way to clear the path to a better understanding.

Claim Self-Acceptance: You will feel more understanding and tolerant when you are feeling confident again. Use positive strokes to feel better.

Feel All Your Feelings: "I find ways to fit in just as I am."

Self-criticisms sound exceptionally rational. They sweet-talk you into believing they are needed to keep you safe from harm.

Self-criticism does NOT HELP you to:

✔ Build a stronger character,

✔ Nor motivate you onward and upward.

✔ It doesn't help you steer clear of immoral things,

✔ Nor protect you from future catastrophes.

Some of us normal neurotics, for many non-normal reasons, contend that a thorough mental thrashing every so often purifies the soul, and self-beatings are a good moral strategy to stay on the straight and narrow and steer clear of sin.

Although self-criticism isn't a sin, it won't get you into heaven either. In fact, self-criticism is an infraction of the mental law that says loving thoughts are more effective than negative ones in rebuilding the self.

Remember, a positive change in attitude will encourage you to unfold who you are for the remainder of your life journey.

How To Stop Self-Criticisms From Getting You Down

Unrestricted self-blame results in a state of mind in which you falsely believe that your worst negative thoughts about yourself are true.

The outcome is always the same — you stop acting assertively in your own best interests because "nothing good or worthwhile will happen anyway." And your life becomes your worse nightmare.

How can you free yourself from unhelpful self-criticism? In doing so, you will march strongly on the path you choose for yourself in life.

1. SAY EVERY CRITICISM OUT LOUD TO YOURSELF.

To Stop Criticizing: Many self-criticisms are sneaky and subvocal. Listening to your inner voices is not whacky. When you are feeling depressed or edgy, listen carefully and put words to what you are feeling.

Start Stroking Your Strengths: The first step toward conquering an enemy is to catch the culprit red-handed.

2. FIGHT THE SELF-CRITICISMS.

To Stop Criticizing: Vocalize persuasive arguments about why the self-criticism is a bunch of hogwash. After all, you're being criticized up and down, so why not get a few good shots in yourself. If you hear, "Who do you think you are?" respond with, "Other people I know have done it, so get off my back."

Start Stroking Your Strengths: The second step toward conquering an enemy is to start fighting back.

3. GET REALISTIC.

To Stop Criticizing: Stick to your goals. If you find yourself entertaining put-downs about a lack — lack of exercise, lack of eating control or lack of religious observances — remind yourself of what you are doing to reach your goals. Your efforts don't need to result in perfect outcomes.

Start Stroking Your Strengths: The third step toward conquering an enemy is to remind yourself that although you aren't perfect, you can still prevail.

4. LISTEN TO CRITICISMS DIRECTED AT YOU DEFENSELESSLY.

To Stop Criticizing: Granted, this technique is easier said than done, but it is worth the effort when you are faced with blaming statements directed at you. Many criticisms are just projections of self-inadequacies. Hearing someone say, "You never listen to me," is changed quite a bit when you hear, "I never listen to me either."

Start Stroking Your Strengths: The fourth step toward conquering an enemy is to admit you aren't the center of the universe.

5. WHEN YOU ARE ANGRY TAKE THE TIME TO THINK BEFORE YOU SPEAK.

To Stop Criticizing: Adult children of self-criticizers can repeat word-for-word the worst things their parents and enemies have said about them. Is it really worth it to say some things in the heat of the moment that will affect you or those you love for years?

Start Stroking Your Strengths: The fifth step toward conquering an enemy is to use anger responsibly, and not as an excuse to say unkind words meant to maim.

6. THROW A PITY-PARTY FOR YOURSELF.

To Stop Criticizing: Really exaggerate your self-criticisms when you are feeling low. Add fuel to the fire by making up outlandish lies about yourself to the point of laughing at the ridiculousness of it all.

Start Stroking Your Strengths: The sixth step toward conquering an enemy is to discard false accusations through the use of humor.

7. CONTRAST EVERY SELF-CRITICISM WITH AN EQUALLY BALANCED SELF-PROCLAMATION.

To Stop Criticizing: If you have a heyday with yourself getting your own goat, try countering every negative thought with a positive one. Rest assured more negative thoughts will result, but you will know better who the real enemy happens to be.

Start Stroking Your Strengths: The seventh step toward conquering an enemy is to put the creep on alert that you aren't going to take it anymore.

8. SAY, "THAT'S ENOUGH... I REALLY FEEL HURT," WHEN YOUR PARTNER HAS GONE TOO FAR AND TRESPASSED INTO YOUR PRIVATE ZONE.

To Stop Criticizing: Criticism isn't as easy to take as it is to dish out. Our partners can usually hit us where it hurts most. By yelling "foul" to low blows, you will encourage caring partners to stand back and take account of their actions.

Start Stroking Your Strengths: The eighth step toward conquering an enemy is to speak openly of your hurt and expect kindness in return.

9. HANDLE A SNAKE IN THE GRASS LIKE IT'S POISONOUS.

To Stop Criticizing: Self-criticizers are notorious for accepting any negative jabs directed their way. Say "No" to intense criticisms that are meant to puncture your ego and poison your will. Don't mince words. Fight back.

Start Stroking Your Strengths: The ninth step toward conquering an enemy is to boldly speak of the good things you have brought to the relationship.

10. TAKE TIME TO LICK YOUR WOUNDS AND COLLECT YOUR SELF-ESTEEM.

To Stop Criticizing: Go ahead and put your mental energy elsewhere — into jogging, aerobics, reading, music, meditation or prayer. You may not have full concentration to devote to the task, but it will help you work off a little of the frustration that is pulling you down.

Start Stroking Your Strengths: The tenth step toward conquering an enemy is to keep stroking your strengths when you are under attack.

Remember, you're not alone on the self-criticism treadmill. It effects every conscientious person.

But blowing your circuits with a lot of self-derisive noise just makes the computer screen go blank and distracts you from using your strengths and focusing on your goals.

MINDPLAY:
HOW HAVE I CHANGED
IN SPITE OF MY OWN RESISTANCES?

Have you ever accomplished changes without thinking much about them? Did you consider the changes a stroke of good luck?

Let's find out how you have been able to change, in spite of disapproval, self-criticism, few strokes, negative self-opinions, no support, depression and little advice.

➤ WHAT TICKS ME OFF ENOUGH TO START CHANGING IS:

➤ HOW I KEEP GOING WHEN I WOULD RATHER GIVE UP IS:

➤ CHANGES EASIEST FOR ME TO MAKE HAVE BEEN:

➤ THE MOST PROFOUND CHANGES I'VE EVER ACHIEVED HAVE BEEN:

➤ ADVICE THAT HAS HELPED ME TO CHANGE THE MOST HAS BEEN:

➤ MY PARENT'S ADVICE THAT HAS PROVEN INVALUABLE TO ME IS:

INTER PLAY:

Are you taking responsibility for your happiness? Get mad enough to start changing. Don't wait to be loved to begin loving yourself.

Take Positive Action Even When You Are Feeling Afraid: Self-acceptance doesn't come from outside, but from inside of yourself. No one can love you like you can love yourself.

Are You Still Waiting for Santa Claus to Come? Why wait any longer? Put a stop to waiting and take positive action today. Don't delay. Start today.

You Can Use Good Advice to Get What You Want: You can get what you want if you turn down self-criticisms. Change-experts keep their radar tuned to any helpful person, information or advice that can help them take more responsibility for their own happiness.

Anger Can Motivate You to Become More Open to Change: Anger is an extremely helpful and valuable emotion when you use it to motivate difficult changes. When you feel angry or mistreated, go back to your original goals and pursue them with renewed vigor.

Just because you are an experienced adult, doesn't mean that you know everything, and needn't choose change. Allow yourself the grown-up pleasures of growth.

SIX REASONS WHY ADULTS RESIST CHANGES THAT ARE GOOD FOR THEM

Freedom and refusal to change are often confused in the subconscious mind. When you perceive others trying to influence you, you may resist whatever idea is being presented. This is why so many times good advice falls on deaf ears.

I want to explain to you how resisting change is a way you try to reassure yourself that your thoughts, decisions and moods are under your own direction — not someone else's.

The Resister Reaction goes like this:

1. "If you want me to...

2. Then I must refuse

3. To prove to myself

4. That you have no undue influence over me."

Do you confuse freedom with refusing to change?

High self-esteemers prefer to focus on ways to increase self-control by choosing to change! Always remember: Your changes are your own to make. No one suffers as much from sitting in your chair as you do.

Here are six reasons you may resist change without thinking much about the real underlying issues:

1. TO PROVE YOU ARE INDEPENDENT OF OTHERS' CONTROL.

The Control Issue: You fear becoming too dependent on a caregiver. You prefer a sense of healthy separateness and identity.

Defeat Self-Criticism: Don't criticize yourself for feeling bad, worthless or weak. You will need more support at certain times. Getting help or leaning into a relationship is not a sign of weakness.

Choose Your Own Changes: Be a careful listener and put caring advice to good use. Healthy dependency means knowing that you have the greatest control over yourself, less control over others and the least control over outside situations.

Value Self-Control: "My personality is uniquely my own."

2. TO PROVE YOU CANNOT BE CONTROLLED BY ANGER.

The Control Issue: You fear irresolvable conflicts. You prefer cooperation, not power plays meant to frighten you into compliance.

Defeat Self-Criticism: Don't use self-criticism to dissipate anger. Express your anger assertively right to the source. Don't be afraid of the constructive forces of anger.

Choose Your Own Changes: Learn that you do not need to fear the anger of others. Stop accumulating resentments and start improving your intimate relationships. Feel free to please yourself and others equally.

Value Self-Control: "My helpful anger is my own."

3. TO PROVE YOUR WAY IS THE BEST WAY TO SOLVE PROBLEMS.

The Control Issue: You fear not having answers to every problem. You prefer to know what to do.

Defeat Self-Criticism: Don't start blaming yourself when you run low on positive strokes. Self-criticism can be an internal way you bathe yourself in negative strokes when positive strokes have dried up.

Choose Your Own Changes: Stop viewing either negative or positive feedback as threatening. Sift through both types of strokes. Use tips that help you the most.

Value Self-Control: "My wisdom is my own."

4. TO PROVE YOU SHOULDN'T HAVE TO BE SUCCESSFUL TO BE ACCEPTABLE.

The Control Issue: You fear that you aren't acceptable if you aren't successful. You prefer to be liked and like yourself with no strings attached.

Defeat Self-Criticism: Don't start blaming yourself when you fail to succeed on the first try. Find ways to accept yourself as a winner.

Choose Your Own Changes: Don't be so pressured to be the best you lose track of your own goals. Think about what you want to change and set out to change it even when you don't have much support.

Value Self-Control: "My success and self-esteem are my own."

5. TO PROVE YOU ARE LOVABLE JUST AS YOU ARE.

The Control Issue: You fear that you aren't lovable when you meet with disapproval. You prefer to be approved of and judged worthwhile.

Defeat Self-Criticism: Don't stop loving or respecting yourself when you have been rejected. When you think you are unaccepted or unloved, you will resist making changes that are good for you. Separate feeling loved from making tough changes.

Choose Your Own Changes: Behave in loving ways even when you don't want to. Make your actions match your promises. Love yourself no matter what.

Value Self-Control: "My good decisions are my own."

6. TO PROVE YOU ARE NOT RESPONSIBLE FOR OTHERS' HAPPINESS.

The Control Issue: You fear you must change to make others happy. You prefer to change to make yourself happy.

Defeat Self-Criticism: Don't rev up the blame when you don't feel okay, important or unconditionally loved. You are okay no matter what lies are told about you — or you tell yourself.

Choose Your Own Changes: Refuse to please others by being who you aren't. Feel self-accepting when you are unaccepted by loved ones. Drop facades, rigid roles and enjoy learning more about who you are inside.

Value Self-Control: "My happiness is my own."

Let go of trying to control others or fight against being controlled — in favor of learning to control your own mind.

Grab back control of your own happiness.

TAKING RESPONSIBILITY FOR YOUR HAPPINESS

Growth is speeded up when you refurbish strengths that have been painted over with the bright red color of rampant self-criticism.

Treat yourself to some self-respect. Take responsibility for your happiness. Accept that there is never a right time to change. Don't wait for the perfect time or until you have explored every option.

Why wait any longer for self-acceptance? Begin again the process of renewing self-respect by setting up communication lines to your inner self. Cooperation between different parts of your personality will radically improve your chances for success.

How should you focus for success? Here are eight key guidelines for you to consider:

1. BE UNWILLING TO BE MENTALLY LAZY.

Respect Yourself: Self-respect requires you to think actively about the quality of your life.

Focus For Success: Set limits to your suffering and seek reasons for your unhappiness. Refuse to let negative feelings or thoughts go on too long before you take corrective action.

Enjoy Being Responsible: Self-esteem is the unwillingness to suffer unproductively.

2. TREAT ALL YOUR FEELINGS AS WORTHWHILE.

Respect Yourself: Self-respect requires that you treat all of your feelings as right, informative and important to analyze.

Focus For Success: Don't discriminate against any emotion, whether you are feeling fear, sorrow, pleasure, anger or sexuality. Embrace your feelings caringly, and don't avoid them.

Enjoy Being Responsible: Self-esteem is dependent on your working cooperatively with all of your emotions.

3. FOCUS INTERNALLY TO FEEL IMPORTANT.

Respect Yourself: Self-respect requires that you fix your life internally and stop trying to quick-fix your life externally.

Focus For Success: Treat your mind like a precious sanctuary. Try to prayerfully fill your mind with permissions, especially when you feel discouraged or defeated.

Enjoy Being Responsible: Self-esteem is operating in the inner world of emotions and the outer world of action.

4. USE GOAL PLANNING TO SUCCEED.

Respect Yourself: Self-respect requires that you set heartfelt goals.

Focus For Success: Desired goals improve your feelings of self-acceptance, self-control and competence during normal or traumatic times.

Enjoy Being Responsible: Self-esteem has to be earned. It's not free.

5. INSIST ON HAPPINESS.

Respect Yourself: Self-respect requires that you insist on your right to be happy.

Focus For Success: Admit that your pain is a natural part of living. Make your satisfaction more important than materialism. Permit a deep, abiding inner respect for your own values and needs.

Enjoy Being Responsible: Self-esteem is expressing thankfulness for your special gifts.

6. BE DISCIPLINED INSTEAD OF DISTRACTED.

Respect Yourself: Self-respect requires that you exert firm discipline over any distractions that keep you from steadfastly moving toward your cherished goals.

Focus For Success: You must actively fight off negative beliefs or moods that bring you down and make you give up hope. Seek to be in control of your own time, goals and energies. Focus your mental energies on excellence.

Enjoy Being Responsible: Self-esteem is appreciating that your energies are limited and that you must protect them.

7. MAKE CONSISTENT MORAL ACTIONS COME FIRST.

Respect Yourself: Self-respect requires that your behavior and daily actions be of the highest caliber to reflect the moral principles to which you entrust your destiny.

Focus For Success: Realize that your inner core of self-love connects you with God. Expect to be treated with respect, and don't be afraid to enter into healthy conflicts.

Enjoy Being Responsible: Self-esteem requires that you do what's right for everyone, instead of what is best for only one person.

8. BALANCE THE PARADOX OF SELFISHNESS/SELFLESSNESS.

Respect Yourself: Self-respect requires that you balance selfishness and selflessness.

Focus For Success: The more you are able to love yourself, the more you are able to share love with others and be empathetically accepting of all human struggles.

Enjoy Being Responsible: Self-esteem means you balance giving with receiving.

Liking yourself is a learned skill. It's not something that magically occurs. Remember, your life is for struggle and celebration!

The opposite of pleasure is the anger and frustration that is brought about by non-change. Lowering frustration makes you demand more pleasure, and makes you insist that problems be resolved and not repeated.

The fear of change resides underneath all of your change resistances. And the way you have learned to deal with the fear of change is by getting trapped in controlling struggles — or power plays — to mask the fear.

Don't indirectly express your anger by resisting change. Resisting change is never a good way to express your frustrations. You can improve your self-worth by mastering negative emotions, busting free from self-prejudices and being free to go ahead and learn what you most need to know.

Are you involved in power plays that are sapping your energy?

They are a common way the fear of change is played out.

BREAKING FREE OF POWER PLAYS

Power plays at home or work are a common way to resist change.

Unfortunately, you can get so wrapped up in the ensuing struggle that you forget to focus on your goals, fail to build your self-esteem or procrastinate in making tough choices that would be really good for you.

The Power Play Stage is the "terrible twos" stage that every good romantic relationship must go through.

Don't get me wrong. Power plays can be vicious. The recipe for the destruction of a relationship is easy to follow: Take several pounds of insecurity, add misunderstandings and resentment, throw in a few threats of abandonment, treat the antagonist like he or she doesn't exist and wait until the concoction boils over and messes up the relationship.

A power play seeks to answer one crucial question: "Do you want me for who I am, or do you just want somebody?"

Here are eight ways to break free of power plays at home or work:

1. STICK TO THE ISSUE AT HAND AS BEST YOU CAN.

Be Powerful: Don't throw in the kitchen sink and unload resentments from years past. Do not allow anxiety to run your life. Although it is natural to throw in all the things that worry you the most — don't do it!

Use Anger Assertively: Steer yourself back on track when you stray.

2. BE HONEST ABOUT YOUR PART IN THE POWER STRUGGLE.

Be Powerful: Proving that you are an innocent bystander proves nothing. Stop trying to find fault, or pick at every relationship blemish until it bleeds. Correct your own crude ways of fighting unfairly.

Use Anger Assertively: Don't harp at yourself for how stupid you are for being embroiled in a difficult relationship.

3. STOP SHORT OF INTERNALIZING HARSH CRITICISMS.

Be Powerful: Easier said than done, I realize. Always remind yourself that the critical comments that spew forth from a volcano of anger are typically illogical.

Use Anger Assertively: Apologize for hurtful words you've said but would never have said had you been feeling confident.

4. REFUSE TO DEFEND THE MISTAKES YOU MAKE.

Be Powerful: Refuse to pay a guilt tax for the mistakes you make. Doing so will keep you making the same mistakes over and over again. Instead, take responsibility for your blunders without coming to your own defense.

Use Anger Assertively: Correct your mistakes as quickly as you can.

5. DON'T MAKE A MOUNTAIN OUT OF A MOLE HILL.

Be Powerful: Trust always dissipates rapidly during power struggles. You will assume the worst about the antagonist's motives, and a few of your psychological concoctions might even be right. So?

Use Anger Assertively: Be realistic about the motives of your confidant.

6. ASSUAGE YOUR HURT FEELINGS BUT DON'T YOU POUT!

Be Powerful: Well, pout a little if you must. Avoid believing that you cannot get what you want during power plays. Ask directly for a small concession that may break the distancing cycle.

Use Anger Assertively: Keep responding competently, and don't betray the relationship.

7. ONLY DEAL IN VISUALS.

Be Powerful: Internally analyze what sets off your insecurity alarm. Always deal with observable actions instead of accusations. For example, it may not mean anything when someone looks out the window when they are speaking to you. Many problems have nothing to do with you.

Use Anger Assertively: Don't use logic to spurn closeness.

8. ASSUME ANY PERSON IS CAPABLE OF CHANGE.

Be Powerful: There are no victims! In this country we all have the opportunity to decide just what kind of life we are going to live. Refuse to believe otherwise.

Use Anger Assertively: Help yourself to a bunch of new changes.

Keep an open attitude toward change.

PERMIT YOURSELF THE FREEDOM TO BE WHO YOU ARE

Here are ten change freedoms that you have no matter how controlled you feel by others' terrible moods or actions.

✔ **YOUR UNIQUE PERSONALITY IS YOUR OWN.**

✔ **YOUR HELPFUL ANGER IS YOUR OWN.**

✔ **YOUR GOALS ARE YOUR OWN.**

✔ **YOUR ABILITY TO FOCUS IS YOUR OWN.**

✔ **YOUR HAPPINESS IS YOUR OWN.**

✔ **YOUR SUCCESSES ARE YOUR OWN.**

✔ **YOUR WISDOM IS YOUR OWN.**

✔ **YOUR SELF-ESTEEM IS YOUR OWN.**

✔ **YOUR GOOD DECISIONS ARE YOUR OWN.**

✔ **YOUR DESIRE TO LEARN NEW THINGS IS YOUR OWN.**

Remember these freedoms when you are feeling like a prisoner who "should" change to feel okay.

Are you resisting being successful by not reinforcing small steps to success? The chapter counterpoint asks just this question.

COUNTERPOINT:

"DO PEOPLE EVER RESIST BEING SUCCESSFUL?"

All the time. Change-experts choose their own changes consciously. This is why they go toe-to-toe with the fear of success. How can you tell if you are resisting success?

★ *You are resisting success when you forget your choices are your own to make.* Nobody can really force you to be different than you are. Make your choices count for more.

★ *You are accepting success when you let changes add more independence to your life.* You can't really be controlled by others forever. Take command of your destiny by allowing yourself to grow and change.

★ *You are resisting success when you forget you are okay whether or not you choose to change.* It's all a trick of magic. You are worthwhile when you allow yourself to grow and change — and when you don't.

★ *You are accepting success when change is thought of as something different from being loved.* Confidence comes from tackling the challenges of change. Your ability to love yourself is not dependent upon who chooses to love you.

★ *You are resisting success when you push yourself too hard and too fast to change.* Start taking all the time you need to change. Don't pressure yourself if you are having trouble recognizing your progress.

★ *You are accepting success when you take responsibility for painful feelings.* Pain is the flip side of happiness. Protect your prized relationships by making them pleasurable.

★ *You are resisting success when you fail to learn something new from frustrations.* Establish a goal to learn something new about yourself from each frustrating person or situation — and chances are that you will.

★ *You are accepting success when you HAVE HOPE — even when you don't.* Success can be deceptive. You might have a breakthrough right at the point that you think you should quit.

★ *You are resisting success when you don't apply every bit of good advice you can.* Search for your own answers and use answers from every source. There are no better answers to be found — bar none.

★ *You are accepting success when you make self-esteem an integral part of your daily life.* Make change a welcome part of your daily life to deflate self-criticisms.

★ *You are resisting success when you deceptively underestimate your progress.* Changers consistently underestimate their progress. One benefit of advisors is to remind you of your progress.

★ *You are in double-jeopardy when you have made the most progress.* Exiting the change process is not necessarily a sign of defeat. You may just be afraid of being so successful.

In the next chapter, I am going challenge you to make a commitment to yourself through using heartfelt goals.

4

USING GOALS
TO SUCCEED

"Happiness, wealth, and success are by-products
of having a purpose in life and setting
specific goals to carry out that purpose."

Dr. Denis Waitley, *Being The Best*,
Oliver-Nelson Books, 1987, p. 119.

BEING THE BEST
MEANS BEING WHO YOU REALLY ARE

If you haven't established your own goals, then chances are
that you are helping ambitious people achieve their goals. There
is no comfortable fence post to sit on when it comes to setting
goals.

The facts: Having goals creates happiness and independence, while refusing to set goals results in resentment and dependence. If you really want to be happy, you must take yourself seriously by setting goals.

Do you let yourself be ambitious without self-censure? Are you trying to be your best, or are you trying too hard to be what a difficult person wants you to be? Ambitious people set ambitious goals to challenge themselves.

Goals help protect and focus your self-esteem. How? The single best way to get rid of negative emotions is to review your goals when you are frustrated. The second way is to take positive steps to implement them to burn off resentment.

Happiness means finding ways to become more comfortable with the ambitious side of your personality.

THE AMBITION QUIZ

How's your competitive edge lately? Razor-sharp or deadly dull? How can you tell if you are competitive enough or too aggressive when it comes to going after what you want?

Let's check how ambitious and goal-focused you are with the following quiz:

YES	NO	
☐	☐	1. Do you feel left out in the cold when someone is promoted over you at work?
☐	☐	2. Do you find it pleasurable to be around physically attractive people at a party?
☐	☐	3. As a parent, do you lose sleep when your child's academic or sports motivation begins slipping?
☐	☐	4. Do you compare your income level to others in your profession?

YES	NO	
❑	❑	5. Does it bug you when a car you are trying to pass surges ahead of you on the freeway?
❑	❑	6. Do your feathers get ruffled when you are proven wrong about something?
❑	❑	7. Do you and your mate prefer being around happy couples and tend to avoid uptight ones?
❑	❑	8. Are you a careful listener to free advice, and do you think most unsolicited advice is valuable?
❑	❑	9. Are you willing to submit work projects when you know they are acceptable, but not up to your true ability level?
❑	❑	10. Do you regularly schedule time for your spiritual and emotional growth?

ANSWERS AND DISCUSSION

The answers below are based on what a person with ideal competitive and ambition drives might say. If you would like to improve your drive — shoot for these attitudes:

1. *No.* I certainly would be frustrated that my work efforts have gone unrewarded and unnoticed, but it's up to me to obtain corrective feedback about what happened to stack the deck against me.

2. *Yes.* I enjoy signs of good health and emotional well-being. It never does me any good to compare my looks to another's.

3.   *No.*   When my child takes a ride down a demotivational slide I'm concerned, but my feeling of being a good-enough parent is not directly linked to a youngster's school performance.

4.   *No.*   I choose to improve my income by becoming an indispensable worker to my employer.

5.   *No.*   Sure, sometimes I get peeved when people don't drive more intelligently, but my attention is riveted on the educational tapes playing in my cassette, planning tomorrow or debriefing from a busy day.

6.   *No.*   It may hurt to be reminded that I'm not perfect, but I'm willing to swallow my pride in order to learn from my mistakes, grow and change.

7.   *Yes.*   Every partnership has disagreements and tough times, but we don't need to adopt a couple-in-trouble to prove just how good we've got it.

8.   *Yes.*   If somebody has a suggestion for me, even if it is one I've heard a thousand times before, I wonder if this may be the time to take it seriously.

9.   *No.*   In a pinch I might be forced to submit inferior work, but I'm never comfortable compromising my work values, or slacking off when it hurts the company.

10. *Yes.*   Self-improvement will always be a strong value of mine.

Avid competitors get the biggest charge from competing against themselves. It's always the best game in town!

Could you hate setting goals because you are afraid to make such a serious commitment to your inner self and your outer potential for success? Could that be true for you?

The reasons for the failure to set ambitious goals?

✔ The fear of commitment

✔ Can make you refuse to set sensible goals.

✔ The fear of failure or success

✔ Can make you avoid the stress of being successful.

What is your change bottom line? Are you willing to do anything ethical to succeed? High self-esteemers solve many problems by setting clear goals.

Monitor your feelings as you read the accompanying change contract.

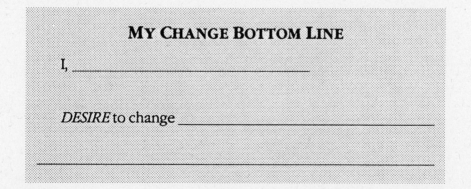

MY CHANGE BOTTOM LINE

I, _____

DESIRE to change _____

_____

Into (the want) _____

_____

by _____. (i.e. "Change my depression into

self-esteem by Dec. 15, 19___")

Despite these odds that stand against me

_____

_____

_____

   (e.g. "A boring job and lack of education.")

   BECAUSE

_____

_____

_____

   (e.g. "I'm tired of being frustrated by lack of money.")

   I hereby vow to use every available resource at my disposal for change, and to remain open to hidden resources. I vow to heal resentments and replace them with satisfactions, genuineness and love.

I request my subconscious mind to be my ally, to stand by me through successful days and tremendous failures, and to come to my aid in unexpected ways when I need encouragement to get up and get going again.

Should I decide to quit changing or fail "accidentally on purpose," I will not blame myself. Nor will I use any excuse or alibi to justify my own disappointment in acting out a script that is not suited to my present life.

I realize that there are no change guarantees, and that change treats every person equally, regardless of race, family heritage, income, intelligence, gender, sexual or cultural issues. Thereby, I give up any special privileges to be or not be successful based upon these issues, and I set about the hard work of getting what I want using my best skills.

Furthermore, I shall do whatever is necessary to confront and to break out of any and all failure patterns in order to be successful. When I am successful, I will express appreciation for the accomplishments and gladly accept recognition from myself and others for my wins.

I vow to do whatever is necessary to achieve my independence and be happy.

Signed:_____

Dated:_____

Witnessed:_____

Do you resist signing on the dotted line, given the no-fault clause? Do you show the same resistance when signing for a loan for a car, a home or a boat?

INTER PLAY:

The fear of commitment will stop you from making warm attachments. Even to yourself! Goals are a key way to love, express and respect yourself.

Your Selfishness and "Selfulness" Is Important: Are you being mindful of your inner self's needs? Keeping your goals forefront in your mind removes many frustrations, power plays and ploys of difficult people.

Goallessness Leads to Frustration and Failure: Failure to set goals results from the fear of making a commitment to a single course of action that will exclude alternative choices.

Is the Fear of Failure Controlling You? You can count on succeeding when you apply your mental energy. Are you afraid of failing if you do focus your energies? The fear of change explains these phenomena.

Your Self-Esteem Is an Important Commitment: Your self-esteem is more important than any of your material possessions, yet you may treat objects more seriously than you treat your emotional needs.

Your Peace of Mind Is Important: The happier you are, the more you will be a healing force for others. Are you taking people along for the ride you'd rather be rid of?

You may need to struggle many months with where you want to go and what you want to do. The time is well spent since your goals dictate your future happiness.

MINDPLAY:
WHAT DO I WANT TO CHANGE MOST ABOUT MYSELF?

As a burgeoning change-expert, what would you most like to change about yourself if almost anything were possible?

➤ I'D LIKE TO MOST CHANGE ABOUT MYSELF:

➤ I'D NEXT LIKE TO CHANGE ABOUT MYSELF:

➤ LASTLY, I'D LIKE TO CHANGE ABOUT MYSELF:

[INTER] PLAY:

Leave out goals that other people contend you "should" want to change about your life. Concentrate on your desires for a change.

THE GOAL-SETTING ESSENTIALS: Remember these essentials of goal-setting so you can use them throughout your lifetime.

✔ **MAKE A COMMITMENT TO YOUR CHANGE GOALS.**

✔ **PERMIT YOURSELF TO MAKE NEW CHOICES.**

✔ **WRITE DOWN YOUR GOALS IN SPECIFIC TERMS.**

✔ **PLACE YOUR WRITTEN GOALS WHERE YOU CAN SEE THEM.**

✔ **JOT DOWN IDEAS DAILY TO MOVE FORWARD ON YOUR GOALS.**

✔ **REVIEW YOUR GOALS WHEN YOU ARE FEELING FRUSTRATED.**

✔ **REPEAT EACH STEP AS OFTEN AS NEEDED.**

Stop hedging your bets and risk feeling fully alive again. Enjoy your life knowing that your life is not a dress rehearsal for a bigger show.

Focus on your changes for a change! Find the time to find your mission.

Five negative results accrue from failing to identify your overriding purpose and goals in life.

The Negative Results Of Goallessness

These negative effects accrue when you don't carefully think about and set your goals, decide on your life mission and move toward the fulfillment of it:

1. LOW SELF-ESTEEM.

Set Your Own Goals: Goallessness makes you lose touch with who you are, and feel tense with the opposite sex. You will falsely believe that low self-esteem can't be altered and high self-esteem is a chore. You will feel lonely and resentful.

Commit Yourself to High Self-Esteem: "I permit myself to focus on my changes for a change."

PERMIT YOURSELF TO FOCUS ON YOUR CHANGES FOR A CHANGE!

2. SHOULDISTIC THINKING.

Set Your Own Goals: Goallessness will make you hound yourself with negative self-talk and feel angry that you can't live out your potentials. You will self-criticize, reject positive strokes and please others to a harmful extent.

Commit Yourself to High Self-Esteem: "I permit myself to think about what I most want."

PERMIT YOURSELF TO THINK ABOUT WHAT YOU MOST WANT!

3. DIFFICULT RELATIONSHIPS.

Set Your Own Goals: Goallessness makes for relationships at work or home that sadden and madden you. Your unsatisfactory romantic and career relationships will be founded more on security than self-expression. Failure patterns will repeat themselves and problems won't be resolved.

Commit Yourself to High Self-Esteem: "I permit myself the courage to decide on what I most want."

PERMIT YOURSELF THE COURAGE TO DECIDE ON WHAT YOU MOST WANT!

4. VICTIM VERSUS EXPERT THINKING.

Set Your Own Goals: Goallessness leads to complaining which replaces changing. You will feel trapped in your current lifestyle, and blame yourself for not getting anywhere. You will feel victimized and shun taking responsibility for your own happiness.

Commit Yourself to High Self-Esteem: "I permit myself goals that reflect my life mission."

PERMIT YOURSELF GOALS THAT REFLECT YOUR LIFE MISSION!

5. LACK OF SUCCESS.

Set Your Own Goals: Goallessness will cause you to be unable to focus on the contributions you most wish to make in your parenting, career and romantic life. You will also be unable to persist in the face of failure. Consistent success will escape you.

Commit Yourself to High Self-Esteem: "I permit myself to focus all my energies on just one goal at a time."

PERMIT YOURSELF TO FOCUS ALL YOUR ENERGIES ON JUST ONE GOAL AT A TIME!

Every significant change begins with a goal which is emotionally significant to you! Yet you've learned to hate setting goals because you are afraid of failure.

In the past, your changes have been outside of your control. That's where goals based on your life purpose come to the fore.

THE POSITIVE RESULTS OF GOALS

Taking time to carefully think about where you are and where you would like to go promotes these positive results in your life:

✔ **INSISTING ON HIGH SELF-ESTEEM.**

✔ **BEING IN CONTROL OF NEGATIVE THOUGHTS.**

✔ **FEELING INDEPENDENT OF OTHERS' NEGATIVE MOODS.**

✔ **CHOOSING TO BE IN CONTROL OF YOUR OWN FEELINGS.**

✔ **CLAIMING THE FREEDOM TO MAKE YOUR OWN DECISIONS.**

✔ **ACCEPTING AND EMBRACING SUCCESS.**

Being who you are and being the best you can be are essentially one and the same thing. Being the best is dependent on carefully selecting your own heartfelt goals that clearly reflect your life mission.

Without goals, change is possible but quite difficult and dreary. With goals, the sky is the limit and your happiness, excitement and self-control reign supreme.

MINDPLAY:

WHAT IS MY LIFE MISSION?

Time has a way of evaporating when you don't pay attention to the purpose of your life and of living. Please furrow your brow and think hard about these lifesaving questions.

➤ MY PURPOSE FOR BEING ALIVE IS:

➤ WHAT I WOULD LOVE TO CONTRIBUTE TO THE WORLD IS:

➤ IN EXCHANGE FOR TAKING UP SPACE ON THIS PLANET I PLAN TO:

➤ AS A CHILD I ALWAYS DREAMED ABOUT BEING:

➤ WHAT I SEEM TO HAVE A SPECIAL KNACK FOR IS:

➤ IF I DIE TODAY, I WOULD REGRET NOT HAVING DONE:

➤ I WOULD DESCRIBE MY HIGHER PURPOSE FOR LIVING AS:

INTER PLAY:

Take the serious time required to discover what you would really like to do. Let yourself THINK about what makes your life worth living.

Loss of Self: When you avoid making a commitment to a

higher purpose, you cannot be who you are or receive what you want. Pain-filled living results.

A Clear Pathway to Success: Goals will help you keep thinking straight in a crooked business and relationship world. Your success is guaranteed within a few years if you've taken the time to review your purpose and establish your goals based on that purpose.

Being Who You Really Are: When you pursue heartfelt goals, you are automatically required to strengthen your character. Facades will be dropped as you reclaim your inner strengths.

"Growing Down": Deeper feelings will surface as you strive to make your life count for more. You will "grow down" into a childlike sense of wonderment and appreciation.

Goal-setting to be your best is the surest route to greater happiness and satisfaction.

Only criticism-minded and mean-mouthed SHOULDISTIC thinking stands in your way. Overcome any "shoulds" that stop you from setting good goals.

OVERCOMING SHOULDISTIC THINKING TO SET GOOD GOALS

Negative emotions are more taxing than most of us care to disclose. Depression, anger, hurt and fear all can take their toll on your self-worth. The Catch 22: The more negative you are feeling without the benefit of goals, the less likely it is that you will feel up to setting good goals.

Ironically, the harder you try to get rid of negative emotions, the longer they tend to persist in your mental life. Self-worth is the process of removing negative labeling — those "shoulds" designed to restrict your emotions.

Self-worth is the fundamental sense of being a deserving human being no matter what emotion you are presently feeling.

It is an internal declaration to accept all feelings as equally important and to learn from each and every one of them.

All "should" messages are authoritarian commands. They come from your family's parent-to-child lectures that said, "You shouldn't be feeling that way. Stop (or change) how you are feeling right this instant."

But trying to stop how you're feeling interferes with accepting the emotion and using it to your best growth advantage. Plus, harsh lectures rarely work.

SHOULDISM is the coercive parent-to-adult way you scold and criticize yourself to move out of painful feelings. SHOULDISM results from a critical belief system that says, "I should be able to pull myself up by the bootstraps and stop feeling bad!"

There are four symptoms that accompany SHOULDISM:

Global Self-Condemnation: You have broad negative thoughts like "I never do anything right. Who would ever want anything to do with me?" You mercilessly pick yourself apart.

Angerphobia: You are afraid of your own anger and afraid that loved ones are fed up with you. You are withholding negative feedback for fear of hurting others. You assume that others are as critical of you as you are of them.

Depressive Memories: You recall your worst failures from the past and say things like, "Why don't I ever learn? Why does this always seem to happen to me?"

Self-Sabotage: You impulsively do things to try and soothe your pain but end up feeling worse. You may make a rash decision, back off from a good health habit or spout off when you should remain quiet.

Are you a SHOULDISTIC person? Here are ten common SHOULDS that must be contained to build better feelings of self-esteem.

I SHOULD FEEL MORE WORTHWHILE.

To Feel Better: Negative feelings attack self-worth.

Feel Free to Use Goals: Set your goal to feel what you do and learn from your feelings.

To Achieve Self-Change: "I'm worthwhile even when I'm not feeling that way."

I SHOULD KNOW WHAT TO DO.

To Feel Better: If you knew what to do, you would have gone ahead and done it.

Feel Free to Use Goals: Set your goal to find out what you need to know to accomplish your dreams.

To Achieve Self-Change: "I give myself plenty of time to learn and grow."

I SHOULD BE HAPPY.

To Feel Better: If you aren't happy, there is no use in pretending that you are.

Feel Free to Use Goals: Set your goal to feel happy some of the time and not worry about unexpected pain.

To Achieve Self-Change: "I should feel what I am feeling."

I SHOULD STOP FEELING SO SORRY FOR MYSELF.

To Feel Better: You're probably not spending enough time bemoaning the fact that life isn't treating you very kindly.

Feel Free to Use Goals: Set your goal to burn off frustrations by complaining and changing.

To Achieve Self-Change: "I'm sad that my feelings are out of my control."

I SHOULD GROW UP AND ACT MORE MATURE.

To Feel Better: You might be taking on too many responsibilities which are resulting in extra stress.

Feel Free to Use Goals: Set your goal to "grow down" and take care of your little kid needs.

To Achieve Self-Change: "I am grown up and do not always have to make good choices."

I SHOULD STOP PROCRASTINATING.

To Feel Better: Maybe you are wisely putting off a decision until you can more thoroughly study the dynamics of the situation.

Feel Free to Use Goals: Set you goal to find out what is stopping you from making a decision or carrying out a goal.

To Achieve Self-Change: "I'll make the decision later at a time best for me."

I SHOULD HAVE MORE WILLPOWER.

To Feel Better: You may need more nurturing and support to acquire the willpower.

Feel Free to Use Goals: Set your goal to show off your strengths.

To Achieve Self-Change: "I'll be good to myself even when I feel undeserving of good treatment."

I SHOULD BE FEELING SOMETHING DIFFERENT.

To Feel Better: Vulnerable feelings are never right or wrong, good or bad.

Feel Free to Use Goals: Set your goal to be alive, open to life and fully feeling.

To Achieve Self-Change: "I'm not going to pressure myself to feel any differently for awhile."

I SHOULD BE MORE FORGIVING.

To Feel Better: You have a right to be fully angry and resentful even over small issues.

Feel Free to Use Goals: Set your goal to be slow to forgive at times of deep grief.

To Achieve Self-Change: "To feel better, I'm going to forgive myself first."

I SHOULD BE BETTER.

To Feel Better: You have a right to be who you are and to define your identity.

Feel Free to Use Goals: Set your goal to learn more about your inner identity and unique self.

To Achieve Self-Change: "I can accept myself even when I'm behaving poorly."

Reversing critical parent SHOULDISTIC expectations has helped many of my psychotherapy clients take a serious look at their goals and enable them to feel good again.

Use reverse psychology to master negative emotions so you won't remain their servant.

MINDPLAY:
WHY YOU'VE LEARNED
TO HATE SETTING GOALS

There is no greater resistance to change then the inner resistance to putting goals down in black and white!

Do you fear setting goals and checking them twice? Answer the following truth or dare questions to find out.

➤ I HATE TO SET GOALS IN THE FIRST PLACE BECAUSE:

➤ I DISLIKE GOING "PUBLIC" WITH MY GOALS BECAUSE:

➤ GOALS FORCED ON ME AS A CHILD WERE:

➤ THE GOALS I KNOW I SHOULD SET BUT I REALLY DON'T WANT
TO ARE:

➤ THE REASON I CAN'T COMMIT MYSELF TO BEING SUCCESSFUL IS:

➤ HOW MY PARENTS WERE CLOSED-MINDED ABOUT MY
CHANGING WAS:

➤ IF I WERE GUARANTEED SUCCESS I WOULD DECIDE TO SET
THIS GOAL:

INTER PLAY:

Why are goals so difficult to set? Put simply, making a
commitment to your self-esteem takes guts. There are a jillion
reasons to fight against change.

Take Plenty of Time to Think about Your Goals: The usual
change fantasy is that setting goals and changing should be natural
and wonderful. It's not. Goal-setting is arduous work.

Your Goals Don't Have to Be Totally Realistic: Let yourself
dream wild dreams for a change. Setting goals can be scary
because they require you to take responsibility for your
happiness.

Use Goals to Overcome the Seductive Victim Mentality: Are you a defeatist in your thinking about what you can have or do? Start assuming that goals mean your changes just might work out right for you this time.

Goals Focus Your Secret Strengths: Reaching for your goals means you must become more real, honest and genuine about who you are. Success makes you showcase your best talents.

Towards what specific goals should you aim? Have you double-checked them for authenticity? Are they truly your own goals to better your own life?

BECOMING YOUR OWN GOAL-SEEKING CHANGE-EXPERT

Maintaining a positive attitude is a challenge for all of us. How do change-experts keep generating a positive attitude toward goals? How do they keep on the alert for new solutions to old problems?

Experts steer clear of using these negative words:

"Yes BUT...": The words used to dispel the good advice that could propel you to new heights.

"I CAN'T": A devious incantation that says setting out to reach far off goals is a waste of your precious time.

"Why Even Try?": Unexpected feelings of sadness when you find out how difficult change can be.

"Why Should I?": The teenage rebuttal to critical parents who say, "Do as I say, not as I do." The response means, "You don't practice what you preach, so why should I?"

Experts also foster these key attitudes to keep an open mind to change:

1. EXPERTS REFUSE TO REMAIN VICTIMS.

Use Goals: Experts create new options. They refuse to quit trying to gain a fresh perspective on stale problems.

To BE Successful: Happiness comes from making meaningful choices that add order to your life.

Achieve High Self-Esteem: "I feel free to make new choices."

2. EXPERTS USE A CLOSE INNER CIRCLE OF ADVISORS.

Use Goals: Experts have a few close advisors who will give them blunt and honest opinions. They even allow their advisors to strongly disagree with them, and don't flinch when they are told they might be in the wrong.

To BE Successful: Sound decisions come from shared wisdom.

Achieve High Self-Esteem: "I feel free to take good advice."

3. EXPERTS USE NEGATIVE EMOTIONS TO FUEL HIGHER SELF-ESTEEM.

Use Goals: Experts act in spite of innate and learned fears of change. They take action despite fears of rejection, commitment, failure or success instead of overreacting to them.

To BE Successful: Self-trust is strengthened when fears are confronted.

Achieve High Self-Esteem: "I feel free to use anger to grow."

4. EXPERTS MAKE THEIR EMOTIONAL ATTACHMENTS MATTER.

Use Goals: Experts value marriage, children, cooperative work relationships and friendships — usually in that order of importance. They value opening up their hearts, and letting others get under their skin.

To BE Successful: Make being loving a higher priority than the fear of being hurt.

Achieve High Self-Esteem: "I feel free to be close to others who value me."

5. EXPERTS EXPLAIN BUT DON'T DEFEND THEIR OPINIONS.

Use Goals: Experts think about issues and conflicts and aren't afraid to take a public stand. They assertively share their true perceptions without putting others on the defensive.

To BE Successful: Gladly undertake the struggle to be more and more accepting of yourself.

Achieve High Self-Esteem: "I feel free to think clearly about my opinions."

6. EXPERTS PROMOTE CLOSENESS AND AVOID CRISES IN LOVING RELATIONSHIPS.

Use Goals: Experts find game-playing to be a waste of time. They take initiative in their relationships, resolve resentments and challenge themselves to pursue large dreams and goals.

To BE Successful: Analyze self first and blame others last is the changer's motto.

Achieve High Self-Esteem: "I feel free to take it easy."

7. EXPERTS OPERATE FROM THEIR STRENGTHS INSTEAD OF THEIR WEAKNESSES.

Use Goals: Experts aren't afraid to tap and showcase their secret strengths. They don't compare their traits to others, but try to find and express their own unique gifts.

To BE Successful: Value listening above speaking or proving a point.

Achieve High Self-Esteem: "I feel free to enjoy my strengths."

8. EXPERTS LET GO OF THE NEED TO CONTROL OTHERS.

Use Goals: Experts mourn the reality that they cannot control what others think or do in this world. They stop trying to gain the conditional approval of critics who use the withholding of praise to manipulate.

To BE Successful: Put high stock in openly giving and accepting praise.

Achieve High Self-Esteem: "I feel free to control myself."

9. EXPERTS WANT TO PLEASE OTHERS AND SELF ABOUT EQUALLY.

Use Goals: Experts value being kind to others. They also value being selfish in healthy ways sometimes. However, experts prefer to give more than they take and always give a little extra along the way.

To BE Successful: Put yourself around people who make you feel worthwhile.

Achieve High Self-Esteem: "I feel free to be selfish sometimes about my needs."

10. EXPERTS ARE POSITIVE PEOPLE TO A POINT.

Use Goals: Experts stop being so giving when they are taken advantage of. They have kindness limits and don't allow displeasers to steal their energy.

To BE Successful: Resist giving angry paybacks. But do set firm and unyielding boundaries around your self-esteem.

Achieve High Self-Esteem: "I feel free to be assertive."

11. EXPERTS DON'T BLAME THEIR PRESENT BEHAVIOR ON THE PAST.

Use Goals: Experts analyze their childhoods to gain power, instead of using traumas to run away from adult responsibilities. They seek to avoid repeating past patterns of failure in their present lives.

To BE Successful: Live your own life. Don't blame your parents for their past mistakes. A payback trap you must not fall into is to refuse to set goals and be successful to pay back your parents for hurting you.

Achieve High Self-Esteem: "I feel free to go forward."

12. EXPERTS USE PERMISSIONS TO REMOVE FRUSTRATIONS.

Use Goals: Experts use permissions and disclosures to give encouraging messages instead of punitive ones. Experts realize that the parental pressures, "You should change!" and "It's all your fault!" seldom work and typically backfire.

To BE Successful: Harvest free advice.

Achieve High Self-Esteem: "I feel free to be really happy."

13. EXPERTS DON'T MIND WORKING HARD TO GET AHEAD.

Use Goals: Experts don't require life to be easy, pain-free or predictable. They accept that learning requires long periods of time and sustained effort to gain new skills.

To BE Successful: Changing your attitudes is the best way to reduce stress. Always look for ways to stretch an outdated attitude to the breaking point.

Achieve High Self-Esteem: "I feel free to be successful."

14. EXPERTS USE PAIN AS A SIGNAL TO CHANGE.

Use Goals: Experts accept that the purpose of pain and rejection is to force them to unleash secret talents that have been denied. Pain is always their cue to embrace change and not fight against it.

To BE Successful: Accepting reality is better than twisting it.

Achieve High Self-Esteem: "I feel free to feel."

15. EXPERTS AIM TO LEARN SOMETHING NEW FROM EVERY FRUSTRATING SITUATION.

Use Goals: Experts know that difficult people are making hurtful choices. They protect themselves from negative people, situations and systems by trying to learn something new from them.

To BE Successful: Seek new insights to add to your awareness about how the world really works.

Achieve High Self-Esteem: "I feel free to change and grow."

Positive people aren't weak people who are easily taken advantage of.

We are people who are committed to building a sense of belonging, self-growth and high self-esteem in ourselves and others we touch as we travel through life.

FOCUSING ON YOUR CHANGES FOR A CHANGE

Are your goals written down and placed on your nightstand for easy review before you retire at night? Or are your goals plastered to the refrigerator door? Mine are. You need to have at least: goals for your self-esteem, goals for your career and goals for your family life.

So where are you headed? Are you just aimlessly bumping along? I hope not.

Do you hate to set deadlines that push you to excel past your self-imposed time frames? And do you hate focusing on doing boring but essential tasks, following through when you don't feel like it or focusing your attention so intently that it doesn't wander?

Human beings are easily distracted, and have a tendency to take the easy way out, instead of making the hard decisions.

I hate the work that setting goals takes. I truly do. But I realize that goals help guide me home when I'm lost, and help me to thrive when new opportunities come knocking at my door.

THREE RULES FOR SETTING GOOD GOALS

Setting goals works. Following through on your goals adds to your sense of competence, self-control and determination.

Here's how you can take your goals for success more seriously:

RULE #1:

TAKE TIME TO THINK ABOUT WHAT YOU WANT MOST.

A Good Choice: If you don't try to achieve your goals, you haven't really lost anything, right? Wrong! A lack of goals keeps you inactive, unassertive and less than ambitious about pursuing what makes you really happy.

Take Charge of Change: If you were in charge of change, what would fire you up to reach your goals? From whom would you ask help?

Go Inside Yourself to Self-Reflect: Find a quiet place to explore what brings you joy. Refresh your memory of what you most love to do. Have you let what you are good at fade into the background?

To BE Successful: TO BE SUCCESSFUL TAKE TIME TO THINK ABOUT WHAT YOU MOST WANT!

RULE *2:

HAVE THE COURAGE TO DECIDE ON WHAT YOU WANT MOST.

A Good Choice: Commit yourself to a single course of action. Encourage your success by knowing what you really want to be doing. Take time to show your courage by making decisions that highlight your self-esteem.

Take Charge of Change: Confess. You really do want to be happy! Don't let guilt and self-criticism keep you stuck in a rut. Whether the criticism is well-deserved or not, it reduces your drive to take yourself seriously.

Go Inside Yourself to Focus: Are you failing to comfort yourself when you need strokes the most? What brings you positive strokes instead of sorrowful memories?

To BE Successful: TO BE SUCCESSFUL DECIDE WHAT YOU MOST WANT FOR YOURSELF!

RULE *3:

FOCUS ALL YOUR ENERGIES ON ONE GOAL AT A TIME.

A Good Choice: Completely engage your efforts to make success appear. Focusing on one goal will give you the energy to jump over most change hurdles. (There will be a great many of them.)

Take Charge of Change: One goal will keep you focused in one area long enough to become really excellent. Focus to keep going when you should quit. Don't let your good ideas come in last nine times out of ten. Take time to enjoy your wins along the way.

Go Inside Yourself to Focus: Where can you focus for the biggest payoff in your life? Do you abide by a rule which says noble suffering procures heavenly rewards?

To BE Successful: TO BE SUCCESSFUL FOCUS ON ONE GOAL AT A TIME!

Focus single-mindedly for success. Take time to think, take time to be tender toward yourself and take time to focus on becoming very good at doing one thing.

THE IMPORTANCE OF YOUR LIFE GOALS

Take all the time you need to consider what goals you want to lead the parade of your life. Search for answers to add a spirit of wild excitement to your life.

I want you to consider the most important areas of your life. Self-esteem, self-nurturing, sex, money, health, career and romantic relationships are the top rated ways to reach happiness. Goals in each one of these areas will add to your happiness equation.

You may have several answers in one area, while another area may be blank. It is best to establish goals in all categories — no matter how small your goals are. Later on, you can rank your goals in importance, and decide which goals will receive the majority of your time.

You can master any challenges when you set your goals high and strive to reach them. Be honest about your goals and you will be able to move your goals from the idea stage to the realm of reality in no time at all.

Let yourself know what you want, even though you might be uncertain how you will be able to attain the goals. Allow yourself to think big, without being totally ridiculous.

SELF-ESTEEM GOALS

My self-esteem could be improved by:

My children's self-esteem could be improved by:

To me self-esteem means:

To respect myself more I could:

Self-acceptance means:

One thing I could do next week to improve my self-esteem:

To improve my self-esteem as a man/woman I could:

What holds me back from hitting my peak of self-esteem is:

**MY GOAL:
TO IMPROVE MY SELF-ESTEEM
I CHOOSE TO ADD THESE ACTIVITIES:**

ROMANTIC RELATIONSHIP GOALS

What I look for from love is:

How I'm unrealistic about romance is:

The type of person who really turns me on is:

How I wish to understand the opposite sex better would be:

I can give more positive strokes by:

Accepting positive strokes is threatening to me because:

Unrealistic expectations I put on men/women are:

Subconsciously I resist being loved for who I am by doing:

**MY GOAL:
I CHOOSE TO INVOLVE MYSELF
IN LOVING RELATIONSHIPS THAT ARE:**

PARENTING GOALS

I believe the role of a good parent is:

What I sacrifice for my children is:

My kids control me by:

I would like to be a better parent in these ways:

The lesson I want my children to learn is:

I wish to pass these strengths to my children:

My children have taught me the most about:

How I need to be a good parent to myself is:

MY GOAL:
I CHOOSE TO BECOME A BETTER AND BETTER PARENT BY:

CAREER GOALS

The perfect job for me would be:

My self-esteem would benefit from a job that:

Work becomes boring when:

Applying my unique gifts and strengths to my work would mean:

In exchange for being successful I will give back:

What I would like to contribute to my field is:

I want my children's attitude toward work to be:

How I resist finding a job that best suits my potential is:

MY GOAL:
I CHOOSE TO DEFINE MY MAJOR CAREER PURPOSE AS:

MONEY GOALS

The amount of money I want to make this year is:

The perfect financial life for me would be:

Hang-ups I would have to give up to earn more money:

More money would make my family-life fuller by:

Money gets confused in my mind with:

I'm skeptical about reaching my financial goals because:

How I stop myself from making more money is:

MY GOAL:
I CHOOSE TO TAKE THESE RISKS TO BETTER MY INCOME:

POSITIVE STROKES GOALS

I would be wise to let go of these self-criticisms:

Positive strokes to give myself each day would be:

Reasonable ways I could rest and relax are:

Taking care of myself is selfish because:

I could receive more touching by:

Silly and fun things I enjoy doing are:

What stops me from loving myself when others don't is:

MY GOAL:
POSITIVE STROKES I CHOOSE TO ADD INTO MY LIFE ARE:

SEXUALITY GOALS

The type of sex I really enjoy is:

The dream sex life for me would be:

Negative ideas that keep me sexually uptight are:

What stops me from being more sexually assertive is:

I block myself from feeling pleasure by:

Sex is confused in my mind with:

Right now I'm resisting good sex by:

MY GOAL:
I CHOOSE TO ADD THESE SEXUAL ATTITUDES INTO MY LIFE:

HEALTH GOALS

What makes me feel healthier is:

My parent's view of health was:

New health habits I would like to adopt this year are:

I could take better care of my mental health by:

Health discipline gets confused in my mind with:

What stops me from adopting better health habits is:

MY GOAL:
I CHOOSE TO ADOPT THE FOLLOWING HEALTH HABITS
IN MY LIFE:

INTER PLAY:

Goals are really challenging, aren't they? You must put your happiness on the dotted line!

Make Sure Your Goals Are Your Own: Don't set goals to please your priest, minister or rabbi. Set goals that are pleasing to yourself and suited to your growth.

Set Your Goals to the Tune of Your Life Mission: Your life mission is the larger umbrella under which every goal falls. Line up your goals under your higher purpose when you are experiencing difficulty accomplishing your goals.

Carry the Yellow Card in Your Pocket or Purse: Carry a bright index card on which you write your top three goals. When you brainstorm ideas during the day to accomplish your goals, write the ideas on the card so you won't forget them.

Add goals for spirituality or goals for where you would like to live. Don't limit yourself by limiting your goals.

Goals are the number one way to take careful aim at your higher purpose. Fire away! Goals are a sure way to arrive at where you want to go.

THE SEVEN CHALLENGES OF HAPPINESS

Since life isn't perfect, it isn't surprising that problems continue to crop up day after day by the dozens. How do some people maintain a good mood, while others succumb to negative feelings?

High self-esteemers make a strong commitment to being happy. Happiness is highly valued.

Do you take pride in controlling your own moods, or do you take in the negative feelings that are displaced by displeasers? High self-esteemers feel all of their feelings and treat each one respectfully.

What are the seven challenges that you must face and overcome to protect your happiness?

CHALLENGE #1:
DEFUSE STEALTHY GUILT BOMBS.

Say Good-Bye To Guilt: Say good-bye to unproductive guilt to change what you have control over. Remove friends who subtly reinforce your self-defeating feelings. Break ties with people and organizations that discount you.

To Be Happy: "I first choose to change myself."

CHALLENGE #2:
RESOLVE OLD CONFLICTS INSTEAD OF REPEATING THEM.

Resolve Problems: Healthy conflicts serve to build, not destroy closeness. Be sure to air disputes and resolve problems. Use anger for assertive and caring purposes.

To Choose Happiness: "The more I blame the less I change."

CHALLENGE #3:
STICK TO YOUR GOALS LIKE GLUE.

Stay Focused: Set goals carefully and follow through on them. Think of human nature as neither good nor bad, but as a mixture of fascinating traits that coexist in the same person.

To Be Happy: "Everyone, everyday, has the same power to choose to be happy."

CHALLENGE #4:
AVOID GETTING BENT OUT OF SHAPE BY STUPID MISTAKES.

Enjoy Making Mistakes: Don't get bent out of shape when you aren't supported the way you want to be. Learn to take care of your own needs. Step out of revenge games that induce dependency, but still enjoy when the bad guys take a good fall.

To Choose Happiness: "Forgiveness protects my prized relationships."

CHALLENGE #5:
CLAIM THE FREEDOM
TO WALK AWAY FROM UNDUE SUFFERING.

Expect Good Treatment: Choose to invest in others who are invested in helping themselves. Give up the need to be needed, but give as much as you can to others. Never consider suffering a saintly activity.

To Be Happy: "Self-change gives me power."

CHALLENGE #6:
VALUE A MIXTURE OF SELF-SUFFICIENCY AND DEPENDENCY.

Enjoy Being Who You Are: Enjoy being able to take care of yourself, while also enjoying being taken care of. Don't let dependency be a word that turns you off. Turn the fear of change into constructive conflict.

To Choose Happiness: "I overcome the fear of happiness by changing."

CHALLENGE #7:
GIVE FIRM CONSEQUENCES TO CHANGE-BACK ARTISTS.

Set Assertive Limits: Don't allow "I'm only trying to help you" types bring you down with their negativity. Instead choose to define who you are and what you are about. Set clear limits and be confrontational when your self-esteem has been violated.

To Be Happy: "Being assertive brings me happiness."

Learn to be both successful and happy. Being happy is one whale of a challenge in a world where feeling bad is so smiled upon.

In short order, you will succeed. Goals will help you keep going through The Five Stages of Change I will be describing in the next chapter.

The unexpected twists and turns of your travels can be smoothed out by sticking to your own personal contract for success.

PERMIT GOALS TO INCREASE YOUR SELF-ESTEEM

I've come to be a realistic optimist about change. Do the same by claiming these permissions as your own:

- ✔ **IMPROVE YOUR SELF-WORTH BY SETTING GOALS.**
- ✔ **USE GOOD ADVICE TO GROW.**
- ✔ **LIVE YOUR OWN LIFE FREE OF RESENTMENT.**
- ✔ **INVEST IN CHANGING YOUR LOVING RELATIONSHIPS.**
- ✔ **ACCEPT YOURSELF MORE — REJECT YOURSELF LESS.**
- ✔ **TAKE POSITIVE ACTION IN SPITE OF FEARS.**
- ✔ **ENJOY YOUR LIFE BY NURTURING YOUR STRENGTHS.**
- ✔ **REINFORCE YOURSELF FOR SMALL POSITIVE CHANGES.**
- ✔ **LOVE YOURSELF EVEN WHEN OTHERS DISAPPROVE OF YOU.**
- ✔ **MAKE NEW CHOICES DESPITE NEGATIVE INFLUENCES.**

Claim your right to high self-esteem by setting goals that are important to you.

You alone are responsible for your happiness!

COUNTERPOINT:

"WHY IS TRYING TO CHANGE MYSELF SO DIFFICULT AND FRUSTRATING?"

Change was meant to be an "uneasy" project. Success means reaching toward your goals.

Changing is so frustrating because:

★ *You must accept that change is a stair-step phenomenon.* You go up two, and down one, before you finally arrive at the top landing. Do not become permanently discouraged by setbacks.

★ *You must set yourself up to be kissed not kicked.* You drop guilt like a hot potato and stop punishing yourself for messing up. Strive to be receptive to affection.

★ *You must set up boundaries or fences around your self-esteem.* You stop being drained by others' controlling behaviors. Accept that the bad choices made by your parents, lover or children do not reflect upon you.

★ *You must depend on yourself more.* You strive to let go of rejections and resentments that keep you distracted from your goals. Let go of the need for approval to feel okay.

★ *You must make mundane practical actions a priority.* You give up any security blankets that keep you acting like an infant. Realize that positive actions lead to positive self-worth (and the reverse).

★ *You must always strive to fill inner emptiness with love.* You unearth your own answers for better living. Rely less on the opinions of authorities to guide your life.

★ *You must learn to master frustrations instead of cave in to them.* You don't use being mistreated or a setback as a dandy excuse to give up. Keep making good choices to change.

Self-esteem means you keep going forward through negative emotions instead of folding under the weight of them.

When events cause you to collapse in a dead heap, you rest, take nourishment and allow yourself to receive help to refuel your spirit to carry on.

Many frustrations are caused by not having a higher purpose, and specific goals that spring from that purpose. You need both. Only then will you be able to fight against long-standing frustrations.

In the next chapter, I'm going to show you how to safely travel through The Five Stages of Change so you won't become lost or wander aimlessly in them.

5

EMBRACING THE FIVE STAGES OF CHANGE

"The experience of change, of unaccustomed activity, of being on unfamiliar ground, of doing things differently is frightening. It always was and always will be. People handle their fear of change in different ways, but the fear is inescapable if they are in fact to change."

The Road Less Traveled, M. Scott Peck, M.D.
Simon and Schuster, 1978, p. 131.

LET GO OF THE NEED FOR TOTAL CONTROL

Change doesn't mean giving up being who you are by role-playing a responsible grown up. Actually, it means just the reverse: accepting those inner talents that have been hidden for too long and put under the destructive searchlight of displeasers' criticisms.

Change means charging into the unknown with a child's spirit, alert as a concerned parent would be to the possible dangers that might be lurking there. Change ultimately means to choose consciously.

What is real change all about? What definition can we use to describe the journey through and mastery of the stages of change? Change requires the eternal DESIRE to undergo challenges and to grow successfully from encountering them.

Change is also the PROCESS of letting go of old anger and hurt, filling the subsequent vacuum with self-esteem and accepting love from others. Change means taking charge of your life and eliminating the frustrations that are weighing you down.

Change always means choice. It is the DEMAND to live a life based on happiness, fulfillment and meaning. Getting through the stages of change is the crucial process by which you make your demands emerge from fantasy into reality.

While you are intensifying your desire to change, I will be teaching you how all changes involve a standard five-stage learning process. To keep going ahead, you must accept these tricky stages of change instead of fighting against them.

To achieve your goals you must give up needing to be in total control of every part of the change process. The result is that in time you will arrive at a different awareness of self-worth, power and pleasure.

The Five Stages of Change operate like clockwork. Any change inevitably has these five stages.

In the change chart, you can see how each stage follows another and needs time to be crossed.

Let's find out what the change stages are, what you can and cannot control in each stage and how you can tell which stage you happen to be in now. Knowledge of these stages will help you anticipate and cope with frustrations much better.

You will be armed with knowledge, and knowledge is power. You will also be encouraged to arm yourself with a healthy sense of self-control.

THE CRISIS STAGE (STAGE I)

The Crisis Stage forces change on you whether you want it or not, and whether or not you are prepared for it. Most of the time you aren't prepared for the event, and experience a substantial loss of control. The dramatic loss of control can create feelings of anxiety, fear, confusion and an array of self-critical complaints.

Crises come in many forms: divorce, unemployment, dealing with stepchildren, affairs, problems with a difficult boss, an unwanted pregnancy, illness, litigation, heavy debts, the kids growing up and leaving home for college, a second marriage, death of a spouse, a heart attack, the stress of relocating, war, etc.

Many crises are externally focused and developmental in nature (e.g. getting married, becoming a first-time parent, blending two families), yet all crises involve a sudden shift in how you see the world. As your external life is changed, you are called upon to change your internal belief systems in healthy ways to keep up (and the reverse).

Unfortunately, crises also can serve to reinforce old negative beliefs about yourself. In fact, bad outcomes often serve as "proof" of your failures and shortcomings which reinforce low self-esteem. Crisis events can be used as incontrovertible proof that you shouldn't try to change.

You can avoid many crises by continuing to grow and change during calm periods when you don't really need to. The more positive your attitude becomes, the more your external life is rearranged to match the template of your positive beliefs.

Heavy crises can make you feel like you are losing your mind. You aren't! The CRISIS STAGE is put under control quickly with brief psychotherapy.

Of course, many crises signal that work toward change has been neglected for too long.

THE CHANGE CHART

THE CRISIS STAGE
(STAGE I)

THE HARD WORK STAGE
(STAGE II)

THE TOUGH DECISION STAGE
(STAGE III)

THE UNEXPECTED PAIN STAGE
(STAGE IV)

THE JOY AND INTEGRATION STAGE
(STAGE V)

CONFLICT:
A CLIENT EXAMPLE OF THE CRISIS STAGE

Peter was a brand new high school teacher who had fire in his eyes and youthful enthusiasm on his side when it came to standing up and delivering "the best kind of education that my kids will need in order to survive in Real Life 101."

Tenured teachers respected Peter and were amused that he took pride in enforcing discipline. The experienced teachers had learned to be afraid of enforcing adequate discipline. They feared being criticized by angry parents who might scold them for excessive or "abusive" discipline.

No one was very surprised when certain parents weren't at all pleased with Peter. In fact, Mr. and Mrs. Glascow lodged several written complaints with the principal and school board against Peter for being "unfair and too critical toward our child."

The parents thought Peter had it in for their child. The parents, who were quite influential, went to the local newspaper editor with the story. The headline "Too Much Punishment?" appeared a few days later. Every imaginable issue group greedily latched onto the crisis to support their particular cause. Everyone watched closely the ensuing battle that took several painful months to investigate and resolve.

Peter was devastated. Although he appeared calm, he was an emotional wreck. He wasn't sleeping well, eating was a chore and he was withdrawing from his wife in order not to bother her with his problems.

Peter was so angry he wanted to resign. Since Peter had made the right choice to be an ethical teacher, why was he so upset by a crisis precipitated by requiring an aggressive child from a wealthy family to behave appropriately in his classroom?

The reasons that the crisis shattered Peter's idealism were uncovered in his psychotherapy and need not be described here. But I do need to focus on the crisis as a call to Peter to grow beyond himself. Here was an opportunity to clarify his values, vision, boundaries and to develop a stronger professional identity.

Crises make you stop, look and listen to your lost needs for self-esteem, your desires to create an interesting life and your needs to make meaningful attachments to others.

ANSWER THESE CRISIS QUESTIONS TO BE SUCCESSFUL

Find out if you are in the crisis stage by answering these questions:

1. **Have you waited too long to change?**

2. **Are you living your life according to the strong values you profess to believe?**

3. **Have you promoted a crisis to force yourself to change?**

4. **Are you really living, or are you just going through the routine motions, as time and opportunity pass you by?**

5. **Are you being too idealistic? Not realistic enough?**

6. **Are you connected with other people or just floating along in life with few emotional ties?**

7. **Is there an alternative way of living, a different call to action that you can't hear?**

8. **What must you freely give up to put your life on a different track?**

9. **Are you using crises as a substitute for intimacy?**

10. **Is the crisis bringing out pain that needs healing that you have been hiding from yourself?**

Are you going to heed the call to be who you are this time? Repetitive crises may be trying to bring a specific change of behavior into your life.

BEING IMPERFECT IS GOOD ENOUGH!

The school crisis forced Peter to answer these questions and learn quickly from them. He had no time to delay, since crises seek to speed up change. Peter now looks back on the crisis as a call he had to heed to take new positive actions.

Sometimes you must choose to say good-bye to unhealthy people, systems, ideas, financial situations, sexual traditions, stroking rules or places that consistently keep you from growing. Is that a shame? No, not at all.

Fortunately, Peter had the courage to stand up for his beliefs, to leave a system he felt wasn't designed for him or the children and switch to a different career that still involved his working closely with children.

Some crises are natural, for example the death of a loved one. Other crises are avoidable, such as distancing oneself from a mate or using conflict destructively. Short-term solutions to problems — like refusing to think about them — increases the risk of a crisis occurring.

You can only stuff so much for so long under the proverbial rug.

In many cases, crises take place because you have been cheating reality of its payment for too long. Sweeping things under the carpet creates the delusion of safety and order. Later, your stumbling can cause a sprained ankle or even a broken neck. Reality does not allow you to maintain your delusion for very long.

How do people act during crises? Do we act like saints? No way! Both great cowardice and grand bravery come from crises.

Your impulse for survival is brought out by crises. Fear can make you respond with offensive behaviors, or make your hidden talents burst forth. Either way, you must keep on learning about your self-esteem after the crisis has passed.

Crises endeavor to force you to grow, fight fair, strengthen your identity and pay more attention to neglected interests that have been put on the back burner for far too long. There's no guarantee that crises will produce change; they can only beckon, urge and invite you to learn important but painful life lessons.

Human beings value being in control. Crises make you feel

puny and small. Loss of control reminds you that superior forces rule the universe. A crisis proves that you are a tiny little being in the scheme of things. This is why you prefer crises to happen to someone else.

Used correctly, crises motivate change through healthy fear. Used incorrectly, crises can make you cower and vow never to go down that road again. Success means getting back up again after you have been knocked unconscious by crises.

The same type of crisis can happen over and over again, until you finally hear the message and learn the lesson, or until reality crushes your self-esteem into smithereens.

MINDPLAY:

PLEASING YOURSELF FOR A CHANGE

Crises signal you should start pleasing yourself for a change. Stop and think about what you might have unknowingly given up in your life that nurtured your self-esteem.

Consider what used to bring you energy, an optimistic bounce to your step, an easy smile. What keeps you from these things now?

Things I could do to get back to feeling I'm a strong, happy person who has control:

1.

2.

3.

4.

5.

6.

7.

Things I could do to stop procrastinating on being the strong, happy person I've always wanted to be:

1.

2.

3.

4.

5.

6.

7.

INTER PLAY:

Start pleasing yourself soon, so you don't become a victim of depression. Being deprived of strokes lowers your self-esteem.

Start Giving Yourself Some Strokes Today: Self-criticism tries to restore lost strokes to add self-control. Have you ever believed, "I must be making this happen to me?" Now how's that for a warped way to try and be in control again?

The Irony of Self-Control: What you don't have control over, you claim you do or should have; and what you do have control over, you claim you can't control any more.

You Can Only Control Yourself: Benefit from admitting what little control you have over any mind, change, decision, emotion, behavior, attitude or thought — but your own! Learn to control what you can and let go of the rest.

Remind yourself that sometimes you aren't responsible for everything that has gone wrong. And what you have pushed under the carpet for too long can be corrected.

Peter learned to control his quick temper so he wouldn't blow up at the accusing parents and lose the respect of school authorities. What he couldn't control was what the vindictive parents might do; and he wasn't able to control the politics that heated up in the community.

Let's summarize what we've tried to cover about the first stage of growth, Stage I: The Crisis Stage.

SUMMARY OF THE CRISIS STAGE OF CHANGE

THE QUESTION:	**"WHAT IS GOING ON HERE?"**
ENERGY FOCUS:	**FEAR OF BEING OVERWHELMED BY FORCES BEYOND YOUR CONTROL.**
GROWTH FOCUS:	**OBSERVATION OF THE QUALITY OF YOUR LIFE.**
MENTAL NEEDS:	**ANALYZING ALTERNATIVES.**
EMOTIONAL NEEDS:	**FOR CONTACT WITH SUPPORTIVE PEOPLE.**
SKILLS:	**TO THINK CLEARLY ABOUT HIGHLY CHARGED EMOTIONAL EVENTS.**

The primary effect of a crisis is to get your attention. Once your attention is riveted on a problem, your goal should be to do anything productive to resolve the problem.

THE HARD WORK STAGE (STAGE II)

The hard work stage makes you roll up your sleeves and get down to doing the dirty work. You don't mind the extensive effort, however, as you are kept busy with interesting and challenging projects. You also gain from acquiring the discipline necessary to learn new skills.

High self-esteemers expect to work hard throughout their lifetimes. They don't like to go around with a chip on their shoulders, saying "Hey, that's me! Take it or leave it!" Nor do they say, "I'm not going to speak to you if you don't give me what I want. You owe me!" To them, hard work is enjoyable.

Goal setting means you break free from unhelpful dependencies, and of relationships that might be encouraging you to stay the same. Some of the very people who complained that you weren't growing enough will do their best to frustrate your further growth. Going back to your goals is a guaranteed way to remove nagging negative feelings.

Changing makes you value yourself and lay claim to your inner strengths instead of disowning them.

Most people aren't afraid of working hard. Still, you may balk at spending money or taking valuable time to learn the information you need. "I've got to be realistic not selfish," says it all. You may feel selfish about allocating limited resources to your own growth, even when your family backs you one hundred percent.

Change-experts keep their radar turned on high to pick up answers that seem to come out of nowhere. Their attitude: "Who or what might I bump into today to help me change?" Experts are walking human sponges who seek to soak up new advice, opportunities and trends.

Education can come from many available sources: libraries, old friends, taking community education classes, radio programs, reading the best works in a field or networking with experts; these are just a few of the ways to tap into the abundance of learning resources.

Beware though: the more you learn, the stupider you can feel. Though at first exhilarating, I remember how difficult it was for me to study basic communication skills for couples. At first, learning was a breeze, but then the concepts got blurred in my mind and I felt as though I were unlearning everything I had learned before!

It can take practice-practice-practice and more practice to get your hands around certain ideas. In fact, in the middle of the learning curve, just before the information comes together in your mind, massive confusion or sliding back to the safety of old habits is common. Stick with the ideas though, and what you need to learn will come into focus.

Learning is the name of the game during The Hard Work Stage.

ASSERTIVENESS:
A CLIENT EXAMPLE OF THE HARD WORK STAGE

Sarah was an attractive accountant who managed purchases for a large company. She was responsible for arranging equipment purchases from outside vendors for several divisions that her boss was responsible for.

Sarah entered therapy to learn how to be more assertive on her job. A crisis had precipitated her coming to me: she had been sexually harassed by her supervisor a number of times. She said, "I don't know how to deal with his awful comments." Her doctor had suggested counseling to reduce her stress. She complied by coming to me.

During the evaluation, Sarah came across like a woman who had it all together. She was competent in her work, positive in her mental outlook and still in love with her husband after twelve years of marriage.

She explained that her supervisor had been sexually harassing her for several months. She then added this painful disclosure: "I feel so ashamed about the whole thing. I know it's not true, but maybe I'm the cause of it all somehow."

Sarah hadn't been provocative. Far from it. She was a caring woman who was serious about doing a good job for whatever boss she was assigned to.

The supervisor was in the habit of making remarks about her when she came to his office. He would grab her and tell her how good she looked, and run his hand up and down her leg while she was on the telephone.

Sarah had heard from others that the boss might fire anyone. Rumor even had it that one female employee had been terminated for unknown reasons. The supervisor was notorious for offering what he called "incentives" to his favorite female workers. Evaluations and promotions also included his special criteria.

Sarah needed the money she earned from her job. Her two kids and her husband depended on her salary. "We're always just one paycheck away from disaster," Sarah informed me. Fear of losing her job had made her keep silent and ate away at her stomach lining.

What could Sarah do? Would assertiveness skills help her confront the supervisor? Would she lose her job if she stood up to him or reported him? Another real fear that was tearing Sarah apart was what her husband might do if he found out about the lewd remarks her boss was making to her. "He's not the kind of guy to sit back and put up with that kind of stuff," Sarah said.

Sarah had her work cut out for her, work that she was very willing to do.

I taught Sarah how to change her victim attitude, to use anger more assertively, how to talk about her feelings without getting into a conflict with her husband and to take stock of her job strengths to feel more in control of herself. The crisis stage passed without notice as Sarah became an expert at handling her feelings and expressing them.

Sarah prepared for her decision to leave by speaking to her women friends, discussing her career options with a colleague in the personnel department, talking with her husband (who was angry only about her silence) and consulting a lawyer about her legal options. She weighed her decision carefully before she decided to confront the supervisor to "make myself feel clean again."

Sarah confronted the supervisor by telling him she was going to transfer to another position. When he expressed surprise and dismay and asked why she was leaving, she told him: "You know why. I've been scared to stand up to you, but not anymore. You're a disgrace as a supervisor."

Sarah walked out the door shaking, but feeling very proud. She had been afraid of what people would think of her for leaving. Her co-workers were sad but happy for her. Sarah went forward with her life, more realistically and more confidently.

Sarah now has the good fortune of working for a normal boss who really appreciates her. Her stress symptoms are all gone. She had worked hard for her new freedom by learning the skills needed to change her self-image and her surroundings. As we said good-bye, she gave me a hug that was filled with confidence and life.

Sarah did not cop out. She didn't run away from her problems, but proudly walked away from a sexist supervisor, the kind that exist in all areas of employment and who prey on vulnerable, hard-working employees who happen to be too unassertive.

ANSWER THESE HARD WORK QUESTIONS TO BE SUCCESSFUL

The questions in Stage II focus on what specifically you must do to improve the long-term quality of your life. Here are some questions to stimulate your success:

1. **Do you let fears of failure hold you back?**

2. **Do you take good advice and run with it?**

3. **Are you taking good enough care of your needs?**

4. **Do you use the fear of the unknown as an excuse?**

5. **Might you be underestimating your partner's support?**

6. **Do you procrastinate to avoid making a commitment?**

7. **How long are you planning to wait until you begin?**

8. **Can you reinforce yourself for small wins?**

9. Do you persist when you run into roadblocks?

10. Are you a careful and caring listener?

You aren't afraid of hard work. But you may still find investing time and money in your own self-esteem difficult to do. Go ahead and invest in yourself anyway!

You Do Have Control Over Your Own Choices!

You do have control over your own choices! Use hard work to gain key skills to help you achieve greater self-control, and to gain greater control of your world.

Sarah boldly decided (a Stage III act) to use her new knowledge to take action. She realized her changes were her own to make. Another person might have continued to suffer from health problems, and conclude, "I'll just have to learn to put up with the frustrating situation."

After a great deal of work, you too will have the option to choose NOT to use what you have learned to improve your life. Recall, you don't have to change yourself! Remember, so you won't stubbornly resist giving yourself what is good for you.

What if you make a bad choice or refuse to change? The good news is that a choice was made, and the learning can be reapplied at a future date. It will be there when you are ready to reenter the change process.

MINDPLAY:
Releasing Revenge Fantasies

You can rechannel frustrating energy into the hard work needed to achieve your goals. How to begin?

Think wickedly for a moment. What would you like to do to get revenge on the person or persons who are frustrating you the most? How could they pay off their debt free and clear for hurting you?

Begin to become friends with your anger now! The fantasy: "My favorite torture tactics."

TORTURE TACTIC ONE:

TORTURE TACTIC TWO:

TORTURE TACTIC THREE:

INTER PLAY:

Do you get uptight just thinking about anger? Have you been trained to think of anger as a "bad" feeling? Healthy anger motivates hard work when nothing else works.

Anger Is a Helpful Emotion Not an Obnoxious Behavior: All right. Don't worry about getting stuck in angry energy. Anger can be your best friend when it is used wisely. Anger is caring energy meant to expand and protect your self-esteem.

Stuffing Anger Results in Depression or Self-Criticism: If you can't fantasize the destruction of your tormentor, are you being too rigid and taking angry energy out on your self or body instead? Quite likely. How caring and kind is that?

Since anger is a friend I want you to be able to:

♦ Gain, not lose, from situations that are frustrating.
♦ Think clearly about your anger.

♦ Feel intense anger without doing or saying something stupid you will regret.
♦ Be confident communicating your anger assertively in your important relationships.

Let's summarize what we've covered regarding the second stage of growth, Stage II: The Hard Work Stage.

SUMMARY OF
THE HARD WORK STAGE OF CHANGE

THE QUESTION:	**"WHAT HAVE I BEEN MISSING?"**
ENERGY FOCUS:	**TAKING CONTROL OF YOUR FUTURE HAPPINESS.**
GROWTH FOCUS:	**PREPARING FOR SIGNIFICANT CHANGE.**
MENTAL NEEDS:	**LEARNING QUICKLY FROM FAILURES.**
EMOTIONAL NEEDS:	**FOR CONTACT WITH CHALLENGING PEOPLE.**
SKILLS:	**TO LISTEN CAREFULLY TO GOOD ADVICE.**

The hard work stage may take many months. Time flies as you are absorbed in learning new skills without being certain whether or not your efforts are going to pay off.

Skills are the tools to get what you want. The primary goal of hard work is to acquire the necessary tools to achieve your goals and thereby receive a richer variety of positive strokes.

THE TOUGH DECISION STAGE (STAGE III)

The Tough Decision Stage invites you to carefully weigh the pros and cons of difficult choices and make the choice that best suits your self-esteem and developmental needs.

Realistically, you stand to make both good and bad choices. However, you may have some trouble telling the difference between the two. Or you may procrastinate until a decision is forced on you. Sitting on the fence post doesn't work in this stage. You are forced to move forward and make new decisions or revert back to tired old habits.

Strangely, the best decision for you may be the one that makes you the most uncomfortable! Comfortable decisions are not always best for your self-esteem. In fact, just the reverse may be so. Uncomfortable decisions are often good for you.

Self-esteeming decisions require you to "grow down" and reach deep inside to grow beyond your current limitations. A good decision makes you take positive action in spite of your fears. Fear of the unknown, fear of failure, fear of commitment, fear of disapproval, fear of success and many other fears must be confronted.

Good decisions are based on your desires and goals and may or may not feel right. They require that you respect your life purpose. Good decisions demand practical and concrete results be returned for your efforts. Independent decisions make you grow and change instead of repeating your problems over and over again.

Is it any wonder then that good decisions are anxiety arousing? After all, as a result of the decision you are venturing into the unknown and trying out behaviors that you have never tried before. No one can predict what will happen! This is why good decisions take a great deal of guts.

Don't let the discomfort of the new stop you from taking action. Don't expect to feel comfortable the first few times you try a new behavior. Instead, bravely set your goal to experiment with the new and learn quickly from your mistakes.

Good relationship choices are important during the tough decision stage because you will need a greater variety of support.

You must challenge yourself to answer these questions:

1. **Shall we be real as a people, close and cooperative in meeting each other's needs?**

2. **Shall we act in ways that make us feel stronger as co-workers, friends, family and individuals?**

3. **Shall we take pride in being a team that strives to win?**

4. **Shall we take positive action in spite of our fears?**

5. **Shall we all have the right to act as competent leaders?**

Changing means more and harder decisions are made, not fewer and easier ones. Your decisions should not be left to chance. Significant choices, such as the choice of a partner or a career, affect the long-term outcome of your life.

CHOOSE TO ACCEPT HELP AND FEEL PROUD OF YOURSELF!

Good decisions are difficult to make and to implement, but feel right in the long run. Bad decisions may feel like a relief, but spell disaster for you down the road. Telling the difference between good and bad decisions is a trial and error process.

The encouragement and feedback of your inner circle of advisors, and positive strokes from other supportive people you love are crucial at this juncture. They can encourage you to go forward when you are afraid, and chastise you when you stray too far from your goals.

Choose to accept help and feel proud of yourself at the same time! New decisions breathe new life into you and your important relationships. Each day choose anew to renew your commitment to change.

Growth means new decisions must be made, whether you like it or not. Many times you may regret needing to make a particular decision. "Ready or not here I come" was the chant of childhood games that is repeated in the adult decisions you make today.

Good decisions clear your life of any debris which keeps you upset, angry or over-focused on your problems instead of your talents. Individuals and relationships that grow go on and on. Relationships that stop growing die. It's as painfully simple as that.

The leading cause of bad decisions is unacknowledged grief. Be on guard: negative emotions can unknowingly contaminate your decisions which results in a lowering of your self-esteem.

UNRESOLVED GRIEF:
A CLIENT EXAMPLE OF THE TOUGH DECISION STAGE

Glenn was a good looking, retired, 61-year-old man. He had been a widower for a few years.

He expressed some grief about the loss of his wife, but claimed, "I'm mostly over it now except at holidays." They had been close as a couple. He had depended on her, and had a hard time handling his loneliness since her death.

Glenn wasn't in a crisis state when he arranged to see me. Rather, he had heard me speak some months previously at a "Choosing Loving Relationships" seminar. Even then he had been wrestling with a decision about whether the woman he was seeing cared more about his money than she did about him.

The dilemma: Glenn had been seeing his new lady friend off and on for over a year, and had enjoyed the female company. His twenty-year-old daughter, who lived with him, claimed that her father was being used by "that woman."

Glenn's rebuttal was, "I think my daughter is just upset because I'm seeing someone else besides her mother." Glenn was a peacemaker who was afraid of the friction that was developing.

His daughter had a point about the money. Glenn was the recipient of a sizable insurance settlement. The money made Glenn feel guilty. He acted like it was "blood money" he should get rid of and bought his lady friend all kinds of expensive gifts.

Glenn's goals were to learn how to deal with the new girlfriend, find out how he could better communicate with his daughter, stop worrying about being a referee between the two women and invest the rest of the money more sensibly.

The girlfriend had something up her sleeve besides good intentions. She had another boyfriend on the side whom Glenn only found out about later. One day she approached Glenn saying, "I desperately need ten thousand dollars to care for my ailing father." Glenn was only too glad to oblige, and didn't consult anyone, including his daughter, about the decision. This was the last Glenn saw of the woman.

So much for the lady. Glenn's grief had controlled his decisions about money and romance. He didn't realize the impact of the previous loss of his wife on his present decisions and behavior.

Glenn was making all the wrong decisions even when he was convinced that he was doing the proper thing. Was he a sucker or stupid? No, not any more than the rest of us. Glenn was unable to make the tough decision to say "No" to someone who claimed to be hurting. To do so would make him face and accept his loss.

ANSWER THESE TOUGH DECISION QUESTIONS TO BE SUCCESSFUL

Good decisions reinforce high self-esteem. Here are some questions about decisions you must make:

1. **Have you made a decision to work on your self-esteem on a daily basis?**

2. **What type of romantic relationship have you decided you want for yourself?**

3. **Have you decided what you want to aspire to in your career?**

4. **What kind of relationship do you desire with your children?**

5. **How can you tell when you are making a good decision?**

6. **Are you being too soft on a bad habit?**

7. **How are you improving your communication skills? Are you working on listening, using conflict constructively or other areas?**

8. **What are your favorite ways to stop procrastinating?**

9. **What choices aren't you free to make? Why not?**

10. **How much money are you planning to make this year? How much would you prefer to make? What is your plan for arriving there?**

Unresolved grief makes you reluctant to go on with your life.

CHOOSE TO FEEL GOOD
EVEN THOUGH YOU DON'T HAVE CONTROL!

Grief or any negative feeling robs you of control and makes you vulnerable to manipulation. You must learn to be a bit paranoid about yourself in this stage, to take back control of your life from the ghost of grief.

Enjoy making good choices in this stage. Take all the time you need to go back and forth in your mind about the decision. Listen to the negative feedback loved ones may be giving you, and take positive action to get your life back in perspective.

Why do you make the same bad decision twice in a row? Unresolved grief resulting from restrictive beliefs is usually the culprit. For example, "Deny your feelings or they will control you."

It isn't that decisions are tough to make, but that tough decisions expose you to old hurts that you have been suppressing. The misfortune: after all the effort of the hard work stage, you may turn right around and blow your chances for change.

Bad decisions both deny and compound painful feelings as was the case with Glenn.

Even therapists cannot predict which way clients will decide to go during this stage of change. "We treat them, but God heals them" is a saying that reflects the fact that the individual alone has the ultimate responsibility to choose what he will make of his life.

Who among us wants to make such dreaded decisions? Your decisions are your own to make. You alone will benefit or suffer from them. But making wise decisions may be a whole lot tougher than you or I care to realize.

MINDPLAY:
LETTING GO OF LOSSES
THAT MAY STILL LINGER

Unresolved losses and hidden anger can silently control your choices. Fear of future losses can make you avoid making new commitments and decisions.

Let's consider losses you may still be carrying around today. Make a list of the people (losses can include roles, ideas or other things too) you have lost.

Lover:

Child:

Parent:

Friend:

Grandparent:

Advisor:

Hero:

Beloved Pet:

Other(s):

INTER PLAY:

Use the following questions to grow. Learn to mourn your losses openly to be successful.

1. DON'T ALLOW LOSSES TO COME OUT IN CAN'TISM.

Listen to Yourself: Is resentment about your losses coming out in CAN'TISM — e.g., "I can't change _____?"
For Success: "I let go of the past by going forward into the unknown."

2. DON'T LET THE FEAR OF FUTURE LOSS KEEP YOU FROM BEING LOVED.

Listen to Yourself: Are you hesitant to make new friends, or pursue your career achievements? Is grief keeping you from focusing on your parenting goals?
For Success: "I stop criticizing myself to change faster."

3. LEARN TO KNOW WHEN YOU ARE OUT OF CONTROL.

Listen to Yourself: Might you have less or more control than you imagine? How might your current struggles be related to a loss that has been incompletely mourned?
For Success: "I am in control of my feelings, including feelings of happiness."

4. FORGIVE PEOPLE THE ERROR OF THEIR WAYS.

Listen to Yourself: Are you limiting your success because you remain angry at a person you've lost? What opportunities are you denying yourself as a result of being mad?
For Success: "I forgive them for not loving me the way I wanted to be loved."

5. STOP BOREDOM FROM DRAINING YOUR ENERGY AWAY.

Listen to Yourself: What are you missing out on today given your present choices? What decisions would make you feel better and add excitement to your life?

For Success: "I don't need to settle for second best."

6. TAKE ALL THE TIME YOU NEED TO LET GO – BUT DON'T STALL.

Listen to Yourself: What do you need to surrender or let go of to go forward with your life? Are you rushing the grief process to your detriment?

For Success: "I do whatever it takes to be successful."

MINDPLAY:
USING A JOURNAL
TO WRITE OUT FRUSTRATIONS

Keep a private journal as you grow, and write about your deepest feelings. Let your frustrations flow out of you as you write.

Here are a few topics to choose from, but better yet, create your own:

TOPIC 1: Write a letter to one of the persons on your list telling how hard it is for you to change right now.

TOPIC 2: Write down the advice the lost person might give you were they sitting with you.

TOPIC 3: How can you use this advice in your change processes?

TOPIC 4: What nurturing words can you say to yourself as you struggle to heal from grief?

TOPIC 5: How can you let others love you more when you are hurting?

TOPIC 6: How do you feel responsible and self-critical for the loss?

TOPIC 7: How would you really feel if this person were to reappear?

TOPIC 8: Are you developing the kind of spiritual relationship you want with God? Why, or why not?

INTER PLAY:

Let your feelings flow as you write. Let anger pour out and tears flow. Release negative feelings that have been stored too long inside of you.

Let's summarize this very important crossroad of change, Stage III: The Tough Decision Stage.

SUMMARY OF THE TOUGH DECISION STAGE OF CHANGE

THE QUESTION:	**"HOW CAN I HAVE WHAT MAKES ME FEEL GOOD?"**
ENERGY FOCUS:	**HOLDING ON, LETTING GO.**
GROWTH FOCUS:	**DECIDING FOR HAPPINESS.**
MENTAL NEEDS:	**TO MAKE GOOD CHOICES.**
EMOTIONAL NEEDS:	**TO BENEFIT FROM CONTROVERSY AND CONFLICT.**
SKILLS:	**TAKING POSITIVE ACTIONS IN SPITE OF FEAR.**

The decision to go on and grow or to withdraw from the struggle and settle for the status quo is usually contemplated for some time.

You can become stuck in the decision stage, or leave it

prematurely, since the benefits resulting from the decision won't arrive until much later. This means that decisions have to be based on pure faith, with no rewards in sight.

The result of the decision stage is to tear down old structures that no longer fit your life. New commitments help you shape a future that more closely resembles your dreams, instead of your dismal nightmares.

THE UNEXPECTED PAIN STAGE (STAGE IV)

The unexpected pain stage is marked by fears of success that torpedo your self-esteem.

Be prepared for a depth charge! Surprising upsurges of panic, pain, disappointment, and disillusionment are a customary part of this stage since you are required to further refine and strengthen your identity.

Ambivalence reigns over your self-esteem. You will feel more successful and frustrated at the same time. You will experience trust and skepticism. You will become convinced that your changes are sinking into a dark abyss.

Since this post-decision stage is a mixed emotional bag (even though on the whole you feel much better), the unexpected pain entailed in this phase can make you back off from integrating your changes and making them final.

Realizing that this stage is a normal phase of changing should give you hope. Promise me you won't be shocked when you hit this stage — keep on going forward with your changes! Keep close track of your goals to be successful.

Each individual must painstakingly chisel out his or her personal definition of the word "success." Success may mean enjoying life, emotional self-control, understanding the opposite sex, starting a business or heightening sexuality to name a few.

The goal at this stage is to challenge yourself to choose success in spite of unexpected disappointments and difficulties.

SYMPTOMS OF THE FEAR OF SUCCESS

A good way to understand the fear of success is to take a closer look at some of the ambivalent feelings that seldom fail to appear at this stage:

1. **Feelings of inspiration and giddiness... alternating with increased anxiety.**

2. **Profound levels of trust and closeness... alternating with stark lonesomeness.**

3. **Unconditional self-acceptance... alternating with shades of old self-critical anger.**

4. **Letting go of negative feelings... alternating with guilt for feeling so good.**

5. **Decreased need for approval... alternating with hunger for positive strokes.**

6. **Higher self-esteem and success... alternating with self-doubt and fears of failure.**

7. **Great faith in setting goals... alternating with pessimism about progress made.**

8. **Enjoying the freedom to be who you are... alternating with resentment at change-back artists.**

What does success really mean? Success means winning the battle of self-control.

Success means that you will become more independent and confident as you surpass old fear limits and start to fly.

It also means that, occasionally, what you had hoped would be great may turn out to be unexpectedly painful or dreary. The more able you are to accept pain as part of reality, the more you are able to tolerate the expanded pleasures inherent in growth.

Pain comes in many forms. You may experience unexplainable physical pain: intense crying jags following a big win, increased sexual desire, existential pain that you can't change any person or just the simple pain when you learn how bored you might be.

True pain: facing reality stripped of all pretexts, fancy titles, posturing or haughty ideals and deciding how best to proceed from that point. In addition, you are confronted with the realization that many limitations are internal ones that are re-enacted in the external world. You stop deluding yourself about the origin of your pain.

You have been taught to avoid pain as if all pain is bad pain. But lasting success is both painful and joyful, just as life itself is a miraculous mixture of pain and joy. The more you wish to be happy and have high self-esteem, the more you must learn to tolerate unexpected pain.

Don't confuse masochistic suffering with pain. Pain is clean, honest, and alerting. Success challenges you to stop complaining and to start constructing your life to minimize avoidable suffering and maximize independence born of pain.

Pleasure/independence and pain/dependence are twins. (As self-esteem and anger are twins.) One would think that independence, satisfaction and happiness are easily accepted. Quite the contrary. To experience joy, you are required to embrace pain and not dilute it. The avoidance of pain limits the possibility of simple happiness.

Successful people are surprised at the challenges in this post-decision success stage. The pain can delude you to think that you are sliding backwards, or have made no progress at all. The solution? Keep the positive strokes flowing and keep hope in living an authentic life.

PRACTICAL WAYS
TO KEEP WELCOMING SUCCESS INTO YOUR LIFE

Success may bring unexpected pain. You must practice being successful, and reinforce yourself for small wins, even when you don't feel like it. Here are some practical ways to accomplish both:

1. ENJOY THE ROLLER COASTER RIDE.

Claim the Freedom to BE Who You Are: Allow your confidence to rise and fall as you struggle to make sense of new decisions. Refuse to be surprised when new successes cause unexpected jolts of disappointment.

To Welcome Success: Your success is a result of your own hard work. Do what it takes! Do what works! Own up to your talents and the effort you've spent to get ahead.

2. LET GO OF NEEDING TO BE IN CONTROL.

Claim the Freedom to BE Who You Are: Let real life be different from your idealistic expectations. Receive more by keeping an open attitude to change. Control only what you can — yourself!

To Welcome Success: Stay open to change even when you feel disappointed. You are smart to have risked so much for the promise of so little reward. Stick with good habits.

3. HONOR THYSELF.

Claim the Freedom to BE Who You Are: You weren't born to put up with crap or swallow a bunch of stinking garbage. Don't let childhood rules dictate all of your adult moves. Get rid of negative beliefs and people once and for all.

To Welcome Success: Stand out in a group by believing in your own selfhood and strong beliefs. Remember, your lot in life is to challenge yourself to be happy.

4. REFUSE TO BE A KNOW-IT-ALL.

Claim the Freedom to BE Who You Are: Stop complaining about the pain if you are doing nothing effective to change. Complaining isn't changing!

To Welcome Success: Learn something new from everyone you come into contact with.

5. PLAY BY THE "DO GROW AND CHANGE RULES!"

Claim the Freedom to BE Who You Are: Don't fall prey to the hidden "Don't Grow Or Change" mentality. Play by new change rules:

Rule 1:	**Think about your life goals.**
Rule 2:	**Tap into your own good advice.**
Rule 3:	**Invest in your own success.**
Rule 4:	**Be yourself no matter what others think of you.**
Rule 5:	**Use every piece of GOOD advice.**
Rule 6:	**Never tolerate emotional, physical or financial abuse.**
Rule 7:	**Compliment instead of complain.**
Rule 8:	**Give thanks when your life comes together.**

To Welcome Success: Create your own rules, and use your own inner wisdom to grow.

6. STOP WAITING FOR THE MAGICAL RESCUER.

Claim the Freedom to BE Who You Are: Remove persons from your life who cause you undue pain. No one is responsible for your life but you. Waiting for a hero to set your life straight is simply silly.

To Welcome Success: Learn to cope with your inconsistent performances and take positive action in spite of fears that tell you to stay the same. Stay enthusiastic to finish the change race.

7. LISTEN CAREFULLY TO CARING NEGATIVE FEEDBACK.

Claim the Freedom to BE Who You Are: Don't avoid feedback that differs from what you think. Your chances for success are strengthened when you listen to controversial feedback.

To Welcome Success: Encourage blunt feedback from change-experts who value you. Contradict bad decisions by learning to change as quickly as you can.

8. TAKE PRIDE IN BEING HUMBLE.

Claim the Freedom to BE Who You Are: Success means becoming friends with your weaker elements and darker sides. Learn to welcome your strengths and correct your weaknesses.

To Welcome Success: Learn to accept and embrace your vulnerabilities. Take pride in doing your best, but don't forget about the less fortunate. Always be the first to forgive, and show compassion to frailty.

Take pride in being who you are. Being selfish in moderation means you have more to give to life and to those your love.

THE FEAR OF SUCCESS:
CLIENTS WHO MASTERED THE UNEXPECTED PAIN OF SUCCESS

Here are some brief vignettes to show how the pain of this stage takes on different appearances.

THE LAWYER: Fred was a 52-year-old lawyer who divorced his wife after repeated efforts to save his marriage had failed. Reluctantly, he started dating and, in spite of experiencing a great deal of guilt, found himself thrilled at meeting many attractive women.

The Fear of Success: Suddenly, he began neglecting his law practice. Fred soon became aware that his hard won successes were being undermined by latent guilt.

Can Lead to Happiness: He chose to become more effective in his business by confronting his guilt and continuing his dating.

THE NURSE: Louise took care of psychologically unhealthy men by making sure that all of their needs were met. Deciding to step out of The Caretaker Script, she became involved with a wonderful man who could handle intimacy.

The Fear of Success: Suddenly, when Louise wanted to become romantically involved with him, she developed a rash over her entire body. She became aware that her body was telling her that she didn't know how to be close with a real man on equal terms.

Can Lead to Happiness: She chose to share her anxieties about intimacy with her lover which resulted in wonderful sexual experiences.

THE HUSBAND: Gene was learning to express his sorrow more openly, instead of turning tears into sarcastic verbal anger against his wife.

The Fear of Success: Suddenly, as Gene was becoming more open about his sad feelings, his wife became more and more distant. They became aware how they were in collusion to avoid sad feelings.

Can Lead to Happiness: The couple chose to reach a new level of closeness by agreeing to share sad feelings.

THE REALTOR: Alice was a terrific realtor. But the more properties she sold and the more money she made, the more insistent her husband became that he control the family budget. In fact, her husband spent the money on "toys for himself and the boys."

The Fear of Success: Suddenly, Alice slacked off from selling homes until she realized that she felt angry about the way her husband mistreated her financial success.

Can Lead to Happiness: She chose to take back financial control of her life.

Finally though, breaking through the pain barrier will take you to the last stage, Stage V: The Joy and Integration Stage.

Let's summarize this growth-period, Stage IV: The Unexpected Pain Stage.

SUMMARY OF THE UNEXPECTED PAIN STAGE

THE QUESTION:	**"CAN I KEEP BEING SUCCESSFUL?"**
ENERGY FOCUS:	**AMBIVALENCE: HAPPY BUT DISAPPOINTED.**
GROWTH FOCUS:	**LIVING A GENUINE LIFE.**
MENTAL NEEDS:	**COMMITTING TOTALLY TO THE POSITIVE CHANGE.**
EMOTIONAL NEEDS:	**KIND CONFRONTATION OF FEARS OF SUCCESS.**
SKILLS:	**PRACTICE MASTERING NEGATIVE EMOTIONS.**

The unexpected pain stage is where panic sets in and you wonder if you've committed yourself to the right course. Barricades are erected that block your success, and your hopes for success begin fading.

The purpose of this stage is to help you better sort out who you are, and how and why you are unique. Inner success fears that have up to now imposed a life sentence of undue compromise upon you are unmasked and conquered.

THE JOY AND INTEGRATION STAGE (STAGE V)

When your life is running along relatively smoothly, and you know exactly why it's going so well, you have probably arrived at the stage of Joy and Integration. From here on, you will be a different person.

Reviewing the route you took to arrive, you probably noticed that everything didn't go exactly according to plan. What you used to consider worthless now seems valuable, and what you used to think was quite grand doesn't seem to matter much.

Most important to you now are positive relationships with real people. You have learned to make warm attachments matter. You like being around people who like you for having the courage to be who you are.

Feeling happy isn't any big deal at this stage. Oh sure, you enjoy feelings of well-being, but you are not obsessed with having to feel any particular feeling in preference to any other "bad" feeling. You accept painful feelings as instructive, instead of something to be eliminated. You recognize that your growth-edge is sharpened when you feel alive inside.

Deep satisfaction occurs only when you live out your aspirations, live by your own values and choose to be who you really are. You realize that when you feel good about yourself, you feel more empathetic and tolerant of others. You don't settle for second best to put your self-esteem to the test.

You no longer demand that life be perfect or idyllic. You strive to learn as much as you can about the difficult game of life. You know the challenges of changing when you are stared down by the ugly face of fear.

Thankfulness: you stop a moment to gaze at a beautiful landscape, smile as a lovely woman or handsome man walks by, and you laugh broadly at the antics of a small child. Tear rivulets mark your face — you are alive!

Your relationships become more meaningful and simple. Most times they nourish, nurture and help you grow when you are holding yourself back. You surround yourself with people and possessions that reflect your identity. During unpredictable crises or periods of conflict you feel more in control.

Living your own life takes you into the unknown. You become comfortable with how little control you have over most situations. The script markers that told you which way to turn, what to say, and how to think or act are gone. You alone accept responsibility for the journey of your life.

Mostly, though, you feel confident, high in self-esteem, real and focused on the present when you are in the Joy and Integration Stage. You have arrived due to your own hard work.

And like other successful people you hear yourself say: "You can do anything you want to in this country, if only you are willing to work hard and change." You have become a model to emulate. You use your strengths and you correct your weaknesses!

But do you care? Probably not, because you still have other goals you are working hard at achieving. You realize that change never stops unless you make it do so.

MINDPLAY:

HOW DO I SABOTAGE MY OWN SUCCESS?

We normal neurotics are consumed with worries about failing as if it were a permanent state.

I like to think of failure as the important flight path, the uncanny zigs and zags that you must take as you home in on your prized destination.

How do you sabotage your own potential for success? Find out any special techniques you use to sabotage your success by completing these phrases:

➤ MY SELF-SABOTAGING THINKING IS:

➤ MY SELF-SABOTAGING ACTIONS ARE:

➤ MY SELF-SABOTAGING RELATIONSHIPS ARE:

➤ MY SELF-SABOTAGING FEELINGS ARE:

INTER PLAY:

Success takes more than hard work. It takes learning from your failures instead of repeating them. High self-esteem means feeling deserving of success.

Here are three rules that successful people live by to conquer the fear of success:

SUCCESS RULE #1: REMEMBER PAST FAILURES IN NO WAY PREDICT FUTURE ONES.

Fight the Fear of Success: Don't defeat yourself before you begin. Instead, remember that each one of your failures is a valuable, discrete event.

Take Positive Action: Start taking the risk to get to know your strengths and apply them.

SUCCESS RULE #2: DON'T LET MEMORIES OF PAST FAILURES MAKE YOU TOO RISK-CAUTIOUS.

Fight the Fear of Success: Failure is never forever. Challenge yourself to take small actions to make yourself happy.

Take Positive Action: Bad memories which make you feel bad must be disrupted by taking new risks.

SUCCESS RULE #3: WORK ON YOUR PRESENT LIFE AND LET GO OF TRYING TO CONTROL THE FUTURE.

Fight the Fear of Success: It is impossible to accurately predict future failure or success. Focus on creating present successes instead.

Take Positive Action: Admit that the future is not yours to know.

Give thanks for all that you have and all that you are yet to receive. Have faith! Your changes will be rewarded.

Let's summarize the final stage of growth, The Joy and Integration Stage (Stage V).

SUMMARY OF THE JOY AND INTEGRATION STAGE	
THE QUESTION:	"HOW MIGHT I SUCCEED EVEN MORE?"
ENERGY FOCUS:	RELAXED CONFIDENCE AND SELF-CONTROL.
GROWTH FOCUS:	HIGH SELF-ESTEEM.
MENTAL NEEDS:	ENJOYING GOOD HABITS.
EMOTIONAL NEEDS:	PEACEFUL EXCITEMENT IN RELATIONSHIPS.
SKILLS:	BEING THANKFUL FOR GOOD THINGS.

The Joy and Integration Stage marks the time when your hard won successes permanently sink in and become a part of your inner nature. The purpose of The Joy Stage is to reward you for being who you are, and for you to enjoy growth as an invigorating process.

The stages of change are a companion to remind you that meaningful change takes time.

Change requires you to become more in tune with your emotions, strengths, thinking, goals, fears of happiness, aspirations, fears of success and a whole lot more.

Changing is the price you must pay to be successful and happy.

COUNTERPOINT:

"HOW CAN I CONQUER THE FEAR OF SUCCESS?"

Use one rule to fight the fear of success or failure:

Challenge yourself to be really happy.

Live an exciting life with the help of these permissions for success:

- ✔ **DO THE DIFFICULT.**
- ✔ **DEMAND TO BE FULLY ALIVE.**
- ✔ **FEEL FREE TO BE WHO ARE WHEN YOU ARE DISAPPROVED OF.**
- ✔ **BE SURE TO BE AT YOUR BEST.**
- ✔ **ACCEPT SMALL SUCCESSES.**
- ✔ **FEEL WORTHWHILE NO MATTER WHAT OTHERS THINK OF YOU.**
- ✔ **LEARN FROM ALL OF YOUR FEELINGS.**
- ✔ **CHOOSE TO BE CLOSE TO OTHERS.**
- ✔ **PURSUE YOUR GOALS WHEN YOU ARE FEELING BAD.**
- ✔ **FIND WAYS TO FIT IN JUST AS YOU ARE.**

Being successful means living the truth of these permissions as fully as you can.

But how can you turn your frustrations into golden opportunities? I'll explore just that question, and many others, in the next chapter.

6

CHOOSING YOUR OWN CHANGES

"Which choice will be made, an actuality, once and forever, an immortal 'footprint in the sands of time?' At any moment, man must decide, for better or for worse, what will be the monument of his existence."

Dr. Victor E. Frankl, WW II concentration camp survivor-psychiatrist, *Man's Search For Meaning*, 1984.

YOUR CHOICES ARE YOUR OWN TO MAKE

You must focus on the importance of choosing. You are not a victim. You are a person who has millions of choices available at this very instant.

You lose whether you choose to procrastinate, or whether you choose to follow through on your own bad choices. Either way, don't blame others for your blunders. Instead, learn quickly from them.

Choice means FREEDOM. The freedom to be who you are is the most precious freedom in the entire world! Are you taking advantage of your right to be who you are? Self-control means making choices that challenge you to be happy.

Resentment is a common form of "stress." Feeling trapped and angry is a good cue that you are not making good choices. Good choices reduce resentment, while having no choices or making bad ones increases resentment.

Change-experts reduce stress by making good choices. They are able to move forward in the direction of their goals by making resentment-reducing choices and attitude changes.

How strongly is resentment impacting your self-esteem? Make your choices count for more to reduce resentment!

THE RESENTMENT QUIZ

Find out how much control you have over stress by answering the following quiz questions.

TRUE	FALSE	
❑	❑	1. People who aren't competent really irritate me.
❑	❑	2. It's hard to forgive myself when I mess up.
❑	❑	3. Kids should be better in sports than their parents were when they were in school.
❑	❑	4. My spouse's bad habits aren't easy to ignore.
❑	❑	5. I should organize my time and life better.
❑	❑	6. My life would be happier if I could let go of my guilt and raise my self-esteem.

TRUE	FALSE	
❑	❑	7. I'm often afraid of making the wrong decision.
❑	❑	8. Typically, I might start, but not finish something important to me.
❑	❑	9. I learn quickly from my mistakes to avoid repeating them.
❑	❑	10. There are flaws in my personality that should be corrected.
❑	❑	11. It's important to express thankfulness for our God-given talents.
❑	❑	12. I believe, "If things are worth doing, they are worth doing right."

SCORING AND DISCUSSION

Tally up the number of answers that you have marked "true." Find out if your choices are fueling high self-esteem:

9-12 TRUE: EXCESSIVE SELF-ESTEEM.

Reduce Stress: You expect more from yourself than is humanly possible to deliver. You are making choices that displease others too much.

Stress Self-Control: Taking excessive control has become a way to wall yourself off emotionally from others or to defend against making needed changes.

Make Good Choices: Friends and loved ones become intimidated by your super-high standards and back away from you.

4-8 TRUE: HIGH SELF-ESTEEM.

Reduce Stress: You manage perfectionism pressures well,

make plenty of good choices and are capable of making more.

Stress Self-Control: You value self-control. When you drive yourself or others too hard, you become aware of that fact and tone down your expectations.

Make Good Choices: You encourage loved ones to be who they are, and you take time to decide what is good for you.

0-3 TRUE: LOW SELF-ESTEEM.

Reduce Stress: You expect too little from yourself compared to your inner potential and need to make more positive choices.

Stress Self-Control: Giving your control away makes you feel out of control of your life. Might you be postponing needed changes that would make your life happier and more satisfying?

Make Good Choices: Loved ones wonder when you are going to stop tolerating frustrations and go after what you really want.

Make more choices — reduce resentment! By using your anger in assertive ways you will be able to unload both past and present resentments.

High self-esteem means you feel free to make new and better choices every second of every day. You don't have to be stuck today with choices you made in the far distant past.

No matter what other people expect from you, you need to set sane standards about what you expect from yourself. The net result: Be proud of who you are, and the rest of life will take care of itself.

THE CONSTANCY OF CHOOSING

Although you are not a victim of a concentration camp like Dr. Frankl was, you too are building a monument to the sum total of your existence this very moment by what you are choosing, what you are avoiding choosing, and what you choose not to choose.

Dr. Frankl knew firsthand the cruelties of concentration camp life. From studying raw suffering he concluded that we each need to: "Just say yes to life!" Remarkably, no matter how bad life gets, God has given us the power of choosing to make it better.

Do your choices make you feel enlivened, more trusting and filled with self-respect? Choosing is the mechanism by which you are allowed to embrace your own unique being. Choosing is a huge commitment to take your self-esteem and happiness seriously.

Are you saying "YES" to a full life right now? If you aren't feeling thrilled to be alive, or your relationships are rocky, chances are that you aren't taking full advantage of the power of choosing — and the corresponding power of unchoosing.

Choice is a constant process. You are always engaged in making choices, even when you aren't aware of doing so. In fact, you are such a powerful choosing animal that you can choose to feel good about yourself even when you choose not to change.

What if all your choices were again open for your review? What different choices would you make? As always, your choices are your own to make. You alone are the beneficiary of good choices, and you are the primary victim of bad decisions.

Much of your pain comes from victim beliefs — those convincing, but error-filled perceptions — that suggest there are no choices available to you. Fears, grudges and frustrations then begin to replace your freedom to choose change.

LIFE'S A CIRCUS AND THEN YOU FLY

The circus teaches us about life. The beautiful trapeze artists and the tricky high-wire acts remind us that real life is exhilarating, dynamic and breathtaking. Life should be no other way.

Each somersault that you perform in midair, or tiny step taken on a slender tightrope, must be carefully decided and expertly done. If you get too far out of balance in any one direction, you will fall. And that's part of the thrill of it all!

Your life is not some boring spectator sport. It is to be lived by joining in and having fun. The point of life is to stretch your talents to their maximum potentials until you fly.

Have you forgotten about the magic in the circus of life? Change opportunities are always flowing around you. Even when you can't see your own change potentials, they are still flowing all about you. Life is never, and never will be, a fixed or constant event.

Your life is in perpetual motion even when your mind, senses and appearances tell you otherwise. Because your mind is so good at simplifying complex data, you have forgotten the fact that life is a dynamic and ever-changing process. Your life is a process that involves a constant series of choices.

Remind yourself of the reality that choices are buzzing around you all day long, and that much is at stake when you slow yourself down from making good choices. Commit yourself to a choice and avoid making choices second-mindedly.

Choice is at the same time a wonderfully uplifting — and terrifying — exercise of free will. You should change what you want to, being mindful that other choices will fade into the background. You should change when you want to, being mindful that you don't have forever. You should change how you want to, being mindful that you must go forward even when you are afraid or unsure of what the outcome will be.

Take charge of your own circus show. Don't put on performances with too little practice or without getting in shape. You are to be at your best under the big top. Make your own choices. Your choices are your own to make.

Do you feel like you have failed to fly high with the greatest of ease on life's trapeze? Have you forgotten how capable of change you are due to making some bad choices and taking a bad fall? Falling into a net of frustrations, and remaining there, is not your style.

Life's a circus and then you fly!

You will be like an accomplished trapeze artist when it comes to choosing your choices. Peak performances appear effortless to the spectators below, who have little awareness of all the smaller steps involved in each larger movement.

They are not aware that you are making split-second decisions, based on hours and hours of practice, that could mean the difference between a breath-taking ending or falling to your death below.

So let go a little, but don't you fall! Remember, change-experts make everything look easy. It's not. You are an expert chooser who must remember this powerful fact.

The circus parable points out that your life is a continuing, constantly unfolding, dynamic series of unending choices that are yours for the taking, if you dare to do so.

Your choices are always your own to make. And your choices will always affect you more than anyone else.

USING YOUR ANGER ASSERTIVELY

Are you frustrated or at your breaking point due to resentment? If you are, then you are making too few choices.

Happiness results from the freedom to choose. Low self-esteem results from anger that has gotten in the way of goal-setting, growing or communicating your needs and ideas well.

You must learn to make anger a friend — but never an outlawed misfit or foe — so you can feel free to enjoy life and gain pleasure from your most important decisions and relationships.

Anger is rarely a neutral force. You can use it assertively, aggressively or passively. Anger even casts the decisive vote for or against most of your self-esteem changes.

FACT: The happiest people among us have learned the secrets of using their anger productively.

Here are eight key ways to use your anger assertively to

motivate higher levels of self-esteem:

1. TREAT YOUR ANGER LIKE YOU WOULD TREAT A FRIGHTENED CHILD.

FACT: Children don't receive proper instruction on the constructive uses of anger. For example, parents who say, "You can just go to your room if you're feeling that way!" are telling children to stuff their anger in unhelpful ways.

Make Anger a Friend: Listen to anger like you would hear out a frightened child to find out what the problem is. Anger results when key needs aren't being met. Learn to slow down the automatic reaction of fearing, avoiding or returning the anger of an angry person.

To Build High Self-Esteem: The purpose of anger is not to browbeat, dominate or control others. Anger is a loud signal to take better independent care of yourself.

2. ACCEPT THAT UNADULTERATED ANGER FEELS "RIGHT."

FACT: No joke: Good sex and good anger have a good deal in common. Why? They each have normal stages of arousal, assertive communication, pleasuring and release. Normal anger feels real good and shouldn't be bottled up.

Make Anger a Friend: Pure anger will make you feel whole instead of split apart. Anger should not be mixed up with "safer" emotions such as sadness, nor suppressed until it comes out in panic attacks or sarcasm. Never unwittingly wed anger to complaining, tiredness, money, the opposite sex, time, jealousy or anything else.

To Build High Self-Esteem: Anger is supposed to help you focus on your goals and aspirations, and help you get up the nerve to solve problems. Healthy anger is energizing, and will help keep you in touch with reality.

3. TREAT GENUINE ANGER RESPECTFULLY.

FACT: You have become accustomed to fearing anger because

you have only seen it used in phony ways to control, scare, manipulate and seek revenge. You can learn to express anger in caring ways without ever raising your voice.

Be Honest with Yourself: Dishonest anger is used by bullies who wish to manipulate your self-esteem. Displeasers must be dealt with forcefully. Sadly, due to poor role modeling, genuine anger has been labeled as taboo, dangerous, unacceptable and quite wrong for grown-ups to feel.

Make Anger a Friend: You must learn to create a valuable place for anger in your life. You must not turn honest anger into refusing to take advice, blaming, nastiness, sexual withholding or any other ineffective behavior.

To Build High Self-Esteem: Anger should hold a special place in your heart without being allowed to take control of you. Feeling angry is not shameful. Take pride in using your anger in assertive ways.

4. USE ANGER AS A CONSTRUCTIVE FORCE FOR SELF-CHANGE.

FACT: Pleasers tend to use anger in self-punishing ways. Destructive anger is acted out in verbal, physical or emotionally abusive relationships. Don't take the anger belonging to displeasers onto yourself in the form of self-criticism.

Make Anger a Friend: Never use anger destructively. Anger wants you to make new and better choices. Refuse to take on angry energy, but when it is forced on you, release frustration through large muscle activity. With practice, you can think clearly and act responsibly when you are angry.

To Build High Self-Esteem: Anger was designed to build high self-esteem. The more assertive you are with you anger, the more able you are to feel happy. Anger can be the push you need to venture into the unknown.

5. EXPRESS YOUR ANGER SAFELY AND QUICKLY.

FACT: Your body wants to release anger verbally and physically in safe ways. When you refuse to express anger at all, your body may take over and create physical symptoms to express it indirectly. Don't be afraid of your anger to the point of ignoring it.

Protect Your Body: Anger is an emotion that you are wise to feel many times during each and every day. You can think angry thoughts to protect your self-esteem without anyone knowing. Even use anger as a cue to slow down or change directions.

Make Anger a Friend: Let your anger come out daily in healthy ways. Don't release your anger indirectly in headaches, ulcers or back problems or in social avenues like reckless driving, infrequent sex or employee tardiness.

Have Fun Outlets: Find safe outlets to release anger, such as frenzied housecleaning, loud singing, dancing to blaring music, yelling in a car with the windows closed or beating a dusty pillow with a tennis racket. Add years to your life and have fun releasing steam at the same time.

To Build High Self-Esteem: Keep in good physical health by working anger out of your body.

6. TO BE HAPPY PROCESS ANGER DAILY.

FACT: Anger is the other side of the happiness and self-esteem coin. You must be able to deal with both sides of the coin to feel well.

Learn to Be Happy: Ask yourself, "Am I feeling angry right now?" The anger scale can range from irritation, to frustration, to anger and finally to rage. Focus on the small ways you feel angry to gain confidence. Don't let the fear of disapproval keep you feeling depressed, helpless or anxious.

Make Anger a Friend: Try to mentally shed frustrations you have collected during the day. The rationale: the ability to let go of resentments leads to satisfaction, happiness and the freedom to choose.

To Build High Self-Esteem: Use anger to energize yourself when you are feeling defeated. Anger needs to be processed regularly to insure that you remain open to choosing change. Unloading anger can become a fun routine.

7. MAKE ANGER A GOOD PART OF ROMANTIC LIFE.

FACT: Romance and sexuality are increased when stored frustrations are decreased.

Don't Make Anger Bad: There is no such thing as "bad" anger, only bad behaviors that are justified and then excused by using the alibi of irresponsible anger. Wise couples express caring anger often. Each partner wants to know what upsets the other partner to keep romance burning bright.

Make Anger a Friend: Caring partners use assertive words to heal hurts and to avoid explosions. They say:

"I'm angry about _____."

"When you did _____, I felt _____."

"Something I've been feeling resentful about and haven't told you is _____."

Feelings are disclosed, not unloaded.

To Build High Self-Esteem: Storing resentments steals intimacy. You and your partner should use non-blaming anger to clarify expectations and restore lost closeness.

8. GET MAD AND GET EVEN BY CHANGING.

FACT: Revenge games will wreck your chances to be really successful and happy. The best revenge when you have been rejected is to go on with your life and be happy. Being happy will haunt your enemies.

Focus on Changing Not on Revenge: Many crises that could have been avoided are caused by playing revenge games. Beat your enemy to the punch by changing! "I don't get mad I just get even," is the self-defeating motto used by change-refusers who don't make wise choices.

Make Anger a Friend: Identify your anti-change victim beliefs and confront them. Don't remain victimized by angry self-beliefs that presume you can't change. Self-criticism is often a sanctimonious way to take anger out on yourself.

To Build High Self-Esteem: Change into the kind of person you want to be. Be assertive and expect the same treatment from others.

Might anger be standing in the way of your changing?

Most change-difficulties are related to secret anger. Use your anger as an assertive ally to insure good health, an optimistic mindset and joyful relationships.

Let the heat of anger thaw your frozen choices and free you to move in new directions.

FROZEN VS. FLUID CHOICES

Remind yourself that you are always free to make new choices. You can choose something new every single day of your life.

Here are some words of *Non-Choice vs. Choice* to help keep you aware of change forces:

Frozen	vs.	FLUID
Static	vs.	DYNAMIC
Fixed	vs.	MOVING
Rigid	vs.	FLEXIBLE
Controlling	vs.	SELF-CONTROLLED
Have To	vs.	WANT TO
Should Do	vs.	WILL DO
Unalive	vs.	LIVING FULLY
Trapped	vs.	FREE

Your choices need not remain frozen in a time and space that you disdain. Let's thaw out your power of choosing change.

You deserve to feel effective and powerful in this world. Having the freedom to make new choices is the only way I know of to accomplish your heart's desires.

When you feel again that your power of choosing is alive and not dead, you will choose to have the type of health, self-esteem, work and relationship life you desire.

MINDPLAY:

I AM FREE TO CHOOSE NEW CHOICES?

Exercise your mind using this format to focus on the idea that your choices are more fluid than you realize:

I'M CHOOSING TO wear these clothes today.
>   What else could I choose to wear?
>   Would I like to change my entire clothing style?

I'M CHOOSING TO feel sexually turned on.
>   How can I really let go and enjoy myself?
>   What else could I be doing with this energy?

I'M CHOOSING TO eat this food.
>   What else could I comfort myself with?
>   Would I enjoy a healthy addiction?

I'M CHOOSING TO make this amount of income.
>   What could I do to double my income this year?
>   Would I enjoy a different job earning less money?

I'M CHOOSING TO think this thought.
>   What else could I be thinking about?
>   Do I nurture my mind with positive messages?

I'M CHOOSING TO feel this feeling.
> What feeling would I prefer to be feeling?
> Why not feel how I want to?

I'M CHOOSING TO live in this home/apartment.
> What area would be more exciting to live in?
> How might I furnish my domicile differently?

I'M CHOOSING TO live in this city.
> What city might I like better?
> Why not move to another state?

I'M CHOOSING TO drive this type of car.
> What type of car might I like better?
> How might I improve my driving habits?

I'M CHOOSING TO work at this place.
> Where might I enjoy working more?
> What can I do to become better at my work?

I'M CHOOSING TO be involved with this person.
> Who else might I rather be involved with?
> Would I enjoy a different kind of person?

I'M CHOOSING TO be a parent.
> How can I spend more time with my children?
> Would I enjoy a different role with my children?

I'M CHOOSING TO read this book.
> What else could I be reading about?
> Would I enjoy joining a discussion group instead?

INTER PLAY:

Yes, you are free to make a new choice right this very instant.
Go ahead and do so!

Open Up All Your Options for Review Again: Brainstorm what all of your options might be. Don't assume you have to remain committed to bad choices.

Your Subconscious Choices Still Count: Whether you make choices intentionally or accidentally, you are still the sum total of all your choices. Don't cop out by keeping your choices out of your awareness.

Volley Back Against Self-Criticisms: Now, when you feel angry, or feel the urge to cop out with additional alibis, say, "I can un-choose whatever I do. I am free to make new choices at any time."

You Aren't Sitting Still in a Moving Car: Life doesn't stand still for you, even when it appears to be doing so. You would never think of jumping out of a moving car just because you felt like you were sitting still. Your choices are always in motion even when they feel frozen.

Go Ahead with Choosing Self-Change: How do you feel flexing your choice muscles and multiplying your choices? You never ever lose your capacity to make new choices, no matter how stuck you feel.

Take Responsibility for Your Happiness: Use frustrating situations and difficult people to help guide you into better choices that make you feel like you matter. Don't stay stuck in angry energy.

Make it a habit to re-experience original choices. All your choices go back to some point in time when your choices were semiconscious acts.

These self-critical ideas drive you away from your strengths, and back into your weaknesses. If you challenge these rigid thinking patterns, you will dramatically improve your change odds.

SIX STATIC IRRATIONAL IDEAS TO AVOID

Are you giving yourself too much "static?" Six irrational beliefs are primarily responsible for stymieing your attempts to choose for change.

Which one of these anti-change ideas blocks you the most when you are caught in the stressful stages of change?

1. _____ I'VE GOT TO BE PERFECT.

2. _____ I'VE GOT TO BE IN CONTROL.

3. _____ I'VE GOT TO BE THE STRONG ONE.

4. _____ I'VE GOT TO HAVE SECURITY.

5. _____ I'VE GOT TO WIN.

6. _____ I'VE GOT TO HURRY PAST MY FEARS.

SIX RATIONAL IDEAS TO USE

More importantly, there are six corresponding *Choice Permissions* that you can give yourself as a change-expert:

1. _____ I CHOOSE TO ADMIRE WHO I AM RIGHT NOW!

2. _____ I CHOOSE TO FEEL GOOD EVEN THOUGH I DON'T HAVE CONTROL!

3. _____ I CHOOSE TO ACCEPT HELP AND FEEL PROUD OF MYSELF!

4. _____ I CHOOSE TO TAKE ACTION IN SPITE OF MY FEARS!

5. _____ I CHOOSE TO VALUE ACHIEVEMENT AND INTIMACY EQUALLY!

6. _____ I CHOOSE TO TAKE ALL THE TIME I NEED TO CHANGE!

These six static ideas dictate that only ideal people are permitted the privilege of self-change.

Irrational ideas keep you from attempting change, and come out even louder and harder to haunt you when you are being successful and changing the most — another paradox of change.

Do you want to freeze up your choices and stop yourself from changing? Then command yourself to *Do The Impossible:*

- Try to be perfect.
- Try to stay in control.
- Try to always be superstrong.
- Try to hold on to your security blanket with a death grip.
- Try to win at all costs — be right all the time.
- Try to do everything faster and more brilliantly than anyone else.

Discover which static idea brings you to a grinding halt when you are changing into the person you want to be.

I'VE GOT TO BE PERFECT!

Keep an Open Attitude: Lack of perfection requires punishment according to this irrational belief. Since you have acted wrongly in times gone by, you must continue to suffer and be punished for your crimes, no matter how well you are behaving today. There is no forgiveness.

Master Negative Emotions: The emotion aroused by this belief is guilt. Since perfectionism tells you to reach for the stars or don't bother reaching at all, you won't try to make even small changes.

Take Pride in Being Imperfect: The Perfectionism Trap stops you from being who you really are. Such a belief will make you fearful of disapproval when you drop your facade in order to succeed at what you most want to do.

The Trick: For example, quitting cigarette smoking is difficult because smokers feel forever condemned for the amount of damage they have already done to their bodies.

Think Rationally: Be forceful and say, "I would have changed sooner if I didn't need this behavior to survive."

To Choose Change: Use this choice permission, "I CHOOSE TO ADMIRE WHO I AM RIGHT NOW!"

I'VE GOT TO BE IN CONTROL!

Keep an Open Attitude: This irrational idea claims you should have control over every internal and external event, and to worry a great deal when you don't. But life rarely goes according to a prearranged plan.

Master Negative Emotions: The emotions aroused by this belief are panic, confusion and disappointment. You may become resentful about events beyond your control, and give up trying to control what you can control.

Take Pride in Self-Control: The Control Trap will make you try to force others to change who won't take responsibility for any changes. It makes you beat your head against status quo walls, instead of thinking creatively about how to get over, under or around them.

The Trick: Many couples are defeated by the "terrible twos" power play stage that every loving relationship must traverse. In this stage, loss of control and severe disillusionment are normal.

Think Rationally: Be forceful and say, "I will let go of needing to control what other people say, think or do."

To Choose Change: Use this choice permission, "I CHOOSE TO FEEL GOOD EVEN THOUGH I DON'T HAVE CONTROL!"

I'VE GOT TO BE THE STRONG ONE!

Keep an Open Attitude: All forms of weakness are sins according to this irrational idea. It contends that you are weak if you need empathy, advice or support during tough times. The person fears being overwhelmed by painful emotions and going insane.

Master Negative Emotions: The emotion aroused by this belief is a numbing depression. Dramatic mood swings are common when sad feelings break through defenses, since the idealistic goal of total self-sufficiency is smashed.

Take Pride in Being Human: The Strong One Trap will make you deny your feelings to a dangerous level. It snares you into thinking that feeling weak is a symptom of going crazy. But power comes from turning negative emotions into positive action.

The Trick: A woman may expect herself to perform at her professional and parenting peak all the time. Likewise, she may always put her self-nurturing needs last.

Think Rationally: Be forceful and say, "I am most sensitive to my needs when I am open to my emotions."

To Choose Change: Use this choice permission, "I CHOOSE TO ACCEPT HELP AND FEEL PROUD OF MYSELF!"

I'VE GOT TO HAVE SECURITY!

Keep an Open Attitude: This irrational idea claims that base-camp security needs should take priority and dominate all of your decisions. Security is considered vital in surviving the stress of the unknown.

Master Negative Emotions: The emotion aroused by this belief is boredom, a "lack of mental or emotional stimulation." Chronic complaining is used to keep fear at bay and to procure badly needed strokes. Stability takes precedence over self-esteem.

Take Pride in Learning New Things: Paradoxically, The Security Trap adds a great deal of insecurity. It stops you from keeping up with the social, occupational and emotional times. The result? Unpredictable disappointments or developmental crises will cause you undue pain.

The Trick: Even though rapid rates of change can make any company obsolete overnight, the loss of a job panics the security-minded person. If you prefer security, you will keep your head buried in the sand and not update your skills.

Think Rationally: Be forceful and say, "I embrace my

weaknesses to learn from them."

To Choose Change: Use this choice permission, "I CHOOSE TO TAKE ACTION IN SPITE OF MY FEARS!"

I'VE GOT TO WIN!

Keep an Open Attitude: Being right and winning is everything according to this irrational idea. It contends that you must succeed, win at everything and be right during a tough dispute despite your better judgement.

Master Negative Emotions: The emotions aroused by this belief are inadequacy and anger. Status, power and wealth are often used to fight off feelings of low self-esteem.

Take Pride in Being Loving: Success-compulsive people reach the top but feel joyless. High self-esteemers know that true success comes from achieving their goals and enjoying relationships. They don't split off the emotions of love and success, but let themselves have the best of both worlds.

The Trick: Successful people work hard to achieve their goals. But some of them become closer to their families in the process, while others drift off into a world of loneliness.

Think Rationally: Be forceful and say, "I can be successful and still be close to others."

To Choose Change: Use this choice permission, "I CHOOSE TO VALUE ACHIEVEMENT AND INTIMACY EQUALLY!"

I'VE GOT TO HURRY PAST MY FEARS!

Keep an Open Attitude: This irrational idea states that you should be able to perform more competently with less learning time than is usually required to master the task. This belief doesn't accept that time is a friend of change, and that pressures to speed up learning can result in failure.

Master Negative Emotions: The emotion aroused is anxiety. Ironically, you will pressure yourself to keep rushing to new heights when at the very same time you need reinforcement for new wins. Self-criticism results.

Take Pride in Small Successes: The Hurry Up Trap emphasizes that counting clock hours is sufficient to realize true change. However, time, in and of itself, rarely heals or teaches.

The Trick: Mourning the loss of a loved one shouldn't be hurried. Good grief work takes time, and the gradual release of sad feelings. Rushing yourself through the process can backfire and slow everything down.

Think Rationally: Be forceful and say, "I can take extra time to learn and grow. All the time I need to heal is available to me."

To Choose Change: Use this choice permission, "I CHOOSE TO TAKE ALL THE TIME I NEED TO CHANGE!"

There are many ways to create a mental atmosphere that fosters openness to change. Stop thinking of decision-making as a chore or a burden.

Hear ye! Hear ye! Your choices are now all open for review! Enter into the change process unshakled and creative.

Make your choices fluid, dynamic and moving; make them an always-in-motion process where life is unfolding around you, and you are an important part of the larger dance.

Whether you choose to bother yourself with this fact or not — YOU are a lean, mean, choosing-machine!

Let's turn your attention to how you can tell the difference between good and bad choices. Learn to feel less confused about which is which.

KNOWING THE DIFFERENCE
BETWEEN GOOD AND BAD CHOICES

Knowing the difference between good and bad choices is crucial for your self-esteem. When you are in doubt as to the wisdom of your choices, ask your inner circle of advisors to give you helpful feedback.

Are you making choices to try and win approval? Are you trying to please others to buy their acceptance? Bad choices result from the pressure to please others until you hurt from the effort. Start today to develop your power of choosing!

GOOD CHOICES ADD UP TO AN OPEN ATTITUDE

How do you know when you are making good choices? Good choices expand your self-esteem when you realize:

1. **Choices don't restrict you — they free you up.**
2. **Nobody else but you chooses your choices for you.**
3. **You alone stand to gain the most from good choices.**
4. **Temporary gain is received from bad choices.**
5. **Long-term gain is received from good choices.**
6. **Self-criticism derails good choices.**
7. **You can claim the freedom to change your mind.**
8. **Today is an exciting day with different choices.**
9. **Avoiding a choice is still a choice.**
10. **Good choices add to your self-esteem.**

Permit yourself to change and have what you most desire.

GOOD CHOICES PROMOTE SUCCESS

Are you taking charge of choices that will make you happy and satisfied? Good choices build your self-esteem and encourage you to:

1. **Feel a stronger sense of self-esteem.**
2. **Expose in safe ways who you really are.**

3. **Realize a good decision is never easy to make.**

4. **Express your hidden capabilities.**

5. **Run your own life.**

6. **Go forward with your goals.**

7. **Know when others are invested in you.**

8. **Neutralize cheap self-criticisms.**

9. **Change perfectionistic ideas.**

10. **Make more and better choices.**

You alone are responsible for making good choices.

Make sure you are using the solid timber of good choices to construct your life!

RULES OF GOOD CHOICES

When you doubt the wisdom of making a particular choice, go down this list to help you decide if you really have made a good choice.

"Yes" answers mean you have made a good but tough choice.

RULE #1:

DOES THE CHOICE REDUCE YOUR FRUSTRATIONS?

The Rule of Good Choices: Good choices subtract more frustrations then they add. Making new choices may teach you that you have tolerated too much stress for too long.

Does Your Choice Reduce Frustrations?: When you feel free to make a new choice, even when outside sources are pressuring you to make the same choice, you are probably exerting your free will independent of outside influences.

The Line Call: Some frustration in life is good. Avoiding all forms of stress is bad.

RULE #2:

DOES THE CHOICE MAKE YOU FEEL FREER?

The Rule of Good Choices: Good choices make you feel unconstrained. They permit you to change back at some later time if you so desire. Bad choices make you feel rushed and afraid that you are going to miss out on something.

Does Your Choice Reduce Frustrations?: You are probably using free will when you feel free to un-choose a previous choice.

The Line Call: Some choices add freedom in the short run only to jail you for a lifetime.

RULE #3:

DOES THE CHOICE CREATE SPACE FOR YOUR IDENTITY TO CHANGE AND GROW?

The Rule of Good Choices: Good choices will make you feel both safe and a bit insecure. Bring out your strengths and unique personality for all to see — including your detractors. An admixture of joy and trepidation may be present.

Does Your Choice Reduce Frustrations?: Exerting your identity at the expense of others is a defensive choice. Equally considering others' needs is a sign that a good choice has been made.

The Line Call: You may sometimes push your identity too hard and ignore the rights of others. Listen to what the people you love have to say when they feel rejected.

RULE #4:

DOES THE CHOICE REQUIRE COURAGE, HONESTY AND GENUINENESS TO BE SHOWN?

The Rule of Good Choices: Good choices make you stand up for what you truly believe — no hedging allowed. Risk being seen for who you are. Risk being disapproved of to find out who really loves you.

Does Your Choice Reduce Frustrations?: You are most free when you take an uncomfortable stand separate from popular opinion. Be separate and take your own stand anyway.

The Line Call: March to the beat of your own drummer, but don't be a rebel.

RULE #5:

DOES THE CHOICE ALLOW YOU TO GIVE MORE FULLY TO YOUR FAMILY AND IN YOUR CAREER?

The Rule of Good Choices: Good choices enable you to give more of your unique talents in your career and family life.

Does Your Choice Reduce Frustrations?: You are freer when you are able to give more to others than you require in return. Challenge yourself to accept all the positive strokes directed your way.

The Line Call: Give more than you should. But never give up yourself to get what you want.

Use these guidelines again and again when you aren't certain if you are making a choice that is good for you. You must remain on guard against reactive choices that make you feel like a helpless victim.

Let's find out how your individuality — and individual choices — affect how free you feel to be happy.

Remember this freedom: you alone sit in the director's chair of your life!

CLAIMING THE FREEDOM TO BE WHO YOU ARE

Give yourself the freedom to be YOU!

Approve of yourself by making your own choices! You have the capacity to create new choices every second of every day to reach high self-esteem.

Do you feel free to make new choices that reflect your best strengths and true individuality? Read the freedoms that change-experts value. Carry these freedoms in your mind wherever you go.

❀ THE FREEDOM TO BE ME ❀

I HAVE THE FREEDOM TO
Heal any hurt that befalls me.

I HAVE THE FREEDOM TO
Hold my own opinions.

I HAVE THE FREEDOM TO
Say hello to new people.

I HAVE THE FREEDOM TO
See a future of health for me.

I HAVE THE FREEDOM TO
Risk new behaviors on my own behalf.

I HAVE THE FREEDOM TO
Love with all my heart and might.

I HAVE THE FREEDOM TO
Say good-bye and let go.

I HAVE THE FREEDOM TO
Be honest.

I HAVE THE FREEDOM TO
Grow and change to suit my needs.

I HAVE THE FREEDOM TO
Be best friends with myself.

I HAVE THE FREEDOM TO
Feel hopeful.

I HAVE THE FREEDOM TO
Persevere during difficult times.

I HAVE THE FREEDOM TO
Learn something new from frustrations.

I HAVE THE FREEDOM TO
Laugh deeply.

I HAVE THE FREEDOM TO
Weep completely.

I HAVE THE FREEDOM TO
Accept reality as it happens to be.

I HAVE THE FREEDOM TO
Let go of unwanted habits

I HAVE THE FREEDOM TO
Correct weaknesses.

I HAVE THE FREEDOM TO
Begin again.

I HAVE THE FREEDOM TO
Finish strong.

I HAVE THE FREEDOM TO
Be who I am.

I HAVE THE FREEDOM TO
Accept myself just as I am.

I HAVE THE FREEDOM TO
Be me!

I GIVE MYSELF THESE FREEDOMS TODAY AND EVERY DAY.

Become the best person you were meant to be!

Remember, there is only one of you, and you and your talents belong in this world. Feel free to be happy and successful.

FIVE FREEDOMS TO BE OPEN TO CHOOSING RELATIONSHIP CHANGE

What can you do to keep choosing change, even when your relationships, or lack of them, are subduing your optimism and enthusiasm?

Virginia Satir in *Making Contact* (1976), contributed an immense amount to our understanding about how entire families can be helped to change. She was a warm, funny and engaging woman.

She left behind her a wealth of wisdom for all of us to share in. I'm going to extend some of Satir's five key change principles for our purposes here. Feel free to enact these freedoms in your daily life.

You Have The Freedom To See And Hear Reality!

Claim The Freedom to Change: Do you feel free to think about the truth? Are you able to take reality into account, no matter how painful the truth might be?

Feel Free to Be Who You Are: Bob's wife, Mary, was so depressed about his dominating style that she moved out and filed for legal separation. Bob entered therapy to try and find out what he had done wrong.

Be Self-Approving: He said, "I haven't really tried to understand a woman before now. But now I'm trying to walk in Mary's shoes."

Manage High Self-Esteem: Can you face reality instead of trying to ignore, cheat or get around it?

Permit Yourself to Succeed: Deal with today, instead of what was once in the past or what might be in the far-off future!

You Have The Freedom To Feel What You Feel!

Claim The Freedom to Change: Are you open to any and all of your feelings? Do you feel free to feel any feeling even when you have been taught that the feeling is taboo?

Feel Free to Be Who You Are: Carol was wrung out and suffering from severe panic attacks. Her husband had confessed earlier to her that he had been having an affair with Carol's best friend for the past year.

Be Self-Approving: She said, "I was taught nice girls don't get mad. Still, I'm just furious at the both of them. The scums don't deserve me."

Manage High Self-Esteem: Do you allow yourself to feel all your feelings without self-criticism?

Permit Yourself to Succeed: Take all the time you need to feel what you feel!

YOU HAVE THE FREEDOM TO
SPEAK UP AND SAY WHAT YOU FEEL!

Claim The Freedom to Change: I'm amazed when sharing feelings that would generate intimacy are stored away in a person's head never to be heard from again. Aren't your feelings important enough to be spoken about?

Feel Free to Be Who You Are: Winny grew up in a dysfunctional family, and her job was to be seen but not heard. When her parent's weren't willing to give her anything, she was still willing to give her all to anybody.

Be Self-Approving: She said, "I used to hold back my good ideas at work for fear of causing conflict."

Manage High Self-Esteem: If you weren't busy pleasing everybody else, what might you find yourself speaking up about?

Permit Yourself to Succeed: Credit yourself for your thinking!

YOU HAVE THE FREEDOM TO
ASK FOR WHAT YOU WANT!

Claim The Freedom to Change: You know that expecting mind-reading is a major mistake loving relationships. Do you expect your needs to be met without asking? Know what you need to feel good, and feel good enough to ask for it.

Feel Free to Be Who You Are: George's ex-wife would pounce all over him when he would bring their ten-year-old daughter back from a weekend visitation with him. She never ceased to find fault with him in front of the girl.

Be Self-Approving: He said to me, "I never feel free to just up and ask her for what I need. Not now, and not during our marriage." He decided to ask his wife to stop criticizing him in front of the girl — but to feel free to ream him out by phone. She agreed to spare her daughters's self-esteem.

Manage High Self-Esteem: Are you waiting for a magic provider to come to your aid and give you what you want?

Permit Yourself to Succeed: To obtain what you want, you must demand encouragement from yourself!

YOU HAVE THE FREEDOM TO
TAKE RISKS ON YOUR OWN BEHALF!

Claim The Freedom to Change: Who will stand behind you if you don't? Who will take a risk on your behalf if you won't? You are responsible for your life. You must take reasonable risks to reach your potentials.

Feel Free to Be Who You Are: For example, Tina was an attractive woman who was married to an insanely jealous man. Her husband would give her the seventh degree whenever Tina would come home late from work.

Be Self-Approving: She said, "I've stopped doing what I love to do. I'm afraid of his anger. The more independent I am, the more possessive he becomes. I'm going to go bonkers if I don't start taking things into my own hands."

Manage High Self-Esteem: Do you encourage others to take risks on their own behalf?

Permit Yourself to Succeed: Demand that you support, encourage and stand behind yourself!

Each of these freedoms is meant to remind you that choosing is a constantly moving, shifting and fluid process, even when you are acting set in your ways.

PERMIT YOURSELF TO KEEP CHOOSING CHANGE

It is okay to talk to yourself about bold new choices before you actually make them. Why not?

- ✔ **CHOOSE TO BE WHO YOU ARE.**
- ✔ **CHOOSE TO USE GOOD ADVICE.**
- ✔ **CHOOSE TO TRUST THE OPPOSITE SEX.**
- ✔ **CHOOSE TO FEEL WORTHWHILE – NO MATTER WHAT.**
- ✔ **CHOOSE TO GIVE PLENTY OF POSITIVE STROKES.**
- ✔ **CHOOSE TO FIND MEANING IN YOUR CAREER.**

✔ **CHOOSE TO BE FUN LOVING AND SPONTANEOUS.**

✔ **CHOOSE TO TALK OPENLY ABOUT YOUR FEELINGS.**

✔ **CHOOSE TO USE YOUR ANGER IN ASSERTIVE WAYS.**

✔ **CHOOSE FORGIVENESS ABOVE REVENGE.**

Live your life free of guilt. Think things through, make good choices and take then take quick action upon them.

COUNTERPOINT:

"WHY IS CHOOSING TO CHANGE SO DIFFICULT?"

The unexpected answer: Change is difficult because the rewards-for-change are so incredibly huge!

Change is great yet grueling. It requires you to be assertive with your anger, let go of the need to control or please others and to say good riddance to bad things that have been around for too long in your life.

Here's why the stakes and positive payoffs are high for your self-image when you choose to change.

★ *Change flips your self-destructive tendencies around into self-instructive ones.* Take every opportunity to learn something new from painful or trying situations until you get your wants right.

★ *Change ends the struggle of: "Am I acceptable enough to be loved by you?"* Strive to love yourself as easily and openly as your children love you.

★ *Change is love of and for life.* Experience deep thankfulness for the small gifts of life.

★ *Change lights up your unique lamp of individuality.* Fashion a self-esteeming life that is built on what you love to do and with whom you love to do it.

★ *Change blesses your goals and self-esteem.* Don't blame God for the condition you're in. Build a better spiritual relationship with God and your spiritual self.

★ *Change sculpts a more tolerant, giving and non-prejudicial you.* Comprehend the humorous and tragic side of human nature, and learn to appreciate how difficult being a human being can be.

★ *Change fosters peace of mind, fun and giddiness.* Begin to glide through life instead of bucking the ride. When you hit the wall of joy, ask yourself why having fun seems so sinful.

★ *Change forces you to be aware of your secret strengths.* Force yourself to remove loser tendencies from your personality by using your strengths.

★ *Change enriches your character and deepens self-respect.* Begin to genuinely like, trust and respect yourself. Feel satisfied with your choices instead of being a victim of them.

★ *Change guarantees you will contribute more successfully in your career.* Make it a good habit to give more than you receive. Go the extra mile to leave something substantial behind after you are gone.

★ *Change fashions you into a sublime, trusting and adventurous romantic partner.* Choose to relate even when you are disappointed, hurt or angry. Let the sexual embrace enliven and refresh you.

Every fairy tale ever written tells a truth: it's never to late to alter self-limiting beliefs and fashion them into the magical stuff of high self-esteem.

In the next chapter, I am going to focus your attention on legal ways to rip off great advice. Why wait any longer to use expensive advice that most people throw away?

7

TAKING GOOD ADVICE

"'Yes, BUT...' is the game most commonly played at parties and groups of all kinds, including psychotherapy groups."

Eric Berne, M.D., *Games People Play*, New York: Grove Press, 1964, p. 116.

USE YOUR OWN GOOD ADVICE

Can you change your whole outlook on life? Almost certainly, when you are wide open to sage advice.

Do you value your thinking to the point of taking your own good advice? No one is more invested in your changing than you are. Why omit a key helper — you and your own great advice — in the process?

No, there's nothing wrong with the advice experts — who have dedicated their lives to obtaining knowledge in an area from which you wish to benefit — share. But if you ignore your own good advice, you won't feel good about taking advice from others.

Good advice is often rejected due to the fear of change. Choosing to try out new behaviors based on good advice is scary because you must travel into the unknown. When you venture into brave new worlds of personal change, fear comes with the territory.

Learn to stay tuned to great advice by keeping your antennae raised up high. Keep asking yourself, "What can I learn from this person?" Or, "What can I learn from this frustration?" You will receive one good idea after another to help you meet your goals and succeed in your quest.

A skill change-experts can't afford to do without is learning to listen to free advice and deftly using it to succeed. Keep an open attitude to advice and benefit from every source of great advice without getting uptight.

Take your own good advice!

THE CHANGE ATTITUDE QUIZ

See how you score on the Change Attitude Quiz. Then check the answers to see who is speaking — the "changer" or the "resister."

YES	NO	
☐	☐	1. I deserve to have what I want most in life right now.
☐	☐	2. I'll pay the price to have my dreams come true.
☐	☐	3. I'll change bad habits to guarantee my happiness, satisfaction and success.

YES	NO	
☐	☐	4. I'll let go of any relationship, no matter how comfortable it might be, if it isn't good for me.
☐	☐	5. I'll update my identity, acquire new skills or seek out a different job if it means I'll feel more relaxed.
☐	☐	6. I'll tackle my fears of being too selfish, too happy or too successful.
☐	☐	7. I'm willing to become more realistic about money, and to live within my financial means to achieve peace of mind.
☐	☐	8. I'm eager to create an exciting sex life that is ultimately gratifying to both my partner and me.
☐	☐	9. I'll freely let go of all my resentments — against parents, lovers and friends — to experience healing and grace.
☐	☐	10. I'm willing to build a closer relationship with God.

ANSWERS AND DISCUSSION

Resisters are quick to say, "Yes, BUT..." Changers say, "Yes, AND..." even when the changes may be painful. Which are you, a resister or a changer?

1. *RESISTER:* **Yes, BUT** I've tried everything, and nothing seems to work. There's no hope. I might as well give up.

CHANGER: Yes, AND I'll try anything. Something will work. There's hope. I've got to keep going.

2. RESISTER: Yes, BUT I think I could be that one-in-a-million who wins the lottery, so why should I work so hard now?

CHANGER: Yes, AND I'm willing to work hard for a long time to make things happen in my life.

3. RESISTER: Yes, BUT I deserve to give myself a reward when I'm down. I'll do something about my behavior tomorrow.

CHANGER: Yes, AND I'll alter any habit that stands in the way of my good health and happiness.

4. RESISTER: Yes, BUT letting go of someone without a replacement in the wings seems foolhardy to me. After all, I need security.

CHANGER: Yes, AND I'm able to feel fine on my own. I'm unwilling to sacrifice my self-esteem for security.

5. RESISTER: Yes, BUT I don't have the time right now to learn new skills. I'm just too busy. Maybe next year.

CHANGER: Yes, AND I'll be sure to make time to improve myself on a daily basis from now on.

6. RESISTER: Yes, BUT I don't have a problem with feeling good. Besides, winners exaggerate when they say goal-setting and hard work are two of the secrets to their success.

CHANGER: Yes, AND I realize my goals take me where I want to go. Goals increase my chances for happiness.

7. RESISTER: Yes, BUT I just had to have that new outfit/car/boat/computer. That's what credit cards are for. I'll just cut back next month.

CHANGER: Yes, AND I know I must respect money. I'll stick within my budget and earn enough money to feel proud of myself.

8. *RESISTER:* **Yes, BUT** I don't want to lose the spontaneity of sex by scheduling planned time for pleasure or by talking about positive strokes too openly.

   CHANGER: **Yes, AND** I really enjoy being responsible about my sexuality and meeting my partner's needs.

9. *RESISTER:* **Yes, BUT** it was their fault.

   CHANGER: **Yes, AND** my negative feelings are under my control.

10. *RESISTER:* **Yes, BUT** most religions are too uptight, and trusting one to be right for me is risky.

   CHANGER: **Yes, AND** giving thanks to God through prayer and worship is worthwhile for me.

Start adjusting your attitude to the "change frequency." Stop trying to find fault with the damnable discrepancy between what most people say and what they actually do.

Instead, find the kernel of truth in every piece of advice that can help you to succeed better. Be among the people who practice what they preach.

Learn to listen to your own inner wisdom as much as you do the wisdom of authorities or your elders — even more to your own advice. Be like a sponge and soak up knowledge to help you change instead of complain.

ACCEPTING HELP FROM EVERY SOURCE

Did you hear yourself in any of the "Yes, BUT.. " answers in the Change Attitude Quiz? If so, you're using the language of resisters. Is it time for you to change into a changer?

Don't remain a victim to your fear of the unknown. Alibis and excuses come easier than the effort required for change. Why cripple yourself before you even get a good running start?

Don't let "Yes, BUT..." become your favorite phrase, or "It's the way it's always been" or "I've spent a lot of years doing it this way" or "It's the only way I can live."

These are merely excuses that keep growth at a standstill and keep a happy, fulfilling life at arm's length.

Get mad at putting yourself through all kinds of BUT-BUT-BUT sputterings! Get anxious to grow by utilizing great advice from any source. If you steadfastly refuse to use standard cop-outs — all those "Yes, BUTs..." — you will succeed!

When you are willing to give up every excuse to achieve worthwhile goals, your feelings of self-worth will increase sevenfold.

EXCUSING YOUR IMPERFECTIONS

Steve Martin, one of the funniest men on the comedy scene, performed an outrageous, tongue-in-cheek loving advice skit during the seventies.

Do you remember the character who would say: "WELL-LL... EXCUS-oooze-ME!" How wonderful.

Mr. Martin would take the ordinary put-down, slap or sanctimonious finger-pointing and give the person a non-guilt filled thrashing with his hallmark words, "EXCUSE-oooz-ME!" In tidy measure he had taken his blemish of character and turned it around into a blessing.

Are you able to take good advice even though you aren't perfect? Do you confront your weaknesses with fun-filled laughter? Are you okay with yourself to the point that you can accept helpful advice? It has taken me twelve years to learn how to be able to listen openly to advice.

Why is it so hard to accept help from every source? Advice gets equated with criticism of your character. But advice is not a put-down. You are not a failure if you accept good advice — just the reverse.

I don't know about you, but Steve Martin's skit also made me laugh at my propensity to jump down my own throat whenever I did something slightly off-right. He mimicked what we all want to say to those criticizers who, with their noses in the air, thrive on pointing out bloopers, blunders and imperfections.

You have learned to automatically use "Yes, BUT..." as a way to protect your self-esteem, because advice is too often used to control and criticize instead of help. But a closed attitude to advice means you cannot benefit from any of it — even good advice given by a criticizer.

Who's perfect? Hilarious. The person who points out a particular flaw or faux pas in my character almost always has the very same flaw, but to a greater degree! Funny. It seems the "Now I've caught you" critical parent attitude of the classic displeaser has got to jump out whenever possible to keep the world from learning to love loads of wise advice.

Truly amazing — all the information you need for changing is all around you for the taking. Just look and see! How able you are to laugh at yourself determines, in large measure, how able you are to be open to new information.

Attitude makes the impossible possible. An open attitude means that you can let go of what doesn't work and try different ideas or alternatives that just might work for you this time.

The freer you are to say "EXCUSE-oooze-ME!... BUT I'm going through the process of change," the better you will be able to accept any imperfection you have and turn it into a new perfection of sorts by using great advice. You will use your strengths and correct your weaknesses.

Information and suggestions about key ways to change are flowing all around you. Great advice not only comes cheap, it's often free-of-charge. Give a careful hearing to advice that pops up unexpectedly around you from unlikely sources.

One small piece of information you casually bump into may work wonders in your life.

AVOIDING "YES, BUT..." VICTIM GAMES

Here are some of the most common ways BUT is used to knock down new changes. Place a check mark by the ones you hear loved ones, colleagues or yourself say most often.

In Chapter 8, I will be giving you plenty of tips about how to overcome the most common "Yes, BUT..." victim games. For now, though, start kicking the butt of BUT!

Learn to challenge these lazy excuses for staying the same. Could one of these rationalizations be getting in your change-success way? I guarantee it.

1. _____ YES, BUT YOU DON'T UNDERSTAND.

2. _____ YES, BUT I DON'T WANT TO TRY AND FAIL.

3. _____ YES, BUT I'M A PROCRASTINATOR.

4. _____ YES, BUT IT SHOULDN'T BE THIS WAY.

5. _____ YES, BUT THAT SUGGESTION HASN'T WORKED BEFORE.

6. _____ YES, BUT I'M NOT FEELING UP TO IT.

7. _____ YES, BUT THERE'S NOT ENOUGH TIME.

8. _____ YES, BUT IT WASN'T MY FAULT.

9. _____ YES, BUT THERE'S NOTHING I CAN DO ABOUT IT.

10. _____ YES, BUT EVEN THOUGH I KNOW WHAT TO DO, I JUST CAN'T DO IT.

11. _____ YES, BUT I'M NOT SMART ENOUGH TO.

12. _____ YES, BUT I'M TOO AFRAID TO TRY.

Read down the list again. Did you hear yourself in any of these self-defeating proclamations? Just reading down this list can have a depressing effect upon the nervous system. True?

My goal is to help you embrace advice, so you can use whatever feedback suits you in learning what you need to learn to get ahead with your life. Sound easy? Don't bet your savings account on it.

Changers do one thing well; they expertly learn whatever is needed to go forward. Changers assume that personal weaknesses are the best way to identify what information must be learned in order to be more successful.

I want you to try to love learning, even when all those around you are satisfied with what little they already know. In fact, I want you to feel excited instead of resentful about needing to learn new things for the rest of your life.

The secret to success is being able to bump into helpful knowledge through keeping an open attitude. An open attitude removes frustrations.

ERASING "BUT" FROM YOUR VOCABULARY

Can you go an entire day without uttering a single "Yes, BUT..?" I doubt it.

BUT — I challenge you to try anyhow! Will you abide by the rules of this change agreement for one solitary day?

MY CHANGE OF ATTITUDE AGREEMENT

I _____,

Vow to go all day on _____, 19 ___

Without using a single BUT,

Without uttering one single solitary "YES, BUT..!"
Without playing any advice-rejecting victim games —
AND without giving away any of my best suggestions to others!

Furthermore, I agree to feel secure and enjoy learning new things —
I also agree to listen open-mindedly to all types of advice —
And faithfully promise to listen particularly closely to my own great advice!
Henceforth, I shall write down the very best advice I come across during each and every day!

BUT!!!

For each BUT I catch myself saying —
I will fine myself an amount of ten dollars. Afterwards, I will donate my change-resistance money..
To _____
A cause that absolutely infuriates and disgusts me.

Furthermore, I will carefully count how many times my cohorts use the word "BUT" to slough off good advice.

I hereby enter into this agreement freely for the sole purpose of finding out how much great advice falls daily on deaf ears.

Learning to listen to good advice thrown at you or thrown away by others will take some getting used to. No problem. Keep finding ways to keep your mind open to advice.

INTER PLAY:

Listening carefully to good advice doesn't mean you have to take the advice. Many advisors never expect their advice to be taken seriously anyway.

Excessively High or Low Self-Esteem Results from Rebutting Good Advice. Don't use "Yes, BUT..." to burn off frustrations. No one knows you better than yourself. Put a stop to esteem-reducing "BUTS."

Beware of Making Suggestions to a Victim: If you hear yourself saying — "Why don't you...?" — than chances are you are giving advice to a victim who is going to frustrate you by rejecting your wisdom. Take a step back from being so helpful.

Chronic Complainers Don't Want to Knock Off the Excuses: BUT-users who reject your prime advice will make you mad. They say, in effect: "You can't tell me anything I don't already know."

Don't Allow BUT to Rain on Your Life Goals: What situations bring out BUT the most? Check across areas of self-esteem, romance, parenting, career, friendships, hobbies, sexual pleasure, the future and so on. Learn to say, "YES, AND...!"

Unconstructive Conflict Is Caused by Rejecting Advice: Success is sabotaged and anger advanced when good advice is rejected. If you despise conflict and crises, you must agree to adopt good advice.

Set yourself up for success by accepting every tasty scrap of advice thrown your way. Be greedy and gobble up great advice!

BUT is the second largest self-change demolishing word that exists in the human vocabulary — following dutifully behind our previous Nemesis "CAN'T." Be serious about catching yourself with your pants down, and your BUT(T) hanging out.

The word "BUT" is short, sickeningly sweet and devastatingly to the point. It is the word most responsible for the inability to listen carefully to your children, customers and lover.

It is the word that magnifies your false pride into a crescendo of superiority and excuse-making when you are dead wrong.

CONTROL WHAT YOU CAN

Don't let the fear of conflict make you back off from giving or taking good advice. Let yourself become a conflict-expert. Remember, let no one have more control over your mind and emotions than you do. Learn to make anger and healthy conflict your lifelong companions.

Begin to think of conflict as a constructive force to help you learn how to please yourself and others on a more equal basis. Conversely, associate refusing to take good advice with incurring the wrath of others and with unending debates that go nowhere.

True, conflict scares each and every one of us. But being able to use conflict constructively will strengthen your marriage, broaden your career skills and instill in your children the idea that anger can be used for rational and productive purposes.

Using conflict constructively is an important way to protect, improve and maintain your self-esteem.

USING CONFLICT CONSTRUCTIVELY

Conflict.

The pain can tear a business or family apart, but it doesn't have to be that way. Conflict can be a highly constructive and motivating force when handled wisely.

How can conflict be positive when so many of us fear being disapproved of? Lessons learned from conflict are the energy sources that keeps companies, teams and human beings changing into more and more effective and successful entities.

Conversely, apathy, chronic complaining, low self-esteem and lack of creativity are present when conflicts are avoided.

Avoiding conflict is often deadly. An ignored employee might reduce productivity levels to pay back a supervisor. Adolescents may be afraid to reach out to parents and ask for help when they need it the most. And mates mangled by blame hide their love away in a cave.

Few of us have been taught how to use conflict to our advantage. Here are some ways to stay positive and creative during times of heavy conflict:

1. TEND TO YOUR WOUNDS.

Use Conflict Constructively: Admit to being hurt when you are hurting. Don't fight back in shock and blind rage when your adrenaline is running on high.

Take Good Advice: Use positive self-talk and relaxation strategies to stay calm.

2. GET YOUR BEARINGS AGAIN.

Avoid Unnecessary Conflict: Communication is nearly impossible when two people are feeling afraid at the same time. Stick to the issues at hand and steer clear of blaming anyone.

Seek Good Advice: Take some time to have fun and to brainstorm new options.

3. FIGHT YOUR FEAR OF CHANGE MORE THAN YOU FIGHT WITH EACH OTHER.

Fight Fair: Unfair fights distract antagonists from the fact that everyone fears change. Since constructive conflict invites changes, fight fair to deal with needed changes.

Stop Listening to Bad Advice: Never allow fear to rule your destiny. To avoid power plays, keep an open attitude toward change.

4. FIGHT THE IMPULSE TO SAVE FACE.

Welcome Healthy Conflict: Anxiety can make you say or do things you will regret later on, and acting tough or distant doesn't replace lost pride.

Give Good Advice: Success means continuing to define and resolve the underlying problems. Most tough problems have solutions.

5. DON'T LAUNCH AN A-BOMB WHEN CRISIS TALKS BREAK DOWN.

Use Anger Assertively: You and your partner probably didn't come from families that modeled good ways to handle anger and hurt. Avoid dropping everything you've got on an antagonist when you are fed up.

Use Good Advice When You Are Afraid: The fall out from angry paybacks is too hard to clean up. Be more giving when both of you are afraid.

6. NEVER DUMP GASOLINE ON A RAGING FIRE.

Blaming Impedes Changing: Don't fuel the flames of existing conflict by causing more trouble. It is far too easy to act out your discomfort in revenge paybacks, gossip, resentment games, blame or self-criticism.

Give Good Strokes: Try holding back negative strokes instead.

7. TRY NOT TO MAKE YOURSELF THE PRESIDENT OF THE DIVIDED STATES.

To Minimize Conflict: Conflict makes you sting from losing control and feeling like you are in the underprivileged minority. Pleasing or displeasing others too much won't force anybody to vote for or against you if they don't want to.

Use Goals to Succeed: Stick to your own mission statement and goals.

8. AVOID A COLD WAR.

Choose to Be Caring: Concrete signs of interest and caring are essential during unfinished conflicts. Politeness and cooperation are needed most when you and your antagonist are feeling rejected.

Value High Self-Esteem: Give good treatment to your cohort during tough times.

9. AVOID THE "IF IT WEREN'T FOR YOU" GAME.

Fight the Fear of Success: Don't wait any longer to be happy. It's a lame excuse to say, "If you would only..., then I would be able to...!" Make changes that are good for you in spite of negative feelings.

Take Positive Action: Fight your fear of happiness and success more than you fight with each other.

10. REMEMBER IT TAKES TWO TO TANGO AND ONE TO GET UNTANGLED.

Be a Good Leader: A good rule of thumb: Put more effort into changing yourself than you do into trying to change others.

Expect Change First from Yourself: Be a role model of teamwork, leadership and cooperation even when you are down or stressed.

11. MAKE USE OF ALL YOUR AVAILABLE SUPPORT.

Use Conflict Constructively: Use books, friends and your inner circle of advisors to help you learn to take healthy conflicts in stride and learn to use them to reinforce your self-esteem.

Take Good Advice: Confront your part of the problem without blaming yourself.

Conflict.

It is the shot heard 'round the world that can set off years of warfare or provide the opportunity for building stronger relationships. The choice is yours.

Self-therapy is the best way to reduce unneeded conflicts and stop BUT from raining on the magnificent parade of your life.

CREATING POSITIVE FEEDBACK LOOPS

BUT expresses two contradictory ideas at the same time — it says "Yes and No" in the same breath.

Nothing like making an unequivocal "Yes and No" decision. No wonder you feel all befuddled when you use the word "BUT."

Here's how the paradox works. Let's imagine that someone has suggested that you take a computer class at a community college in order to upgrade your employability skills. And let's assume the suggestion is a solid gold piece of advice.

You sandwich the change-blocker BUT inconspicuously in the middle of your excuse about why you "can't" attend school. For instance, "YES, I would like to be able to go back to school, BUT I have too little time to spend with my kids as it is."

My point: BUT cancels out the entire sentence, and in one easy breath you aren't permitted a chance to succeed. Even worse, the very reason you use to stop yourself from going ahead with a new behavior is the best reason you have to permit yourself to go ahead.

For example, taking a computer class might mean you will be in line for a better paying job, earn more money to meet your children's needs and eventually have MORE time with your family as a result of your increased earnings.

BUT is a fast and easy way to avoid facing your fears of change.

THE NEGATIVE LOOP OF CAN'TISM

Learn to catch on to the paradox of *"Yes, BUT..." Victim Games:*

1. Yes, it would be wise to
2. BUT...
3. No, I can't do it because of x, y, z reason.

Be wise to the BUT trick that makes you think you don't have any choices when in fact you do. Challenge any BUT excuses that keep your life at a standstill.

BUT is Anti-Change in this way:

1. YES, I WOULD LIKE TO
   {The Agreement}

2. BUT...
   {The Excuse}

3. NO-O! I WON'T BE TRYING ANYTHING NEW.
   {The Outcome}

Make a commitment to your self-esteem to say "YES" to good advice.

THE POSITIVE LOOP OF SELF-CHANGE THINKING

You must learn to internally challenge CAN'TISM. Start thinking of yourself as a capable, take-charge type of person.

Learn to say, "Why can't I?" or "Why not?" Don't allow anything to stand in the way of your success and happiness. Here's what you can say to challenge "Yes, BUT...":

1. WHY NOT? WHAT'S STOPPING ME FROM...?
   {The Challenge}

2. (I CAN'T BECAUSE...)
   {The Fear}

3. BUT I DESERVE SUCCESS AND HAPPINESS!
   {The Permission}

4. I CAN FIND A WAY TO CHANGE!
   {The Decision}

Think of "Yes, BUT..." as the emissary of the fear of change. Make "BUT" march to your tune for a change. Begin to think of BUTTISM as complaining — not changing.

The less you complain the more you create change. For example, "Why not take the computer class? What's stopping me? My family obligations? Absolutely not. My entire family can benefit from my education!"

Just say YES!

ISSUING THE SELF-CHALLENGE

Challenge yourself to take good advice even when you are feeling helpless, lost or angry. The time to stand up for yourself is when you are feeling negative.

Here is the four-step format I recommend to challenge yourself to listen carefully to solid gold advice:

STEP ONE: WHY DON'T YOU...?
                   {The Good Suggestion}

STEP TWO: YES, BUT I CAN'T BECAUSE...
                   {The Excuse}

STEP THREE: REALLY? WHY NOT?
                   {Issue the Self-Challenge}

STEP FOUR: YES, I WILL!
                   {Proceed in Spite of the Fear}

Be your own therapist and confront the "BUT" excuse. Use a positive feedback loop during a difficult conversation or during unproductive self-talk.

Here is the format I recommend you use to create a positive feedback loop in your thinking in order to keep an open attitude to each and every bit of change advice you might hear.

USING SELF-THERAPY TO FIGHT THE FEAR OF CHANGE

Learn to fight your fears with self-therapy. Use self-challenges to grow.

Verbally correct yourself and checkmate what you are saying when BUT makes a move. Replace BUT with this therapeutic sequence:

STEP 1.

CHALLENGE YOUR EXCUSES TO A DUEL.

Assume You Are Capable: Ask, "Why not?" or "So what?"

Demand High Self-Esteem: Challenge the victim reasons you habitually use to avoid creating the kind of life you want. Direct your anger to your anti-change alibis.

Fight the Fear of Change: For example, "Why not find the time I need?" Or, "So what if I haven't been able to be successful before now?"

STEP 2.

ASSUME YOU CAN LEARN ANYTHING WITH TRIAL AND ERROR.

Make a Commitment to Yourself: Say, "Yes, AND..."

Demand High Self-Esteem: Begin assuming that you can learn anything. All you need to know is what skills are necessary to succeed, and how you can spend the least amount of time acquiring them.

Fight the Fear of Change: For example, "Yes, AND I can learn to use better time management skills." Or, "Yes, AND I might be successful this time with my new skills."

STEP 3.

LEARN TO CONTROL NEGATIVE EMOTIONS TO BE HAPPY.

Choose to Be Self-Approving: Ask yourself, "How can I mentally challenge my excuses to be happy?"

Demand High Self-Esteem: Never presume that you are incapable of learning to be happy. Question your motives and your moves when you are being run over by alterable frustrations.

Fight the Fear of Change: For example, "What keeps me from using my own advice on better time management?" Or, "Am I afraid to be really successful by going after what I want?"

STEP 4.

STICK UP FOR YOURSELF FOR A CHANGE.

Step into the Unknown: Do yourself a huge favor and Practice!/ Practice!!/Practice!!! interrupting negativity.

Demand High Self-Esteem: Give yourself the freedom to fail in big ways. To interrupt self-criticisms you don't have to be perfect or mean what you say. You just have to stand up for yourself. Interrupting the power of BUT is what counts.

Fight the Fear of Change: For example, "I may not believe what I'm saying, but I deserve to be happy in every area of my life." Or, "I don't have to make myself suffer any longer by using my time unwisely."

Challenge your anti-change excuses to a duel. Go ahead and take positive action in spite of any fears that caution you to stick to the status quo.

PRACTICE USING GREAT ADVICE

Start practicing putting great advice to good use.

Now, I'm going to walk you through different practice situations so you can get used to hanging out with friendly advice.

You know the change rule: Listen carefully to all advice to be successful. Sifting out and applying good advice is the only way to reach your heartfelt goals. So put you antennae up — and listen!

SITUATION #1:

SOMEONE IS BESTOWING A GREAT IDEA ON YOUR MENTAL ESTATE.

STOP the BUT: Yes, BUT I've tried that idea before and it hasn't worked.

Use Self-Therapy: So what? The idea hasn't worked before AND I still need to find a solution to the problem. Maybe I can modify the idea and make it work this time.

To Have a More Open Attitude: What am I overlooking to be successful? Did I persist long enough with the new idea to give it a fair trial run? What part of this advice might I use to my advantage?

Go Stroke Yourself: Find a way to win this time!

SITUATION #2:

YOU HEAR YOURSELF USING TIME AS AN EXCUSE TO FORESTALL GOING FORWARD WITH YOUR GOALS.

STOP the BUT: Yes, BUT I don't have the time to do...

Use Self-Therapy: Why not make the time? There's never enough time AND I need to free up some time to commit to my self-esteem as soon as possible.

To Have a More Open Attitude: I wonder how I could budget my time better to reach my goals? Am I looking at the big picture in my life, or getting caught up in the details?

Go Stroke Yourself: Use your time to obtain nurturing strokes!

SITUATION #3:

YOU DON'T HAVE LEGITIMATE CREDENTIALS AND FEEL INFERIOR.

STOP the BUT: Yes, BUT I don't have a college degree.

Use Self-Therapy: So what? I'm not degreed AND I need to have more confidence in my learning abilities. I can learn what is necessary to excel.

To Have a More Open Attitude: In what ways might I be smarter than I'm giving myself credit for? What must I know to be one of the best in my chosen field? Why do I stop myself from beginning my own reading program for success?

Go Stroke Yourself: Being smart means keeping an open attitude!

SITUATION #4:

YOU FEEL GUILTY OVER A "STUPID" MISTAKE.

STOP the BUT: Yes, BUT I feel rotten for messing up.

Use Self-Therapy: Why not make mistakes? It may be all my fault AND I need to be responsible for what I've done without punishing myself.

To Have a More Open Attitude: How can I learn to avoid making the same mistake twice? Why do I conclude I'm a bad person when I fail? Am I messing up to express anger at someone? Where has it been written that I am the person most likely to screw things up?

Go Stroke Yourself: Being imperfect is good enough!

SITUATION #5:

YOU NEED TO COMPROMISE AND FIND BETTER RULES AND ROLES TO GUIDE YOUR BEHAVIOR.

STOP the BUT: Yes, BUT that's not the way it was done in my family.

Use Self-Therapy: So what? My parents' rules were right for them AND I need to decide what rules are best for me and my family.

To Have a More Open Attitude: What sane standards must I create to live a happy life? How do I know when I'm being too stubborn for my own good? How can I be more nurturing to my mate?

Go Stroke Yourself: Decide what rules and roles are the best guides for your life!

SITUATION #6:

YOU DON'T WANT TO HURT ANYONE WITH YOUR DECISIONS.

STOP the BUT: Yes, BUT I can't make up my mind about what to do.

Use Self-Therapy: Why not wait a little longer? I'm a born procrastinator AND I need enough time to make the right decision in order for me to feel confident.

To Have a More Open Attitude: How do I fear my own success and happiness? How can I make decisions faster and better? Why am I willing to hurt myself to make others happy?

Go Stroke Yourself: Stop waiting for a magical rescuer to appear and bring you happiness!

SITUATION #7:

YOU ARE FEELING HURT AND ANGRY TOWARDS YOUR MATE.

STOP the BUT: Yes, BUT my lover doesn't understand me.

Use Self-Therapy: So what? My mate may not be supportive of me AND I need to learn how to be more supportive of myself.

To Have a More Open Attitude: Who else can support me? Why do I withhold caring during power plays? What individual issues am I acting out on the relationship stage?

Go Stroke Yourself: Rely on yourself first to make you feel okay!

SITUATION #8:

YOU ARE AFRAID TO STEP INTO THE UNKNOWN.

STOP the BUT: Yes, BUT it would mean giving up my security blanket and stepping into the unknown.

Use Self-Therapy: Why not? I might be afraid of the unknown AND I can learn how to cope with it just fine.

To Have a More Open Attitude: How can I cope better with the unknown? What do I stand to gain from this change? Which strengths of mine can be used to succeed?

Go Stroke Yourself: Take small steps in the direction of your most urgent goals!

I'm sure by now you know how to self-challenge the word "BUT." Great job.

Be open to yourself. Be kind and patient with yourself. Be as open as you can be to yourself. Be cautious when you utter a BUT that means: "I don't have the right to do what would really make me feel successful and happy."

Challenge every area of your life when you hear BUT cutting in on your dance of success. You will gain a new feeling of freedom, and renew your sense of being a chooser — not a loser!

GLEANING ALL YOU CAN FROM GOOD ADVICE

How can you develop the most positive attitude toward advice? How can you listen to free advice without getting all riled up and defensive?

Here are some tough rules to adhere to in order to make sure you are gleaning all the wisdom you can from advice:

RULE #1:

STOP AND SUMMARIZE ADVICE.

Take Advice: When you hear yourself say "BUT" to an advice-giver, stop in mid-sentence and summarize the advice you've just heard.

An Advisor Says: "Why don't you try interviewing at Johnson labs. I understand they have some openings."

Use Self-Therapy: "Yes, BUT I don't have any contacts at that company." (You can't believe you just heard yourself get in your own way of a good idea.)

Stop and Summarize Advice: Repeat aloud, "I hear you saying that it would be wise for me to interview for new jobs. Is that right?" Then say: "I think I'll go ahead and do just that."

Stand Back: Your advisor's mouth should drop open right about now. Why? Advice-givers don't really believe that anyone is going to take their advice seriously.

RULE #2:

TRY TO UTILIZE ALL ADVICE.

Take Advice: When you catch yourself rejecting good advice, ask yourself why or how the advice might work out this time.

The Advice-Giver Says: "You would be wise to improve your listening skills."

Use Self-Therapy: You hear yourself saying: "Yes, BUT I took a communications class and the teacher wasn't very good." (You dislike hearing yourself say you are a hopeless case.)

Try to Utilize All Advice: Inwardly say, "Why am I being so quick to reject a good idea? Might this advice work out right for me this time?" Then ask, "What classes do you recommend for learning listening skills?"

Stand Back: The adviser may jump for joy when you ask for a specific referral. Why? Rarely does an advisee seek out and seriously agree to take additional good advice.

RULE #3:

PRACTICE TAKING ADVICE.

Take Advice: When you hear yourself cautioning: "Yes, BUT I can't really do that," apologize to the speaker and ask the person to continue talking.

The Advice-Giver Says: "Juliet, why don't you let me set you up for a date with Romeo. I know he is available."

Use Self-Therapy: You hear yourself say, "I think it's a great idea for me to date somebody like Romeo, BUT I can't really do that." (You flinch upon hearing yourself sound so scared.)

Practice Taking Advice: Stand up to fear, and say: "I'm sorry for being so negative. I didn't mean to reject your offer to help me. Would you tell me more about Romeo?"

Stand Back: It's tragic how quickly sensible people dismiss good ideas due to the fear of change.

RULE #4:

APPLY GOOD ADVICE.

Take Advice: When you feel resentful about being unsuccessful, ask for help identifying your weaknesses in order to correct them.

For High Self-Esteem: Ask for negative feedback, by saying: "Could you tell me what you perceive my weaknesses to be? I won't hold what you say against you. I would really like to know. I plan on using your good advice to grow."

Use Self-Therapy: The listener responds, "Since you've asked, you could manage your time much better." (Suddenly, you realize how often you've complained about how little time you have.)

Apply Good Advice: Embrace the advice and do not run from it. Think about the options you have to obliterate the weakness. For example, you could sign up for a course in time management.

Stand Back: The criticizer is going to faint when you listen carefully to the blunt feedback. Helpful discussions about obvious weaknesses are normally disallowed.

RULE #5:

CHARGE FOR THE GOOD ADVICE YOU GIVE.

Take Advice: Don't let your solicited advice be dismissed by co-workers (or anyone) as if your expensive wisdom is cheap.

You the Advice-Giver Say: "You should talk to the boss directly about being cut off during the meeting. He's always open to hearing what people have to say."

Use Self-Therapy: The "Yes, BUT..." player says: "Sure, BUT his star employee is the one who interrupted me. He's going to take sides." (You know the conclusion is false and notice your irritation is growing.)

Charge for the Good Advice You Give: Since you expect your advice to be employed, say: "You seemed to dismiss my advice rather abruptly. Are you just trying to blow off some steam about the boss, or are you planning to resolve the issue?"

Stand Back: The complainer will do a double take and apologize. Remember, your wisdom is priceless.

RULE #6:

GO ADVISE YOURSELF.

Take Advice: Determine if you are taking advice to please yourself, or refusing to take advice to prove you cannot be controlled by others.

Think Clearly about Control Issues: Counsel yourself, "Did I just say BUT because I'm afraid to please myself?" Or, "Am I using BUT as a way to prove I'm an individual who cannot be controlled?"

Advice-Giver Says: "You are one of the best employees in this company. Have you given any thought to moving up into a higher paying job with more responsibility?"

Use Self-Therapy: You say back: "BUT my boss would be lost without me. I'd like to move on but I'm pretty secure here." (You cringe hearing your response knowing you aren't pleased in your present position.)

Go Advise Yourself: Thank the speaker and say: "I'm really going to think long and hard about your suggestion. Maybe I'm slowing myself down because I'm afraid pleasing myself will hurt others."

Stand Back: Co-workers will quickly admire your candor and ability to listen to their helpful feedback.

Choose when and how to improve yourself.

Tell yourself: "I won't give BUT as an excuse — or tussle with other people who use the same word — to avoid doing what I really don't want to be doing in the first place."

Outrageously, the hidden purpose of BUT is to let you find fault with every suggestion in order to avoid taking necessary action on any of them.

"BUT it won't work..." "has been tried before..." "to new/out-moded..." etc. are wet-blanket ways that the power of ideas are smothered before being fully explored.

EIGHT LOVING CHANGE-ADVICE PRINCIPLES

Soon the BUT will jump out at you from every sentence and you will challenge it to a duel. Fantastic.

I know it's not easy to remove an overused word that has such uncommonly negative side effects from your daily vocabulary. But you need to think clearly to free yourself up to change.

What should you feel or do when you hear BUT in response to the good advice you bestow on others? Why, frustrated, of course. BUT doubles frustration in every loving relationship. Your frustration results from the realization that someone isn't about to use your profound advice to improve their life.

Are you in the right if you choose to get mad? Let's take stock: each and every person in this democratic society of ours has the right to refuse to use any helpful information. Strangely, we Americans are entitled to the inalienable right to refuse to take good advice.

The major symptom of "Yes, BUT..." frustration? Chronic complaining. Just because people complain doesn't necessarily mean they wish to change. Many complain to burn off pent-up energy, but stop short of changing what frustrates them the most.

Do your best to avoid becoming a help-seeking, but advice-rejecting complainer, who makes everyone around them miserable. Instead, seek out and listen to good advice. And give good advice when you are asked, and only when you are willing to take your own good advice.

Remember, frustration is nature's way of encouraging you to change. These are tough standards to follow I know. In fact, accepting advice may be the all-time toughest task of adulthood.

Using advice lovingly is a tremendous challenge. Here are some ways to be diplomatic and caring at the same time:

1. GIVE ADVICE TO YOUR PARTNER ONLY UPON REQUEST.

Take Your Own Good Advice: Do you ask your partner if they want to hear what you have to say? Or do you just blurt out your comments in anger? Don't look for minor flaws in your partner in order to make a federal case.

Insist on High Self-Esteem: Practice changing more than you preach about change.

2. GIVE ADVICE TO YOUR PARTNER ONLY WHEN YOU CAN FOLLOW THE SAME ADVICE YOURSELF.

Take Your Own Good Advice: Are you a good role model of success? Do your actions speak louder than words? Are you advising a course of action that you can't follow yourself? Be a genuine person not a hypocrite.

Insist on High Self-Esteem: Learn to listen to your own great advice.

3. GREEDILY GOBBLE UP GREAT ADVICE.

Take Your Own Good Advice: Do you accept advice that will help you reach your goals? Do you seek out the kernel of truth in every piece of advice your partner gives you? Stop being so suspicious of great advice.

Insist on High Self-Esteem: Find out how great advice can benefit you.

4. ALWAYS USE NEGATIVE FEEDBACK TO IMPROVE.

Take Your Own Good Advice: Do you try to use criticisms to improve more than you try to win or be right? Are you able to feel cared about when you are criticized? Don't shut down your thinking when you are being questioned closely.

Insist on High Self-Esteem: Appreciate opinions that are different from your own.

5. STOP TRYING TO PROVE YOUR POINT.

Take Your Own Good Advice: Do you behave obnoxiously to court rejection? Do you reject others before they have a chance to reject you? Make your partner feel worthwhile and acceptable, and stop trying to take the upper hand of control.

Insist on High Self-Esteem: Drop safe facades to be close to others.

6. ENCOURAGE LOVED ONES TO BREAK FREE FROM NEGATIVE THINKING.

Take Your Own Good Advice: Do you offer advice to help your lover and children improve? Do you realize when remnants of childhood expectations are being repeated in your current relationship? Self-esteem benefits everyone.

Insist on High Self-Esteem: Don't let hurt feelings reinforce negative thinking.

7. USE ADVICE TO RESOLVE STICKY PROBLEMS.

Take Your Own Good Advice: Do you believe that there is a great wealth of knowledge to be tapped for resolving any type of problem? Are you an ungrudging giver? Take pride in what you contribute to your family life, marriage and to your career.

Insist on High Self-Esteem: Be the first one to be giving.

8. BUILD UP YOUR CONFIDENCE AND SELF-ESTEEM.

Take Your Own Good Advice: Do you talk with your partner

about better ways to meet the needs of both of you? How are you and your partner trying to achieve self-esteem? Feel free to ask directly for your individual needs to be met.

Insist on High Self-Esteem: Working daily on your self-esteem is best.

Be humble. Take pride in your own good advice!

PERMIT YOURSELF TO TAKE GOOD ADVICE

Take pride in learning from everyone. Take great advice and run with it! Permit yourself to:

- ✔ **STOP LISTENING TO BAD ADVICE.**
- ✔ **CHOOSE TO GIVE ADVICE INFREQUENTLY.**
- ✔ **KEEP AN OPEN MIND TO UNEXPECTED ANSWERS.**
- ✔ **STEP BACK WHENEVER YOUR BEST ADVICE IS REJECTED.**
- ✔ **LEARN HOW TO BE OPEN TO GOOD ADVICE.**
- ✔ **PLACE HIGH VALUE ON YOUR INTUITIVE HUNCHES.**
- ✔ **STAY OPEN TO THE UNKNOWN.**
- ✔ **LISTEN COURAGEOUSLY TO FAIR CRITICISMS.**
- ✔ **BE THANKFUL FOR HELPFUL ADVICE.**
- ✔ **ALWAYS LISTEN CAREFULLY TO YOUR OWN GOOD ADVICE.**

Get the best mileage possible from good — and great — advice. Value good advice from any source!

You may be wondering, "Look, isn't there ever a time to reject advice?" There most certainly is. The following chapter counterpoint tells you why.

COUNTERPOINT:

"WHEN SHOULD I REFUSE TO TAKE ADVICE?"

Many times! Much advice is bad advice. In fact, bad advice usually seems easier to hear and accept. Zounds! Feel free to be picky about advice. Select advice that works best to pick up your self-esteem.

Here are some straight ways you can respond to crooked statements you may hear from bad advice-givers:

★ *"BUT isn't it true you would be better off if you would just...?"* This is a leading question meant to make you agree to a conclusion that might not be true at all.

Fire Back: "I might be better off, but what makes you think I want to be better off?"

★ *"Now, I don't want to hurt your feelings by what I'm about to tell you BUT..."* This is a set up for unloading preachy or hurtful advice.

Respond Assertively: "Thank you for your consideration. I don't want you to hurt my feelings either. Let's talk about something else."

★ *"BUT you do want to know what I'm thinking, don't you?"* This is one way to get you to agree to being unfairly criticized in advance, and to give up your constitutional rights for rebuttal.

Say Firmly: "Actually, I've already made my decision. I don't really need to know what you think at this point."

★ *"BUT wouldn't you agree with me that...?"* This leading question tries to get you to agree with the speaker before you have time to fully evaluate an opinion.

State Opposition: "Apparently, that is what you think. I'm not certain I agree."

★ *"It really hurts me to have to tell you this, BUT..."* This is a coy set up for angry comments to be delivered that are laced with the poison of helpfulness.

Say Quickly: "Since I don't want you to be hurt, why don't we just omit the comment?"

★ *"You really aren't serious about doing that are you?"*

Say Confidently: "BUT I'm proud of the decision I've made." "BUT I've thought this out completely." "BUT this would be good for me and our relationship." "BUT I do know who I am and what I want." "BUT I have the right to make my own choices."

Do use the BUT word to defend good changes you have made. Stand up for your rights when you are being unduly pressured to unmake your hard-won decisions.

BUT. Use all types of advice to feel fine! You deserve it!

In the next chapter, I'm going to explore with you why complaining is a completely different game than changing.

8

CHANGING INSTEAD OF COMPLAINING

Misery doesn't love company; it only loves itself.

EXPERTS DON'T BLAME OR COMPLAIN — THEY CHANGE

Chronic complaining means you are passively putting up with changeable life frustrations and taking too many unfair punches on the chin with a grin.

Complaining is a highly superstitious act meant to magically bring about new changes in your life without any hard work. Chronic complaining must never again be confused in your mind with changing.

Suppressed anger is at the root of most complaints. Therefore, the better able you are to use your anger assertively, the less often you will complain, be the victim of a chronic complainer or please too much when a complaint is filed against you.

Always set your goal to change more than you blame or complain. Remember: Complaining isn't changing.

THE ANGER QUIZ

Are you able to use anger assertively? Or does your anger come out indirectly in chronic complaining? Test your knowledge of the positive uses of anger with the following quiz:

TRUE FALSE

☐ ☐ 1. Anger is often taken out in misdirected ways without knowing it.

☐ ☐ 2. Refusing to keep an open attitude to good advice is a major cause of chronic complaining.

☐ ☐ 3. Most Americans can't identify the different levels and types of anger.

☐ ☐ 4. A typical communication mistake is to become angry at people who are expressing anger at you.

☐ ☐ 5. Complaining can be a useful tool to bring co-workers closer together as a team.

☐ ☐ 6. Genuine anger is the jet fuel for rapid change.

☐ ☐ 7. Many people feel afraid of feeling angry.

☐ ☐ 8. A paradox of change: people who have every right to complain don't speak out enough, while people who should refrain from complaining never stop.

TRUE	FALSE	
☐	☐	9. Angry blaming can be a cover up for more sensitive feelings such as sadness or hurt.
☐	☐	10. Vengefully trying to get even with your enemies hurts you far more than it hurts them.
☐	☐	11. Happiness and anger have an inverse relationship: as one goes up the other comes down.
☐	☐	12. Game-playing results more from anxiety than anger.

ANSWERS AND DISCUSSION

1. *True.* Behaviors that lower self-esteem result from anger. Self-criticism, poor listening skills, giving negative strokes, time mismanagement and procrastination are just a few ways to indirectly express suppressed anger.

2. *True.* Suppressed anger is a major reason so much good advice is given and rejected. Rejecting advice and complaining are angry behaviors.

3. *True.* Anger varies in intensity on an increasing scale: irritation — frustration — anger — rage — violence. Rejection, resentment and revenge paybacks are the three basic forms of anger.

4. *True.* Tremendous skill is required to listen with an open mind to anyone who is expressing a legitimate gripe about you.

5. *True-and-False.* The answer is true when complaining is used to work out problems, motivate superior performances and make tough decisions to risk change. The answer is false when complaining gives a false sense of intimacy, but poisons initiative.

6. *True.* Healthy anger can make you so fighting mad that you won't let anything stand in the way of accomplishing the good goals you have set for your self-esteem.

7. *True.* The fear of anger and conflict can make speaking up about angry feelings a frightening event. But stuffing resentment, or taking resentments out in unending complaints, leads to blow ups and power plays anyway.

8. *True.* Pleasers and chronic complainers both use anger inappropriately to reinforce non-change. Unnecessary or prolonged suffering is a symptom of denied anger.

9. *True.* Sadness usually lurks behind insensitive comments. Verbal browbeating and intimidation are used to force you to conform to controllers' wishes by placing their pain on your shoulders.

10. *True.* Giving revenge paybacks — in contrast to having revenge fantasies or giving tough consequences — is the fastest route to certain failure and negative fall out across all areas of your life.

11. *True.* Lack of pleasure results from chronic anger. In fact, one definition of anger is: "The feeling of

extreme displeasure." To feel pleasure you must learn to deal assertively with your anger.

12. *True.* Games are played to avoid feeling deeper anxieties about the meaning of love, time, money, sex, death or life itself. Complaining seeks to increase feelings of self-control to bolster self-esteem, but it backfires.

SCORING CATEGORIES

9-12 Correct: **ANGER EXPERT.** You know that anger is not a behavior but an emotion. Consider yourself an anger expert who isn't afraid to use anger assertively and appropriately.

5-8 Correct: **ANGER AVOIDER.** You are stuffing resentments or complaining in ineffective ways. Your self-esteem will improve greatly as you learn to use your anger assertively.

0-4 Correct: **ANGER PHOBIC.** You are afraid of healthy anger. Take charge of your frustrations and begin to change them one at a time to improve your self-esteem.

You must learn to keep chronic complaining from interfering with your changing and being happy. Remember, complaining isn't changing. Be a changer not a chronic complainer.

The change rule: The less you complain the more you will change and the more happy you will feel. Change more than you complain!

ANALYZING COMPLAINING TO REFUEL YOUR SELF-ESTEEM

Did you know that the ultimate positive purpose of complaining is to establish a supportive lifeline to people or resources you fear you have lost? Absolutely true.

Complaining seeks to recreate lost human CONTACT that threatens your sense of well-being and self-control. Someone who complains a lot is saying in effect, "Please draw closer to me and reassure me that everything will be all right."

We all look to authority figures, loved ones and friends to tell us we are special, important and worthy of validation. Why? We need to know when we are wanted and that we belong to this world. When we are rejected, treated unfairly or ignored we want it to be made right by those who value us.

Your complaints are meant to signal loved ones that you feel out of control and are in need of additional reassurance, praise and positive change. It is natural to want more contact — not isolation or criticism — when you have lost control to assure you that you are competent and important in the scheme of things.

But unknown to you, constant complaining can have the reverse effect. It pushes people further away. Too much complaining can result in your misery being reinforced.

DO YOU CHANGE MORE THAN YOU COMPLAIN?

Learn to listen to your own complaints and use them in constructive ways to get up the nerve to solve problems. Don't feel down on yourself for losing control. Use anger against your problems instead of yourself.

Refuse to use complaining as an end in itself. Change more than you complain. Also, be wary of being around people who complain nonstop. Negative feelings are transferred to you through the airing of unending complaints.

Do you become a compulsive pleaser when complaints are directed at you? I hope not for your sake. Your job should be to solve your own problems not the world's. Many displeasers seek to control your moods, thoughts or actions through the vehicle of blameful complaints. Don't let them.

Chronic complaining is helpful anger used in unhelpful ways. Complaining creates CAN'TISM, "Yes, BUT..." victim games and distance — not warm attachment. Complainers reject all kinds of good advice to shift their anger over to you.

Of course, complaining isn't all bad.

Complainers may just want you to listen to them — and that's all. Rarely, though, do you hear a complainer say, "I just want you to listen to me gripe for awhile. I don't need any sympathy or advice."

Should you lend a sympathetic ear to a chronic complainer? No, not necessarily. You don't want to end up being filled up with their negative feelings.

You must learn when to create a boundary between your self-esteem and the unfocused anger of complaining.

ARE YOU A CHRONIC COMPLAINER OR A CHANGER?

How can you tell if you are complaining too little or too much?

Humorously, clients of mine who think they complain too much don't complain that much at all, while clients who complain the most don't think of themselves as being the complaining type. So stop and think about the truth.

CHANGING INSTEAD OF COMPLAINING MEANS

Are you a changer or chronic complainer? Changing means:

1. **Accepting success and happiness.**
2. **Tackling life's transitions instead of resisting them.**

3. **Accepting responsibility for what you can control.**

4. **Opting for freedom instead of helpless resignation.**

5. **Increasing self-esteem instead of self-doubt.**

6. **Making good choices.**

7. **Feeling attached instead of feeling detached.**

8. **Choosing loving relationships.**

9. **Making a meaningful contribution to life.**

Change-experts have learned that many good things come from conquering complaining.

To make new choices, use complaining in constructive ways to open up your attitude and unblock yourself from the generic fear of change. Demand the freedom to change even when you don't feel you have any control.

Complaining reinforces the message, "Don't you dare be who you are." Resolving complaints means you stop being a pleaser who desperately searches for approval. It means you stop complaining as a way to disguise or give up what is best in you.

COMPLAINING INSTEAD OF CHANGING MEANS

Complaining is always equated with trade-offs, compounded frustrations, pressures, losses and enforced restrictions. "I can't be who I am!" sums up the painful crying and fussing of chronic complaining. Resisting change means:

1. **Putting up with changeable life frustrations.**

2. **Avoiding positive strokes.**

3. **Being an approval-seeker.**

4. **Being afraid of change.**

5. **Giving up your self-esteem rights.**

6. **Taking your goals for granted.**

7. **Resisting your own inner wisdom.**

8. Squelching the strengths that make you most lovable.

9. Engaging in a false sense of intimacy.

Chronic complainers must face many negative consequences. Negative change-attitudes will make you stay in situations that are bad for you, and inevitably make you give up hope and stop growing and changing. And what outlet will remain for you to reduce your frustrations?

Why, complaining, of course. You will complain to protest the unfairness of forfeiting your needs to the insanity of desperately needing to receive approval and avoid anger. Stand up for your right to enjoy your life even when you are feeling bad.

Learn to love your anger for a change.

To begin to conquer the bad habit of complaining, let's take stock of the benefits complaining tries to bring to your self-esteem.

POSITIVE ASPECTS OF COMPLAINING

Complaining has many positive intentions.

The primary positive intent of complaining is to obtain badly needed strokes and to restore lost human contact. When positive strokes aren't available though, which is frequently the case, the negative strokes of complaining come into play.

Be honest. Are you a habitual praiser or complainer? You must learn to value praising and receiving praise above complaining. After all, the secret to conquering the fear of success is to be able to openly and genuinely accept compliments.

Here is a summary of the benefits complainers hope will accrue to them. Your complaining seeks to:

1. INCREASE YOUR SENSE OF SELF-CONTROL.

To Be Successful: Know who and what you can and cannot control to feel more in charge.

Use Self-Control: Sharing complaints tries to give you a greater feeling of mastery over difficult situations that seem beyond your meager coping resources and control.

Change More Than You Complain: Complaining can make you feel more in charge of your destiny. So can changing.

2. RESTORE A SENSE OF COMPETENCE IN YOURSELF.

To Be Successful: Be good at what you do and use positive strokes to be a fast learner.

Value Self-Competence: You need to feel you are lovable and capable and can weather any relational or occupational setback with a little help from your friends.

Change More Than You Complain: Complaining can address grievances and increase hopefulness. So can changing.

3. REDUCE YOUR FEELINGS OF LONELINESS AND ALIENATION.

To Be Successful: Demand that you live an exciting life and contribute something to this world instead of being bored.

Encourage a Sense of Belonging: You need to feel you are not alone or rejected. Find ways to fit in and refuse to be bored or suffer in silence.

Change More Than You Complain: Complaining can reassure you that you are not drowning all alone in the ocean of life. So can changing.

4. ALLOW YOURSELF TO RECONNECT WITH IMPORTANT SOURCES OF LOVE.

To Be Successful: Stay attached, but when you detach due to resentment, try to reconnect as soon as you can.

Let Go of Resentments to Stay Attached: You need to resolve resentments, not dump your frustrations. Healthy complaining should be the first step in resolving tough problems.

Change More Than You Complain: Complaining can renew a sense of teamwork, family togetherness and intimacy. So can changing.

5. SAFELY RELEASE YOUR PENT-UP FRUSTRATIONS AND ANGER.

To Be Successful: To get out anger, physical activity and hard work is by far a better way than complaining.

Release Emotions Appropriately: Accumulated anger festers and tears down your self-esteem. Don't let anger come out in cutting remarks, a closed attitude or procrastination.

Change More Than You Complain: Complaining can erase the slate clean of festering resentments. So can changing.

6. IDENTIFY TOUGH CONFLICTS YOU NEED TO RESOLVE.

To Be Successful: Relationships without problems aren't real relationships. Don't let idealism rob you of real love.

Develop Insight: Harping about problems is meant to put needed pressure to bear on finding solutions to the problems. Listen carefully to complaints, and then brainstorm solutions to them.

Change More Than You Complain: Complaining can challenge you to be at your best. So can changing.

7. UNLOAD HURT FROM YOUR SELF-ESTEEM.

To Be Successful: Stay sensitive and vulnerable when you are hurt and don't wall yourself off from others. Expect a caring response.

Trade Hurt for Peace of Mind: There is usually a deep hurt that is hard to handle at the root of complaining. Crying is necessary to release hurt and should not be outlawed.

Change More Than You Complain: Complaining can open you up to emotional closeness and stronger attachment. So can changing.

Learn to change what gripes you the most.

Complaining about your work woes or love fiascoes is a culturally permissible avenue to get rid of anger, receive badly needed strokes and to try to improve your sagging self-esteem.

But adopting a complainer lifestyle actually creates what you want least: unhappiness, rejection, resentment and low self-esteem.

Are your complaints getting you where you want to go? If not, learn to control complaining by clearly expressing what you want and why you feel mad, sad or scared. Always change what you have most control over — yourself!

Don't let complaining drain you of your most important resource — feeling that you and your talents belong in this world, and that your existence and potential are heartily welcomed.

Refuse to remain a victim to any person, place or thing. Keep chronic complaining to a minimum — and changing to a maximum.

MINDPLAY:
WHAT YOU COMPLAIN ABOUT
IS WHAT YOU DON'T GET

Ponder these questions to increase your awareness of your particular complaining style.

➤ Which topics do you complain the most about?

- ❑ Money
- ❑ Children
- ❑ Work
- ❑ Men
- ❑ Women
- ❑ Weather
- ❑ Myself
- ❑ Mate
- ❑ Physical Problems
- ❑ Self-Esteem
- ❑ Goals
- ❑ Habits

❑   In-laws
❑   Opportunity
❑   Energy
❑   Other

➤ How does complaining typically make you feel?

❑   Better
❑   Worse
❑   Indifferent
❑   Bored
❑   Irritated
❑   Depressed

➤ How do you PRAISE equal to the amount you complain?

➤ What do you think complaining should accomplish?

➤ How do you push away what you complain about not having?

➤ Do you feel it is your responsibility to correct a problem that a family member complains about? Why do you feel this way?

INTER PLAY:

Learn to deal with anger in a forthright and assertive manner. Refuse to remain a victim to your own or others' chronic complaining.

Refuse to Remain a Victim of Circumstance: Don't change-experts ever complain and feel like victims? Of course they do. But they don't stop there and assume that changing frustrations into self-esteem is an impossible feat.

Build Self-Esteem by Solving Problems: Why solve problems you hear yourself complain about? Confidence is acquired in the process. Complaining not only makes you feel bad, it can make you think you are bad.

Misery Is Lousy Company: Real intimacy is squashed when complaining becomes a way of life. When you complain, ask, "How does complaining put up a wall between us?" or, "What can we do differently to bring about more closeness?"

Good Advice Is Flowing All Around You to Help You Solve Problems: Take your own or any free advice and run with it. Open up your attitude by closing down complaining. Go ahead and take the time to try something new and different.

Praise More to Complain Less: Positive or negative strokes pack the same wallop. Complaining is a low-risk way to obtain strokes to help you survive. Positive strokes keep you going and get you where you want to go.

Complaining is a major obstacle to change. And yet, we all indulge in complaining when we are caught up in "Yes, BUT..." victim games. Complaining can work for or against you, since it is the verbal method used most often to draw your attention to a problem that needs resolving.

Deep down chronic complainers know that their gripes won't magically alter a bad situation. They don't expect anyone to take their carping seriously. Chronic complainers know you and I tune them out after just a few sentences.

Remember, use your complaints to spur on new actions, since positive actions lead to significant changes, and change adds to your success and happiness.

BE ASSERTIVE ABOUT COMPLAINING

Can you take time to tame the bad habit of complaining, and learn how to enjoy complaining at the same time? You bet. How?

Analyzing and correcting your complaint style will help you cope with frustrations better and use your anger more assertively. Ideally, almost all of your complaints should serve as an impetus to change.

Use complaining to get to know what really bugs you. Use any one of these principles to avoid becoming an unwitting victim to complaining that promotes low self-esteem.

1. DECLINE TO BE A PATSY OF COMPLAINING.

Be Assertive: Don't remain a victim to your own or someone else's complaints. Take a stand for change.

Do the Difficult: You are not in this world to solve everyone's problems, absorb negative feelings or to be a super-tolerant listening post if you don't wish to be. Change what you hear yourself complaining about the loudest.

Enjoy Complaining: Feel free to stay in a good mood when you come into contact with a chronic complainer.

2. GIVE UP TRYING TO CONTROL OTHERS THROUGH COMPLAINING.

Be Assertive: Don't sink so low that you try to control others through complaining. You must take control of your own goals and gripes.

Learn to Love Your Anger: Don't pass on your anger or anger dumped in your lap as if it were a hot potato. The more you complain the less you will gain. Learn to make anger a responsible part of your life.

Enjoy Complaining: Feel free to let go of frustrating people and move on.

3. FIND OUT WHAT IS AT THE ROOT OF YOUR FRUSTRATIONS.

Be Assertive: Complaining will be reduced when you dig at the roots of your frustrations — the frustrations that are choking out your secret strengths and unique talents.

Be Good to Yourself: Take time for self-reflection, review your self-esteem goals and seek to listen to what your inner self might be trying to get across to you.

Enjoy Complaining: Feel free to take responsibility only for your own frustrations.

4. LEARN TO PLEASE YOURSELF WHEN YOU ARE TREATED POORLY.

Be Assertive: Be a good role model. Don't complain about how poorly you are treated, and then turn around and treat yourself just as poorly.

Be Free to Be Who You Are: Be giving toward yourself, as much as you are a caregiver to others. When you lose a sense of control — be extra-giving toward yourself.

Enjoy Complaining: Feel free to expect loved ones and colleagues to take charge of their own happiness and success — just like you do.

5. STICK TO YOUR LIMITS SO YOU WON'T FEEL BAD.

Be Assertive: Set boundaries and use limits to protect your self-esteem from being damaged. Don't give past the point that you know will make you feel frustrated.

Be Attached: Keep your word and fulfill your agreements to foster healthy attachments. However, don't stick with people, jobs or habits that bring you down or betray you.

Enjoy Complaining: Feel free to set your assertive limits in the short run to avoid feeling bad over the long haul.

6. COMPLAIN TO YOUR ADVISORS, BUT USE THEIR ADVICE.

Be Assertive: Your advisors need to be appraised of all of your complaints. Don't hold back.

Use Good Advice: Advisors will help you sort out realistic from unrealistic complaints. After all, sometimes you aren't complaining enough about what you should be complaining about.

Enjoy Complaining: Feel free to expect your advisors to give you practical advice you can use quickly.

7. FOSTER CLOSENESS BY SELF-DISCLOSING.

Be Assertive: Complaining is a false way to feel loved and understood, and serves as a substitute for real intimacy.

Be Intimate: The less afraid you are to be close, the less complaining will be able to consume your life. Don't keep your feelings to yourself when you can help it.

Enjoy Complaining: Feel free to volunteer information to foster closeness and reduce distance.

8. GIVE OUT TWICE AS MANY COMPLIMENTS AS YOU DO COMPLAINTS.

Be Assertive: Complaining reinforces the status quo through the use of negative strokes. Use positive strokes to encourage change, even though you may be perceived as a pushover.

Accept Compliments: Unleash the positive strokes and stand back. Be sure to snarf up great compliments, and pat yourself on the back. Don't let complaining be a safe outlet for receiving badly needed attention.

Enjoy Complaining: Feel free to expect to hear lots of positive strokes.

9. DON'T ALLOW COMPLAINING TO RUN DOWN YOUR SELF-ESTEEM.

Be Assertive: Never fool yourself into thinking that complaining doesn't try to control the listeners' mood. Take charge of your own good feelings. Change what you complain about to improve your self-esteem.

Be Giving to a Point: High self-esteemers complain to a preset point and then stop. The stopping point? Never complain about a problem you don't intend to change. Not fair!

Enjoy Complaining: Feel free to reinforce your strengths and succeed in your goals.

10. LEARN TO APPRECIATE THE STRUGGLES OF THE OPPOSITE SEX.

Be Assertive: Men and women need the same emotional things. Don't polarize the sexes by complaining about your different, but equally difficult roles, and stop blaming your struggles on the opposite sex.

Be Open To Success: Stop expecting the opposing gender to change solely for you. Expect your romantic life to be one of equality, one filled with more treats than tricks.

Enjoy Complaining: Feel free to get along with the opposite sex when they are mad at you.

And how should you relate to others' complaints when you are changing instead of complaining?

Learn to listen to others' complaints without getting all bent out of shape. You don't need to offer some fantastic "Why don't you..." advice-solution to their struggles. Instead, try listening more carefully to feelings, and have fun getting underneath the complaint and making contact.

You will be saving yourself a great deal of time and frustration by being more empathetic and less preachy.

After all, most of your advice has been rejected with a "Yes, BUT.. why don't you just go jump in the nearest lake," anyway.

Let's find out how male and female styles of complaining

differ, and how each gender impacts the other with complaints.

HOW COMPLAINING STYLES VARY BETWEEN THE SEXES

Have you ever had the experience of listening to a member of the opposite sex harangue you on some issue only to find yourself no longer listening and turning away? Of course. Who hasn't felt frustrated about the complaints of the opposing gender?

I tire easily of arguments meant to prove which gender is more difficult, different, or superior. Psychologically, I believe men and women have the same basic needs.

Men and women are alike in needing:

- Honesty
- Fun
- Successful communication
- Great SEX
- Tenderness
- Growth
- Forgiveness

Too much complaining causes the skin to crawl with irritation and may make you ready to launch angry counter-complaints. Or you may want to jump up and run away from the complainer. Distancing patterns between men and women are promoted through the use of compulsive complaining.

Stereotypically, when running away happens between men and women, it is usually the "I've got to be the strong one" man who runs away from the "I've got to be the perfect one" woman. Realistically though, the partner who is most afraid of anger will do the running away. The abandoned partner then feels resentful, and intimacy is lost.

Unfortunately, human nature plays a nasty trick on men and women by making it easy to receive reassurance when our self-esteem is shipshape, but extremely difficult when it has crashed upon the reef of life. This means you and your partner are least able to receive emotional support during the times you most need positive strokes.

The solution? Give support when you are hurt by the opposite sex, and accept support to feel better. Stop expecting the opposite sex to be perfect. Don't turn misunderstandings into sex-role warfare. Be sure to be good to yourself and trust the opposite sex.

Men and women deserve to get along as friends, co-workers, lovers and brothers and sisters. We deserve to appreciate the strengths, weaknesses and differences of each other free of game-playing.

Just because we were raised differently, think differently and have separate value systems doesn't mean we can't get along!

Listen carefully to the men and women you value to find out what they really feel. I guarantee you will discover deeper feelings that lurk under the superficial surface of complaining.

MINDPLAY:

MEN AND WOMEN CAN COMMUNICATE?

Free up with the opposite sex regarding complaining. Learn to laugh a little about the stupidity of your own sex role. We men and women must learn to talk more — and complain less!

"Talk about what?" you may ask. Take time to talk about the following questions with an open mind.

➤ My biggest complaints about your gender are:

➤ How I think your gender has it made is:

➤ My sex role tells me to handle your complaining by:

➤ What your gender would be wise to learn is:

➤ What I would enjoy if I were your gender would be:

➤ What I really envy about your gender is:

➤ How I feel sorry for your gender is:

➤ My own role says I should only complain when:

➤ What I feel saddest about my own gender is:

➤ What I feel most proud about my own gender is:

➤ What I magically wish to change by complaining is:

INTER **PLAY:**

Men and women indirectly express anger at one another through chronic complaining.

You Deserve to Be Happy Not Sad: Both genders need to learn more effective ways to efficiently meet needs, while also being able to caringly express conflicts and disagreements.

Learn from the Opposite Sex: We all have a great deal to teach one another about what it really means to be a well-balanced human being. Complaining keeps us in the dark ages.

Learn from the opposite sex instead of feeling controlled by their stereotypical complaints.

CURING THE TOP FOUR VICTIM GAMES

You learned all about the "Yes, BUT..." victim games in the last chapter. And now you know that complaining reinforces victim thinking, non-change and encourages unassertive behaviors.

Now I want you to take control and change what many people only complain about:

1. **Fear of the Unknown**
2. **Procrastination**
3. **Time**
4. **Listening Skills**

To that end, this section is loaded with many practical tips to help extricate yourself from the four most common "Yes, BUT..." anti-change complaint ruts.

COPING WITH THE UNKNOWN

Hang onto your self-esteem hat. The unknown is waiting to greet you and show you new sights. I suggest you practice coping with the unknown in fun ways to prove you can cope with uncertainty.

Why bother? You will become increasingly self-critical shortly before and after you enter the unknown. Just when you are changing the most, I predict you will conclude you haven't changed at all. So be sure to use positive strokes when you succeed!

There are four symptoms that indicate you are probably being controlled by the fear of the unknown:

Your Mood Fluctuates Between Anxiety and Boredom: You quickly lose confidence in trying something new, and are bored to tears with the same old tried-and-true routines.

Alibis Are Used Excessively: You use alibis about time, money or energy to avoid venturing out to new places or events, and you complain about the lack of pleasure in your life.

Beneficial Changes Are Resisted: You deny how your future is determined by the choices you make today and rarely live in the present moment.

You Are Close-Minded about Alternatives: You refuse to think you have the courage to embrace different and better ways of doing things.

How can you develop the habit of facing the unknown, while staying open to change, and safely venturing out into new areas?

Here are some simple experiments to help you learn how to cope with the universal fear of the unknown. Try one or two that tickle your funny bone.

1. DRIVE A NEW ROUTE TO WORK.

Take a longer or more scenic route, or try to come up with as many new ways to get to work as you can.

2. ALTER YOUR TRADITIONAL TIME SCHEDULE.

If you are a night person, put yourself on a day schedule, or exercise in the morning instead of the evening.

3. DETERMINE THE BEST THING THAT COULD HAPPEN.

Focusing on the benefits of change instead of the potential costs can build up your courage.

4. ATTEND A DIFFERENT PLACE OF WORSHIP.

Go to a synagogue, an evangelical meeting or attend a mass different from your norm.

5. WEAR A DIFFERENT CLOTHING STYLE.

Listen to the compliments or criticisms you receive for changing with a smile.

6. WRITE A HATE LETTER IN CARE OF THE UNKNOWN.

Analyze how you are holding the unknown to blame for your present choices.

7. ASSOCIATE WITH PEOPLE OF A DIFFERENT RACE.

Imagine what benefits or costs you might acquire if you were a different color.

8. SPEND AN AFTERNOON ON A COLLEGE CAMPUS.

Gain a fresh perspective by going to a place where new trends are adopted feverishly.

9. ARRIVE TO WORK EARLY OR STAY LATE.

You might be surprised what you will learn about your place of employment and the employees who work there.

10. DEVELOP YOURSELF SPIRITUALLY.

Read classics in psychology, religion, literature or history.

11. EXPERIMENT WITH PLEASURING YOUR SEXUAL PARTNER.

Be receptive to new expressions of sensuality, fun or intense sexuality.

12. TRAVEL WHERE YOU NORMALLY WOULDN'T GO.

Go through new areas of your office building and chat with people about their jobs as you walk by.

Have some fun whipping the universal fear of the unknown.

The unknown is nothing new—not for long!

MINDPLAY:

TREATING YOUR LIFE AS AN ADVENTURE

Treat your life as an adventure! Answer this question: "This week I'm going to try out these three new pleasurable activities":

ADVENTURE #1:

ADVENTURE #2:

ADVENTURE #3:

➤ The most threatening experiment for me would be:

➤ By venturing into the unknown I'm afraid I'll find out:

➤ By venturing into the unknown I might obtain:

➤ Good ways my mother handled the fear of the unknown:

➤ Good ways my father handled the fear of the unknown:

➤ Good ways I've coped with the unpredictable in the past:

INTER PLAY:

Give yourself more credit!

Just Blame the Fear of Change: The fear of change is to blame for your fear of the unknown — not you. So stop blaming yourself to start changing yourself.

OVERCOMING PROCRASTINATION

Waiting.

Waiting for the perfect time to come. Procrastination is a sure-fire way to resist growing up and becoming your own person.

The procrastinators' battle-cry: you don't want to take small steps when you can make one gigantic leap to influence mankind. So you end up waiting, sometimes for your entire life, until your success stars are aligned just right in the sky.

You weren't born to be a procrastinator — you were trained to be a procrastinator. The fear of failure, the desire to receive approval and a history of making bad decisions will encourage you to back off from making your own timely decisions.

Procrastination bids you to wait forever until you have a signed, sealed and delivered contract that you can succeed in something new before you waste your precious time trying it out part-time.

Are you waiting for a guarantee of success or for your star chart to be just right before you BEGIN? Fess up. And use some of these tips to march out of the procrastination trap.

1. BREAK THE TASK DOWN.

Take Action Today: Use the assembly-line approach.
Demand High Self-Esteem: Break down large changes into small units that you can handle without undue anxiety. Go in the right direction and you will eventually arrive.

2. START TODAY.

Take Action Today: Even when you don't know if you can handle something by yourself—start today.
Demand High Self-Esteem: Getting forward movement going will help you feel encouraged. A little effort goes a long way.

3. REMOVE STRESS.

Take Action Today: Use a mental high-pressure gauge to measure the undue stress certain people or situations place on you.
Demand High Self-Esteem: Don't keep rotten people in your

life to avoid relaxed living. If you can't remove yourself physically, try to remove yourself mentally from their negative impact.

4. BE THE FIRST TO CHANGE.

Take Action Today: Don't wait for your cohort to change. Change yourself first.

Demand High Self-Esteem: Your changes will put healthy pressure on the other person to change. Learn to be an individual in a world crowded with look-alikes.

5. LOVE YOUR ANGER.

Take Action Today: Learn to love your anger and use it productively.

Demand High Self-Esteem: Stay off your high horse. People don't have to be more supportive or reasonable for you to go ahead and do what's best for you to do.

6. STAY AS RELAXED AS YOU CAN.

Take Action Today: Enjoy doing something new for the first time without having to do it well.

Demand High Self-Esteem: Never expect yourself to be perfectly calm when you try new behaviors. Give yourself plenty of opportunities to fail in big and small ways.

7. HAVE TRUSTED ALLIES.

Take Action Today: Refuse to protect your ego from hard-hitting advice.

Demand High Self-Esteem: Form professional alliances with people who aren't afraid to tell you kindly what must be changed about your personality or work performance to make your life take off.

8. BE A SMART RISK TAKER.

Take Action Today: Step out of your own personal closet —

the one that stores away your strengths.

Demand High Self-Esteem: Openly risk disclosing your hidden childlike aspirations. Do not be ashamed about your ambitions, passions and fiery dreams.

9. FIGHT DOOM AND GLOOM THINKING.

Take Action Today: Admit that you do not have a crystal ball to predict a future full of bad consequences if you change into a newer and more powerful you.

10. AVOID THE TRAP OF BEING TOO SERIOUS OR TOO CARE-FREE.

Demand High Self-Esteem: Schedule time to work hard and concentrate on your new goals, and time to clear your mind completely through fun activities.

Procrastination thinking encourages you to stay the same when your higher self is screaming for you to have the courage to take on new changes.

USING TIME WISELY

Don't stand idly by as you avoid having the time of your life. Choose to find novel ways to free up some time.

You must master time or become the victim of lost opportunities. Ask yourself, "How can I get more work done in the same amount of time?" And, "How can I spend enough time with my children, lover and friends and still enjoy my work?"

Time-management methods help you squeeze ten hours' worth of effort into an eight-hour work day and still allow you to go home feeling refreshed (or close to feeling refreshed) from a full-day's work.

If you find yourself feeling like you are sitting on the sidelines of life, or running around frantically in circles in the middle of the playing field, then you may find some solace in the following time saving tips:

1. ANALYZE YOUR PEAK PERFORMANCE PERIODS.

Certain times of day will be most suited for basic tasks, creative work or boring duties. Use low energy times for the least important requirements.

2. SWITCH TO DIFFERENT TASKS WHEN YOUR ATTENTION WANDERS.

Build excitement into your work pace, add variety to your day and mix up types of work to be done so you can maintain intense levels of concentration.

3. BURN YOUR BASIC MISSION INTO YOUR MIND.

Ask yourself, "How does what I'm doing right now fit into the big picture?" Or, "Am I using my time on efforts that will provide the biggest payoff?"

4. AVOID PLAYING PHONE TAG.

Leave specific times you are available and can be reached, or ask when is the best time to reach your party. Don't let your time be chewed up holding onto a telephone.

5. WHEN YOU WORK—ONLY WORK.

Daydreaming, personal calls, social pastimes or getting strokes in other ways cuts into productive time. Assertively say, "I've got to get back to work now," when co-workers hog your time with socializing.

6. EAT ON OFF-HOURS.

Traffic jams, fast food lines and time spent away from your work location will chew up badly needed time. Eating alone while taking stock of your goals and accomplishments is a good way to go.

7. BLOW OFF SOME TIME WITH A VENGEANCE.

Find a place to close your eyes, listen to soothing music, read some passages from a favorite book or try out some new joke material. Goof off for awhile and let your mind take a break and vegetate.

8. USE SLOW-PACED MEETINGS TO GET SOME WORK DONE PRIVATELY.

You can rough-draft memos, quick-scan research or be creative in other ways during meeting down time when little work is getting done.

9. USE POSITIVE INFLUENCES WHEN YOUR ENERGY WANES.

Use role models from history, inspirational writings or caring people to pick yourself up when you are fatigued. Talk to yourself in nurturing and encouraging ways.

Be the master of your time instead of a victim to it. You'll feel better and get more done.

MINDPLAY:

USING A "TO DO" LIST TO STICK TO SCHEDULE

Make a list of essential tasks to be done as soon as you arrive at work. You will sidestep many distractions by having your own agenda. Always keep the *To Do List* in your visual field.

TO DO TODAY:

1.
2.
3.

4.

5.

6.

7.

INTER PLAY:

Even when you haven't gotten very far, give yourself encouragement for the small steps you have taken to reach your larger goals.

Use Time Lovingly: On your drive home, review in your mind how well you have — or have not — measured up.

KEYS TO BEING A GOOD LISTENER

I think the most difficult skill to acquire is the ability to listen open-mindedly and judgement-free to another human being. Just listening. Taking in. Trying to understand the person's frame-of-reference free of blame.

Judgemental listening produces this result: "Nobody really cares for or appreciates me." Such words are spoken bitterly and with an air of tragedy. A gnawing sense of loneliness begins forming, and resentments collect making it impossible to accept love.

Careful listening means you try to hear what the speaker means to say — instead of what you would like the words to mean. There is no more loving gift you can give than trying to understand the ever-changing inner world of another human being.

Careful listening is an invaluable skill that you can sharpen with some practice and patience. Good listeners have learned to listen to their own inner urges too. Serious communicators use seven keys for effective listening and ask open-ended questions to encourage more talking.

Here's how you can do both:

1. CLEAR OUT YOUR MIND.

Listen Openly: Empty your mind of daily worries and remove any preconceptions about what "should" be discussed.

Opening Gambit: "What have you been thinking about this issue?"

2. SHY AWAY FROM GIVING ADVICE.

Listen Openly: Good listeners heal what ails a speaker by seeking to understand, instead of trying hard to come up with a quick-fix solution to pesky problems.

Opening Gambit: "How have you solved problems like this one in the past?"

3. ACCEPT ALL FEELINGS EQUALLY.

Listen Openly: No feelings are better or superior to others, so listen fairly across different emotional frequencies.

Opening Gambit: "Which feelings are the hardest ones for you to handle?"

4. PERMIT DIFFERENT THINKING.

Listen Openly: Your job is to be a semi-neutral sounding board for the speaker to sort through his or her own pain, confusion and mixed-up ideas.

Opening Gambit: "What confuses (hurts, angers, scares or delights) you most about this situation?"

5. EXPRESS DISAGREEMENT SPARINGLY.

Listen Openly: Moralizing, preaching and arguing are symptoms of anxiety that shut down communication and judge feelings to be right or wrong.

Opening Gambit: "How would you argue against your own opinions?"

6. WALK IN THEIR MOCCASINS FOR ONE MILE.

Listen Openly: Empathy and compassion are developed when you flex your mind to grasp how others perceive.

Opening Gambit: "What would a wise person in your shoes do right now?"

7. DON'T BE TOO SMART OR HELPFUL.

Listen Openly: Advice may be cheap, but respecting a speaker who is struggling for solutions is priceless.

Opening Gambit: "What might the answer to this problem be?"

Truly understanding another human being is one of the most precious gifts you can ever give.

Listen carefully to what people mean to say, instead of what they say they mean.

WAYS OF TAMING COMPLAINING
BETWEEN THE SEXES

As you have seen, although complaining seeks to address grievances and give you a greater feeling of self-control and mastery, it can also backfire and cause others to feel angry and distance themselves from you.

Complaining is productive when it increases human contact, acceptance and creative problem-solving. Complaining is unproductive when opportunities for self-improvement go by the wayside.

What can you as a woman or man do to change complaints into more constructive actions?

1. OFFER A SOLUTION TO THE PROBLEM AT HAND.

Think Clearly: Try to solve what you find yourself complaining about. Specify why a situation is bothersome to you and try several alternatives to remedy the problem.

Tame Complaining: Brainstorming reduces defensiveness in yourself, a listener or a team; it also reassures others that they are not the cause of your discomfort.

2. REFRAIN FROM PLAYING "YES, BUT..." VICTIM GAMES.

Think Clearly When You Are Frustrated: All problems have solutions. Keep brainstorming. Solutions don't have to be ideal — they just need to work.

Have Hope Even When You Don't: Aren't you being too pessimistic when you believe that no one can devise any useful solutions to the problems that plague you? No problem is that tenacious.

Tame Complaining: Give old solutions to problems a new try. Accept good advice and give good strokes. Persist until you find a solution that works.

3. BE HONEST ABOUT FEELINGS THAT EXIST UNDERNEATH THE SURFACE OF BITTER COMPLAINING.

Think Clearly When You Are Hurt: Real feelings aren't as easy to come to terms with as faked, replaced or denied feelings. Hurt and fear are complex human emotions easily misread in the midst of misery.

Tame Complaining: Share what is hurting you down deep so people know what is really bothering you.

4. LIST THE PERSONAL COSTS OF COMPLAINING TOO MUCH.

Think Clearly When You Are Afraid: Have you noticed that complaining can turn off other people from listening to you when you need them the most? Stop pushing people away with a negative attitude.

Tame Complaining: Don't force other people to feel responsible for your problems. Complain only about things you plan to change, and express thanks for what you take for granted immediately after complaining.

5. BE STRAIGHT ABOUT ASKING FOR SUPPORT TO AIR GRIPES.

Think Clearly When You Are Vulnerable: Be upfront about the need to complain. Ask, "Would you be willing to listen to some things that are bothering me? You don't have to solve these problems, just listen to them."

Tame Complaining: Be flagrant about complaining, and gripe with a flair for fun. Getting permission to gripe freely can free everyone up to get things out into the open.

6. SCHEDULE AN OFFICIAL TIME TO COMPLAIN.

Think Realistically about What Works: Family and business meetings would run more smoothly if a ritual time period were used to air complaints. Schedule complaining and stick to the schedule so complaining won't eat up all of your productive time.

Tame Complaining: Learn to exaggerate problems to end up laughing at them. Humor is the best stress-reduction strategy going.

7. GIVE AS MUCH AIR TIME TO YOUR SUCCESSES AS YOU DO TO YOUR FAILURES.

Think about Your Wins: Try to balance your comments about how bad things are with an equal number of comments about how successful and satisfied you are. Take responsibility for creating a positive work and home atmosphere.

Tame Complaining: Be sympathetic to problems, but don't be a sucker. Don't tolerate a lot of carping or fishing for sympathy. Never forget about your previous successes when your stress is high.

8. CREATE ONE DAY THAT IS COMPLETELY FREE OF COMPLAINING.

Think about Your Happiness: Live one full-day without the anger-reduction strategy of habitual complaining. You will be required to develop new coping strategies. Prove to yourself that complaining can be a deceptive habit that depresses more than it helps.

Tame Complaining: Enjoy working closely with others free of complaints. You will find surprising new sources of positive stimulation and energy.

9. AVOID BLAMING OTHERS FOR PROBLEMS THAT CONFRONT YOU.

Think about Your Self-Esteem: Blaming others for low self-esteem is the cowards' way out of an essential life dilemma. How can you grow if you don't deal with the things that pressure you? You can't.

Tame Complaining: Use this change rule: Change first and blame later.

10. REMAIN VULNERABLE DURING TIMES OF DISAGREEMENT AND CONFLICT.

Think about Feelings to Master Them: Speak of your hurt when you are hurting. Do not speak hurtfully when you are hurting. When you do blame, apologize and correct the offending behavior.

Tame Complaining: Hurt should not be a four letter word. Never let yourself become too lonely without talking to somebody. Changing will provide you with a lot more positive strokes.

Remember, complaining is an indirect way to ask for more positive strokes.

PERMIT YOURSELF TO CHANGE MORE THAN YOU COMPLAIN

Are you willing to have what you complain about lacking? Then permit yourself to change your complaints into new changes using these permissions.

✔ **RESOLVE COMPLAINTS BY TAKING ACTION.**

✔ **GIVE YOURSELF WHAT YOU MOST NEED.**

✔ **BE ASSERTIVE WHEN YOU FEEL RESENTFUL.**

✔ **TAKE TIME OFF FROM THE WORK OF COMPLAINING.**

✔ **ENJOY THE IMPERFECTIONS OF THE OPPOSITE SEX.**

✔ **LISTEN CAREFULLY TO LEGITIMATE COMPLAINTS.**

✔ **LISTEN TO THE DEEPER FEELINGS COMPLAINING CONCEALS.**

✔ **BE GENEROUS WITH YOUR POSITIVE STROKES.**

✔ **GO INTO THE UNKNOWN TO OVERCOME NEGATIVE FEELINGS.**

✔ **FEEL FREE TO CHANGE WHATEVER YOU COMPLAIN ABOUT.**

Use complaining to claim high self-esteem.

COUNTERPOINT:

"HOW CAN I STAY CALM AROUND A CHRONIC COMPLAINER?"

You can't! Just joking. You CAN remain calm and unfrustrated around a heavy complainer. Here are some mental tricks to stay relaxed:

★ *Remember you are not responsible for the problem.* Learn to listen to a person's struggle without becoming a rescuer who tries too hard to help. Define caring as the ability to listen without giving advice.

★ *Notice any beginning signs of irritation.* The person who ends up frustrated at the end of a conversation is the loser. Complaining seeks to control your mood. Set a goal to stay relaxed around the complainer.

★ *Give plenty of empathy, but a paucity of advice.* Give not one shred of advice — not one bit. Instead, make summary statements by repeating back what you hear the complainer saying. Often people are shocked to hear you echo back how negative they have been sounding.

★ *Switch the topic to another subject.* Unassertive people must learn to feel free to abruptly switch the topic of conversation when they are feeling bored. No one has the right to dominate a conversation through complaining.

★ *Daydream.* Tune out and have a sexual fantasy, or recall a wonderful vacation you took. Use creative ways to remain calm whenever your frustration elevates.

★ *Don't take in negative feelings.* Sensitive people absorb others' negativity too easily. Notice when you are feeling depressed, and remind yourself that your sensitivity and kindness must have limits.

★ *Complain along with the complainer.* Waste some time in a gripe session and unload your complaints free of guilt. Let yourself really go. Moan, groan and whine to your heart's delight. You may end up laughing uncontrollably.

★ *Ask questions to make the complainer stop and think.* Show interest by asking, "What do you think the solution is to your problem?" "Does your complaining usually lead to your changing?" "Do you feel better when you get gripes off your chest?" "Have you been complaining about this problem for very long?" These questions encourage new thinking.

In the next chapter, I'm going to challenge you to break all the rules and use positive strokes to insulate your self-esteem to withstand the heat of rapid success.

9

ACCEPTING POSITIVE STROKES

The person who dies with the most joys wins.

KEEP STROKING YOUR STRENGTHS TO SUCCEED

Rejection happens. But when miscommunication and negative strokes happen to you, you must learn how to take charge. And somehow, some way: Keep stroking your strengths to move forward successfully with your goals.

Putting strokes to good use reduces the five fears of change, and helps keep your energy high when you are undergoing tough changes. In particular, the fear of disapproval is removed when strokes flow freely and no family or team member is starving from a lack of strokes.

Difficult people thrive during difficult times when the demand for strokes is high and the supply is low. When displeasers plow your strengths under with harsh words, you must acquire more positive strokes — by stroking your own strengths — to regain control of your self-esteem.

Displeasers gain mental control over your mind by making you feel ashamed of your most "stroke-able" strengths. Putting positive strokes under your conscious control is a great way to deal with the sly tricks of difficult people.

How aware are you of how strokes affect your life? Find out by taking the following 'Stroke' I.Q. Quiz.

WHAT IS YOUR 'STROKE' I.Q.?

Let's determine how worthy you feel of praise, and how likely you are to act in a praiseworthy fashion.

TRUE	FALSE	
❑	❑	1. If I have to ask for positive strokes, they really don't count for much.
❑	❑	2. Hidden anger is disguised by dishing out excessive praise.
❑	❑	3. Competent workers shouldn't have to be told when they are doing a good job.
❑	❑	4. Men give fewer positive strokes than women.
❑	❑	5. High self-esteemers need fewer strokes to feel good.
❑	❑	6. Lavish praise makes children lazy, egotistical and less responsible as adults.
❑	❑	7. Giving verbal strokes to my mate is an artificial way to build intimacy.

TRUE   FALSE

❑   ❑   8. High praise types often receive less attention than chronic complainers.

❑   ❑   9. Talking to your peers about your successes may cause resentment.

❑   ❑   10. The positive strokes you hear today could dry up and go away tomorrow.

ANSWERS AND DISCUSSION

1. *False.*   Assertively asking for positive strokes shows you are working on high self-esteem. However, you shouldn't have to always tell loved ones what you need. Some mindreading is all right.

2. *True.*   "Gee you're wonderful" strokes are phony and dripping with anger. Syrupy compliments should be tasted with suspicion. Don't bite into bad strokes.

3. *False.*   Competent workers need to hear good strokes for a job well done. People change jobs to receive more recognition and get rid of resentments. Job dissatisfaction occurs when the loyal efforts of workers go unrewarded.

4. *True.*   Men have been trained to believe that giving positive strokes is a sign of weakness, while women have been reared to believe just the reverse. The truth: men and women need non-controlling strokes from one another to feel good.

5. *False.*   Actually, high self-esteemers require greater variety and a larger amount of positive strokes. However, they aren't as panicked when strokes dry up because they are good self-encouragers.

6. *True.*   Unearned praise or unjust criticism makes children lazy and indolent. Children who learn to feel adequate do so when their talents are realistically recognized. Encourage your children to enjoy a diet rich in positive strokes, but give helpful criticisms for good balance.

7. *False.*   Stressed marriages are so affection-starved that even basic courtesies are absent. Resentment doesn't justify hoarding away positive strokes. Why? Negative strokes will escalate when a partner feels forgotten.

8. *True.*   Hard to please individuals take up a disproportionate amount of time and attention. We may think they are promising a pot of gold at the end of their rainbow, but all we find are empty promises. High-praise types need to stick together.

9. *True.*   Excessive self-praise is a sign of game-playing. High self-esteemers share their useful talents, but are cautious about bragging when their peers' strengths aren't likewise acknowledged.

10. *True.*   Depression results from ignoring, turning around or minimizing compliments that come your way. There is no sense in trying to stave off a future letdown by refusing to enjoy your present-day successes. Painful times will come

whether or not you guard against them.

YOUR SCORE?

9-10 Correct: **GENIUS.** You are a genius when it comes to balancing the use of positive and negative strokes.

7-8 Correct: **ABOVE AVERAGE.** You could add more self-encouragers.

5-6 Correct: **AVERAGE.** You could improve your stroke economy, both giving and receiving.

0-4 Correct: **DULL.** You are not receiving as many strokes as you need or deserve.

YOU ALWAYS GET WHAT YOU STROKE

The change rule: You always get what you stroke! If you tell somebody they can't, they will oblige. And if you stroke somebody by saying: "You can do it!" they won't stop long enough to figure out they can't.

The best ways to use positive strokes to build lasting high self-esteem? Follow these three powerful stroke rules for developing high self-esteem:

RULE #1:

**TO ACHIEVE HIGH SELF-ESTEEM
STROKE YOUR STRENGTHS TO SUCCEED.**

RULE #2:

**TO MANAGE HIGH SELF-ESTEEM
STROKE YOUR STRENGTHS WHEN YOU SUCCEED.**

RULE #3:

**TO MAINTAIN HIGH SELF-ESTEEM
STROKE YOUR STRENGTHS AFTER YOU SUCCEED.**

Time now to turn your attention to why strokes are so important to your changing, and how to use positive strokes most effectively for speedy growth.

POSITIVE STROKES ARE NEEDED
FOR HIGH SELF-ESTEEM

Many of my clients believe praise is artificial, fleeting and insincere. They have come to learn from experience to expect more critical than positive feedback, and to reject positive signs of approval as phony, covert attempts at manipulation.

However, you must receive positive strokes to build a mountain of high self-esteem. I know that a lack of appreciation for your best efforts is too often the normal routine. Worse yet, your strengths may go unrecognized and undetected by you too.

Praise, or strokes, can be about as tricky to handle as money and just as important to your basic feelings of changeableness and self-esteem. A positive stroke is any form of genuine recognition that adds to your self-esteem.

Each day you begin with a balance sheet of surplus or deficit strokes and expectations for receiving additional strokes. A solid savings account of strokes helps you act effectively and feel confident.

When you become depressed, burned out or quick-tempered, you are suffering from stroke hunger, and you will search for signs of affection. Complaining will be one safe way you try to obtain strokes.

A search for affection can turn into a desperate search for approval and you may hurt your self-esteem in order to obtain strokes. Negative strokes are any type of recognition that subtracts from your self-esteem. Such disapproval comes in many forms: harsh criticism, rejection, power plays, avoidance, blaming anger or other negative strokes.

You were taught as a child to fear negative strokes, disapproval and anger. As an adult you will resist making needed changes for fear of being rejected and made to feel like a little helpless child again. But refusing to change guarantees you will receive tons of negative strokes.

Both positive and negative strokes are used for manipulative purposes. You have learned from getting burned to filter out positive strokes because you fear the person giving the praise might be after something. Unfortunately, many times you are right.

Paranoia about strokes between the sexes is not without justification. Men and women fight against and manipulate each other in the arena of strokes all the time. Both parties know what the other gender needs to hear to feel good.

Too many people feed your ego to steal from your pockets. As a result, you've learned to ignore or ridicule positive strokes to avoid being controlled or used. But blocking out positive strokes also means you close down the bridge to building high self-esteem.

SELF-CONFIDENCE IS MEASURED IN STROKES

Miscommunication could be greatly reduced if we all were required to compare our stroke "bank accounts" at the start of the day. People low in stroke funds would be treated more kindly, and people high in stroke reserves could put out extra energy without being depleted. We would all know just how confident we were.

Praise is the daily exchange of invisible emotional currency, with big spenders and tightwads existing along the continuum. Resentments and negative feelings occur when we don't get enough strokes.

Pleasers are high-praise types who give away their positive strokes freely, but too often end up feeling taken advantage of. Low-praise types utter few words of encouragement, but when they speak, everybody listens.

High-praise types give until it hurts, and they don't really think their words are worth very much. Low-praise types perceive high-praise types to be weak, gullible, indiscriminating and easily used. Displeasers who are takers have a great time sucking these kindhearted givers dry.

Displeasers are low-praise types who give little, but expect a lot. They believe that starving others of positive reinforcement helps build character. High-praise types perceive low-praise types as nasty and stingy, but fear their disapproving anger.

No matter what your praise type, you will tend to compliment others for the very things you would like to have complimented in yourself. For example, the types of strokes your friends give you are the same kind of strokes that your friends probably prefer to receive from you.

Pay attention to strokes. Experiment with giving a wide variety of strokes, and give out more strokes than you get. Strokes should be given freely and not hoarded, especially when people are hurting or lack confidence.

Give your confidence a boost by learning to give positive strokes.

GIVE POSITIVE STROKES BUT SET ASSERTIVE LIMITS

Don't be too free with your positive strokes.

Your strokes are valuable. Don't let the guilt of hurting someone else keep you from speaking up. Set assertive limits to protect your self-esteem even when you may hurt the people you love.

The assertive stroke rule: Don't let your good positive strokes go down the "Yes, BUT..." tubes. Confront people who refuse to acknowledge your strokes. Ask, "Did you hear the stroke I just gave you?" Or say, "Could you repeat what I just said I liked the most about you?"

Either make people be accountable and accept your strokes, or stop giving them. Positive strokes are like precious gold. Although you should give unto others the strokes you would like given unto you, don't go overboard and give to the point of frustration.

Do people play games to get negative strokes? Absolutely, and many of these crooked games are played outside of your control. Beware: Positive strokes are used as a set up to get rid of anger. For instance, a good stroke may be followed by a "BUT" poke.

Stop giving until it hurts. Some people just want to be rejected and kicked around because they are afraid to be close. So? You can still learn to target your self-esteem with positive strokes and hit the bull's eye every time.

In marriage, grudges occur when one spouse gives more than the other spouse. Marriage operates as a reciprocal agreement. Each spouse keeps silent count of the number of strokes and favors received. Strokes in unequal amounts lead to anger, hurt and power plays. Negative strokes result in negative behaviors, but are better than no strokes.

None of us like to be cheated of our rightful paycheck, and couples must be realistic when paying each other for favors received. Wise couples discuss what physical and verbal strokes are most important to them, and how to schedule the valuable time to deliver these strokes.

Your nervous system doesn't discriminate between negative and positive strokes. Both types of stroke give you the needed jolt to keep going. When positives fall flat, negative strokes always rush in to replace them.

Learn to prefer positive strokes.

BE SURE TO STROKE YOURSELF WHEN NOBODY ELSE WILL

You must remember that displeasers try to pass along their negative feelings to you by giving you plenty of negative strokes. Don't agree to take on others' bad feelings. Rejecting yourself when you are already stinging from a rejection fuels self-criticism.

Self-criticism is the low-down way you resist change. When you are self-critical, you are feeding yourself a harsh diet of negative strokes. Negative strokes strongly promote failure, unless you get mad enough to say: "I'm not going to take failure and negative strokes anymore."

No one can make you reject yourself — but you. Rejection by others wounds, but the worst rejections occur at your own hands. Do you compliment yourself when you feel down? Probably not. Most of my clients even fail to praise themselves when they are going great guns.

Couples argue in circles instead of learning how to risk giving romantic strokes. Leaders and team members may be too shy to stroke one another for success. Your most negative behaviors will come out when you aren't receiving enough attention.

Ignoring or withdrawing from another human being is the cruelest kind of psychological punishment. Lack of recognition leads to unhelpful anger and depression. Hate hath no fury as a person scorned from lack of strokes. Withholding strokes invites revenge paybacks.

How can you tell when your sources of positive strokes have dried up? You will feel out of control, a bit crazy, quick to make harsh judgments, self-critical and sad. You will fear change and fight against improving yourself. You will avoid trying the new, feel goal-less, off-balance and without hope.

Stroke depressions can be corrected. When feeling low, let yourself know what you need to feel better. Give yourself the permission to change negative feelings into positive feelings by obtaining needed strokes.

Give yourself good strokes especially when others won't.

How can you survive a stroke famine when there aren't any surplus strokes to go around? To survive a stroke famine you must learn to accept a wider variety of alternative positive strokes.

SURVIVING A STROKE FAMINE

Stroke depression results from the difference between the amount of strokes you need to feel good and the amount you have received so far today.

When fear is high, and your ability to control your life is low, you are bound to feel stressed out. When rewards are low, your energy will be gradually sapped until you have trouble acting positively on your own behalf.

Paradoxically, the times you most need strokes are the times you are most likely to ignore or discount any small strokes that are available to you. Stroke depression causes self-criticism, or an "I don't really deserve any praise" attitude.

Here are some things you can do to survive a stroke famine:

1. ADD NOVELTY TO YOUR STROKE DIET.

Survive a Stroke Famine: Create a change of pace in your lifestyle by pursuing something different. Try a new restaurant, travel to a new city or play a new sport. Change your routine to create new mental stimulation.

Accept Positive Strokes: A mixture of novel strokes can carry a big wallop.

2. DIG OUT OLD STROKES.

Survive a Stroke Famine: Start keeping a stroke file to fill with touching cards, caring letters, verses and drawings. Pictures, post cards, vacation mementos and anniversary photos all have a positive impact.

Review Previous Strokes: Strokes collected yesterday are just as good as strokes received today.

3. GIVE YOURSELF SOME STROKES.

Survive a Stroke Famine: Nurture yourself when you are down and out. Go back two years in time and judge your current accomplishments from that vantage point. A hallmark of high self-esteem is the ability to feel okay about yourself even when things are rotten.

Accept Positive Strokes from Yourself: If you can't seem to muster up any positive thoughts, simply say, "I am an important person who deserves to be loved."

4. GIVE MORE COMPLIMENTS THAN CRITICISMS WHEN YOU FEEL DOWN.

Survive a Stroke Famine: Stroke depression makes you go into hiding and be less available to new sources of reinforcement. Or, you will lash out and give unfair negative pokes. Get active in life again and don't use hurtful words when you are hurting.

Stay Focused on Stroking Strengths: Noticing your own and others' strengths when you are in a bad mood will force you to get into the good habit of giving good strokes.

5. ASK FOR THE STROKES YOU NEED.

Survive a Stroke Famine: It's hard to ask for anything when you feel like a big nothing, but the surest way to remove a stroke depression is to do just that. Requested strokes are just as good as strokes that come your way accidentally — maybe even better!

Request Positive Strokes: Refuse to resent people who don't give you the strokes you want. Remember, anyone you ask for strokes has the right to say "No."

6. MAKE SURE TO DIGEST YOUR STROKES SLOWLY.

Survive a Stroke Famine: When you are depressed, you will tend to let good strokes pass you by without realizing it. Learn to make your accomplishments into a big deal, take in every good stroke that comes your way and chew your strokes carefully.

Accept Positive Strokes Thankfully: Make your small successes into big productions. Be humble when you are feeling good, but be thankful when you receive something really important to you.

7. PUSH AWAY NEGATIVE STROKES TO A LATER DAY.

Survive a Stroke Famine: You are most susceptible to unfair criticisms when you are stroke deprived. Even outlandish lies about your character seem true when you are depressed. Let criticisms pass right through you, and try not to focus on them. Tough to do, but necessary.

Accept Positive Strokes but Refuse Negatives: Remember a paradoxical stroking rule: When positives are gone, negatives rush in to take their place — especially self-criticisms. Do anything to cut out the self-criticisms. They do more damage than good.

8. REMIND YOURSELF YOU CAN SURVIVE THIS STROKE FAMINE.

Survive a Stroke Famine: You will be hit at different times by loneliness and unexpected pain when you are growing and changing. You must keep learning to keep going. Remind yourself that you are serious about resolving the fear of success to acquire what you want.

Accept Positive Strokes for Changing: Survive as graciously and effectively as you can when you don't have anyone to lean on, or when you are treated like you don't exist. Faith can overcome any adversity.

Don't expect yourself to be at your best during a stroke famine. Who can be? But do survive by taking in a variety of nourishing positive strokes.

As you change, you will be forced to come to terms with your hidden strengths. Wonderful!

Learn to accept all of your strengths to succeed.

OWNING UP TO YOUR STRENGTHS

Resisting change means ignoring a hidden strength until it becomes a weakness. For example, a caring man may criticize his strength of sensitivity, and remove himself from relationships. Or, an ambitious female may feel guilty about her aspirations, and lose self-confidence.

I believe most people don't know what their real strengths are. In fact, my clients get downright embarrassed when I point out their strengths to them. Unacknowledged strengths try to get your attention by kicking your butt as a weakness.

Every person has been given unique gifts and strengths from the universal talent pool. Identify your strengths. Stop taking them for granted!

Using your strengths for success means you:

1. **Own up to your strengths.**
2. **Stop transforming your strengths into self-criticisms.**
3. **Learn to accept your strengths.**
4. **Use positive strokes to build high self-esteem.**
5. **Operate from your strengths and not your weaknesses.**

When you begin admitting the power of your strengths, you will no longer be controlled by negative people who try to dominate you by criticizing your best strengths.

MINDPLAY:
THE STRENGTHS I HAVE TO STROKE?

Scan this list to find your top ten strengths. Rank order your strengths from one to ten. Which of these assets do you have the most trouble accepting?

I possess these strengths:

- ❏ Sexy
- ❏ Brilliant
- ❏ Sensitive
- ❏ Intuitive
- ❏ Ambitious
- ❏ Caring
- ❏ Bold
- ❏ Aggressive
- ❏ Thoughtful
- ❏ Organized
- ❏ Spontaneous
- ❏ Passionate
- ❏ Fun-loving
- ❏ Non-judgemental
- ❏ Nurturing
- ❏ Creative
- ❏ Healthy
- ❏ Relaxed
- ❏ Humorous
- ❏ Sincere
- ❏ Charming
- ❏ Persevering
- ❏ Open-minded
- ❏ Quick learner
- ❏ Family-oriented
- ❏ Curious
- ❏ Diplomatic
- ❏ Determined
- ❏ Clear-thinker
- ❏ Entrepreneur
- ❏ Confident
- ❏ Lovable
- ❏ Loving

- ❏ Considerate
- ❏ Sympathetic
- ❏ Understanding
- ❏ Deep
- ❏ Insightful
- ❏ Analytical
- ❏ Dependable
- ❏ Enthusiastic
- ❏ Visionary
- ❏ Practical
- ❏ Skilled
- ❏ Honest
- ❏ Fair
- ❏ Discreet
- ❏ Optimistic
- ❏ Regal
- ❏ Brave
- ❏ Natural
- ❏ Gentle
- ❏ Loyal
- ❏ Imaginative
- ❏ Stable
- ❏ Leader
- ❏ Rational
- ❏ Realistic
- ❏ Generous
- ❏ Zany
- ❏ Inventive
- ❏ Attractive
- ❏ Achieving
- ❏ (You do have more...)
- ❏ (Even more...)
- ❏ (And many more...)
- ❏ (And yes, even more...)

INTER PLAY:

Do you laugh off your strengths like a bad joke? Choose to get all charged up — give good positive strokes to yourself!

Make Your Strengths List and Check It Twice: Take out a sheet of paper and start writing down as many of your strengths as you can. Appreciate how your strengths are unique. Are you too close to your strengths to be able to think clearly about them?

Doodle Permissions During the Day to Stay Strong: Write about your strengths in a notebook during business meetings when you are bored. Everyone will think you are absorbed in the work at hand. And you are! Does your work bring out your strengths or conceal them?

Search Endlessly for Your Strengths Each and Every Day: Refocus on your strengths after you have to deal with a difficult person or frustration. Ask yourself, "How do I ignore my strengths which adds to my frustration?"

Ask a Friend to Speak Up About Your Strengths: Ask a trusted friend to review your strengths. Which strengths of yours do they envy? Why? Listen to, and absorb, all of the positives free of judgement. Might the strokes be true?

Low self-esteemers believe that focusing on strengths is a waste of time. Quite the contrary: Keeping your strengths foremost in your mind makes you less likely to act out your weaknesses.

USING POSITIVE STROKES TO CREATE FAST CHANGES

You will be going against the social grain when you practice how to receive positive strokes. That's just fine by me. You will be violating the social norm that says you shouldn't be self-approving. Good for you.

A cautionary note: Never, never, ever use positive strokes for manipulative purposes. If you do, you will be falling right into the pattern of using positive strokes to get something in a crooked way. Be genuine no matter how strong the temptation to be phony.

To create rapid change, liberally apply the following six stroking strategies:

STROKE STRATEGY #1:

"I LIKE YOUR _____."

The Goal: To keep positive strokes from becoming a scarce commodity.

Be Successful: Hunt down and expose everything that you like about someone you care about.

For Example: Easily say, "I like your warm smile." Or, "I like your enthusiastic attitude."

Use Strokes for Fast Change: Give positive strokes even when you don't get any back! (But don't be a total sucker.)

STROKE STRATEGY #2:

"I DISLIKE YOUR _____."

The Goal: To be assertive about what you would like to see changed.

Be Successful: Be specific about what turns you off. Avoid complaining, whining or indulging in guilt trips.

For Example: Firmly say, "I dislike the fact that we haven't made love tonight." Or, "I dislike your coming late to this meeting."

Use Strokes for Fast Change: Give negative strokes even when conflict or hurt could result! (But don't seek revenge through blaming.)

STROKE STRATEGY #3:

"WILL YOU TELL ME WHAT YOU DISLIKE ABOUT MY _____?"

The Goal: To stay ahead of angry paybacks that can catch you off guard.

Be Successful: Don't fear, but freely engage in negative feedback. Stay open to learning something new from every criticizer.

For Example: Ask, "Could you tell me how you would like me to be more romantic...?" Or, "Will you tell me what you disliked about my performance?" Smile at the person, and take a deep breath. Don't start shaking!

Use Strokes for Fast Change: Seek to learn equally from your successes and failures! (But don't let displeasers get their kicks by harming your self-esteem.)

STROKE STRATEGY #4:

"WILL YOU TELL ME WHAT YOU LIKE ABOUT MY _____?"

The Goal: To call the bluff of a chronic complainer.

Be Successful: You are an important and worthwhile human being. Find caring ways to confront someone who finds nothing right about you.

For Example: Ask, "What do you like most about being with me?" Or, "How am I important to you?" Look the person straight in the eye, and wait for an answer. Don't start giggling!

Use Strokes for Fast Change: Do not reject yourself when you are rejected by those you love! (But don't keep hoping to be loved by those who disapprove of you.)

STROKE STRATEGY #5:

"I LIKE OUR _____."

The Goal: To be clear about what mutual activities or goals are most gratifying to you.

Be Successful: Be a role model of leadership by rewarding teamwork at home and work.

For Example: Offer, "I like the values we are teaching the kids."

Or, "I like our new product."

Use Strokes for Fast Change: Set mutually beneficial romantic and career goals that nurture everybody! (But don't make it a practice to give more than you receive.)

STROKE STRATEGY #6:

"I LIKE MY _____."

The Goal: To stay independent of manipulative attempts to control your self-esteem.

Be Successful: Stand up for yourself when negative strokes are flowing your way. Assertively reveal your real opinions.

For Example: Say respectfully, "I like my boss." Or, "I like my attention to details."

Use Strokes for Fast Change: Promote your own and others hidden strengths and never take them for granted! (But don't lose track of correcting your weaknesses.)

If you want to change quickly: "No excuses. Use positive strokes!"

Why do you have such a tough time finding or taking in positive strokes? There are six irrational rules that keep strokes in short supply.

THE SIX IRRATIONAL STROKE RULES

Claude Steiner wrote about "The Stroke Economy" in *Scripts People Live* (1974). He first described the stroke rules that most interfered with high self-esteem and being loved. I want to adapt his work for our purposes here to help you use positive strokes to succeed in your change goals.

Steiner defined positive strokes as any stroke which feels good to the recipient, and negative strokes to be any stroke which feels bad. The subjectivity factor explains why strokes that sound good, or strokes that may be readily enjoyed by another, may not feel very good to you.

I have chosen to add "Don't give any negative strokes" to his original five rules. I've done this because pleasers are notorious for withholding valuable negative feedback from colleagues and loved ones.

The following *Six Irrational Stroke Rules* interfere with success:

RULE #1: DON'T REFUSE TO TAKE IN NEGATIVE STROKES.

RULE #2: DON'T GIVE YOURSELF GOOD STROKES.

RULE #3: DON'T GIVE ANY NEGATIVE STROKES.

RULE #4: DON'T EVER ASK FOR POSITIVE STROKES.

RULE #5: DON'T GIVE POSITIVE STROKES.

RULE #6: DON'T ACCEPT POSITIVE STROKES.

I will explore each of these self-limiting rules in turn with you.

I hope you will grant yourself the permission to disobey each and every one of them.

IRRATIONAL RULE #1:
DON'T REFUSE TO TAKE IN NEGATIVE STROKES.

DO REFUSE BLAME: You have been conditioned to believe that when someone is angry with you, you must listen, because that person is right.

The Fear: If you refuse to take in negative feedback, you will become uncontrollable, bad or arrogant.

The Irrational Idea: "I'm unlovable when someone is angry with me."

The Choice: You don't have to absorb the angry comments of someone who is belittling you. Why not refuse negative strokes you do not want? There's nothing wrong with being finicky about your stroke diet. You have the right to say "No" to bad strokes.

Choose Success: Block out negative strokes you do not want. Focus on positive strokes instead. Refuse to repeat negative strokes given to you. Reject negative strokes, by saying, "That comment doesn't fit me. I'm unwilling to accept it."

Fun Tasks:

• Be assertive about negative strokes.

• Point out a negative stroke you dislike.

• Let go of hateful comments you resent.

Where to Draw the Line: Don't block out bits of helpful advice just because the advisor is mad at you.

IRRATIONAL RULE #2:

DON'T GIVE YOURSELF GOOD STROKES.

DO GIVE POSITIVES TO YOURSELF: You have been conditioned to believe that what others think of you is more valuable and important than what you think of yourself.

The Fear: Giving yourself good strokes will cause you to become selfish and vain.

The Irrational Idea: "I'm not supposed to think too much about what I want or give it to myself."

The Choice: Self-acceptance results from learning how to control your own negative opinions of yourself. Why not praise yourself? Why not accept yourself, especially when you have been rejected by others?

Choose Success: Give yourself good strokes. Search out your strengths and expose every last one of them. Find the balance of strokes that feels best to you.

Fun Tasks:

• Give yourself pep talks when you are driving to work.

• Talk to a co-worker about what sets you apart from your peers.

• Tell your lover what you think makes you special in bed.

Where to Draw the Line: Check out your thinking with your advisors when you are feeling too confident or inferior.

IRRATIONAL RULE #3:

DON'T GIVE ANY NEGATIVE STROKES.

DO GIVE NEGATIVE FEEDBACK: You have been conditioned to believe that you should not hurt others by being too honest.

The Fear: Telling the truth will cause unneeded hurt or rejection and end a relationship.

The Irrational Idea: "Conflict is always bad."

The Choice: True caring means telling the truth even when you stand to lose something from doing so. Do you let people know what you really think? Constructive criticism invites change. Why not be bold about your preferences?

Choose Success: Unruly conflict does ruin many a good relationship. No excuses! Give out some negative strokes before you explode.

Fun Tasks:

• Tell an authority figure of your worth.

• Ask your lover, "Will you listen to some of my gripes about our sex life?"

• Ask your boss, "I've been collecting some hard feelings about this project. May I tell you about them?"

Where to Draw the Line: Don't give negative feedback when a person doesn't want any or refuses to listen.

IRRATIONAL RULE #4:

DON'T EVER ASK FOR POSITIVE STROKES.

DO ASK FOR POSITIVE FEEDBACK: You have been conditioned to believe that if you must ask for a stroke, then the stroke doesn't amount to very much.

The Fear: You fear that needing to ask for positive strokes from a loved one proves you are unloved.

The Irrational Idea: "To be loved I must give up my individuality to please my partner."

The Choice: Wise partners try to please each other about

equally. Why not ask for strokes tailored to your changing needs? Give your partner the opportunity to please you by telling them what you want.

Choose Success: Let yourself know what type of positive strokes you need. Loving relationships should involve mindreading sometimes, but ask straight for positive strokes most times. Insist good strokes be delivered your way.

Fun Tasks:
• Ask for the help you need when you're stressed.
• Ask to organize one fun day of activities.
• Trade off taking turns pleasuring your partner.

Where to Draw the Line: Don't confuse asking for what you want with harassment.

IRRATIONAL RULE #5:
DON'T GIVE POSITIVE STROKES.

DO GIVE POSITIVE STROKES, PLUS SOME: You have been conditioned to believe that positive strokes are insincere and controlling.

The Fear: Giving positive strokes will make many people want to be close to you and you won't know what to do.

The Irrational Idea: "I shouldn't have to explain what I like about someone."

The Choice: You are free to choose who you want to be close to. Don't let a lack of confidence show up in a lack of giving strokes. Withholding positive strokes is a form of control. Why not give good strokes if you have them to give?

Choose Success: Give positive strokes if you want to be close to others. Don't make anyone work hard for your strokes. Say the same small stroke, day after day, to a loved one. Use positive strokes to instill independence.

Fun Tasks:
• Compliment each person you come into contact with today.
• Give at least three sincere compliments to close associates.

• Ask, "How did you like the stroke?"

Where to Draw the Line: Don't give positive strokes as a devious way to obtain what you want without taking risks.

IRRATIONAL RULE #6:
DON'T ACCEPT POSITIVE STROKES.

DO ACCEPT WHAT YOU WANT: You have been conditioned to believe that nothing good can last forever.

The Fear: The fear of success results from the inability to accept positive strokes.

The Irrational Idea: "I can't be hurt if I don't get my hopes up."

The Choice: Enjoying success doesn't mean you will end up more hurt later when strokes dry up. Do you really believe that you don't lose out when you don't accept positive strokes? When you refuse to accept positive strokes you are being controlled by negative feelings.

Choose Success: Why not accept the strokes you want? True, many strokes are designed to sell you something. No excuses! Don't buy the merchandise, but do accept the gift of strokes.

Fun Tasks:
• Listen intently to every positive stroke you hear.
• Let the strokes sink in.
• Breathe deeply as you think about the stroke.
• Thank the speaker.

Where to Draw the Line: Don't use positive strokes for purposes of seduction, or let yourself be seduced by a smooth talker.

Do you want to bolster your self-esteem? Then stay open to positive strokes, start rejecting unfair negative strokes and break every single last one of the irrational stroke rules.

Now I want to more specifically explain how you can use positive strokes in four very important areas:

1. **Building Self-Confidence**
2. **Being a Successful Leader**
3. **Building a Spirit of Teamwork**
4. **Keeping Romance Alive**

You must become an expert in all of these areas in order to reach the pinnacle of self-esteem.

USING STROKES TO ACHIEVE HIGH SELF-ESTEEM

How do you spell success? Are you a model of leadership and responsibility? What type of team player are you at home and work? How do you keep the fire of romance burning bright in a long-term relationship?

All of these are important areas rich in strokes. Achieving high self-esteem means you are willing to stroke everyone you come into contact with.

Free yourself up to bathe your mind internally with plenty of positive strokes that cleanse low self-esteem.

Maintaining a good relationship with the inner self is extremely important to high self-esteemers. Why? Self-insight builds a strong sense of self-confidence.

BUILDING SELF-CONFIDENCE

When you enter a new stage in your life such as getting a big promotion, moving into the home of your dreams or finally getting your kids raised and off on their own, you may experience mixed feelings.

Your feelings might include natural excitement sprinkled with more than a dash of unnatural fear, soul-searching or stomach churning.

Have you ever heard yourself say, "I know I should be happy, but what a letdown." Or, "If they really knew me, they wouldn't like me?" If you start to worry when you become successful, the fear of success is in control of your confidence.

Self-doubt occurs when good fortune outpaces your self-esteem. The dastardly psychological result: You are unable to drink deep of your successes and enjoy them to the fullest.

Worse yet, you may feel edgy or on guard, because someday, someone is going to march into your life and shout out to the whole world, "You're really nothing special. You're just a fake."

The fear of success can make you feel like an impostor. The fear of positive strokes creates the fear of success.

The following symptoms can result from **LOW SELF-ESTEEM**:

Split-Screen Emotions: You feel ambivalent, split, equally placed between pleasure and anxiety.

Self-Doubt: You feel guilty, "just lucky," skeptical of your future abilities to handle responsibilities.

Fuzzy Identity: You feel unglued, adrift without a feeling of rootedness and dubious about your integrity.

Strange Experiences: You feel unable to judge whether your feelings are right or wrong, good or bad. Self-doubt and low self-confidence absorb your energies.

You also may run the risk of stripping yourself of your own successes or undermining your enjoyment of hard-earned wins due to the fear of success.

The result? Success can become a punishing experience filled with guilt or unhappiness. Set your sights on being both success-ful and happy!

KEEPING YOUR CONFIDENCE UP

Success seeks to help you become more accepting of your genuine strengths. Self-approval unleashes your best traits to be expressed in your work and family life, and in the world.

How can you learn to accept your successes without panicking? Being able to accept compliments protects you against the fear of success. Be a shining beacon to your children that confidence means self-approval and accepting positive strokes.

Here are some practical ways to learn to celebrate all of your SUCCESSES:

S. SELF-ESTEEM. Being a genuine achiever means you acknowledge your strengths, hunt for your secret talents and give your best to the world without being a braggart.
Build Self-Confidence: Learn from your failures.

U. UNDERSTANDING. Achievement means you are an intense person who expresses who you really are while staying open to growing and changing each and every day.
Build Self-Confidence: Thrive on responsibility.

C. CHILD DRIVE. You pay attention to inner urges that speak to you about what work you love to do and what insights you have to give to the world.
Build Self-Confidence: Make work fun.

C. CURIOSITY. You talk, talk and talk some more to people to find out what makes them tick. You soak up information like a sunbather taking in sunshine.
Build Self-Confidence: Take good advice.

E. ENERGY. You maximize your energy by eating, sleeping, exercising and working in recognition of our own special rhythms.

You do what makes you feel most alive.
Build Self-Confidence: Keep your energy high.

S. SET GOALS. You dignify life with long-term goals and mark your progression toward them.
Build Self-Confidence: Choose commitment.

S. STAY FOCUSED. You intensely focus single-mindedly on the most important tasks to accomplish, and say "No way!" to nifty distractions.
Build Self-Confidence: Accept self-discipline.

E. ERRORS. You make errors every day and know that if you aren't failing at least once a day than you aren't succeeding. You try again to hit the mark after you've missed it.
Build Self-Confidence: Never accept failure as a permanent state.

S. SATISFACTION. You endorse yourself for your wins, follow a consistent set of values and take humble pride in all of your accomplishments.
Build Self-Confidence: Feel gratified.

Permit yourself to be a genuine achiever instead of an impostor. Real people aren't impostors — we are the genuine article. Take the risk and be the real McCoy!

BEING A SUCCESSFUL LEADER

Are you able to be a successful leader at home and at work? Can you take initiative and get the job done? Good leaders love to take charge of change.

The constant theme that surfaces in studies of leadership is: A good leader must always seek out other people's opinions and give workers due recognition to get the best results. Plus, you must get people to talk to one another as equally valuable team members up and down the chain of command.

Motivation stays at its peek when leaders make people matter. Be a leader who makes everyone feel included.

Here's how to become the type of leader who makes every individual matter.

1. GET EVERYBODY INVOLVED.

Give Due Recognition: Foster human connectedness. Use a positive attitude to touch every person you come into contact with. Discuss new ideas that stimulate thinking.

To Achieve Success: Make everyone reach beyond the fears that restrict achievement.

2. KNOW WHERE YOU ARE GOING AND GO THERE.

Give Due Recognition: Use a long-term focus. Think of your goals every day. Go for smaller payoffs instead of the big take. Make decisions based on what is good for all parties involved.

To Achieve Success: Actively analyze social trends, negotiate wisely and plan for the future.

3. BREAK FREE FROM A TOO PRESSURED PACE.

Give Due Recognition: Regularly use self-care strategies. Make relaxation and "vegetation" time rejuvenating for you. Nurture your body, mind and spirit.

To Achieve Success: Moderate the pace of your day. Give spontaneous strokes that bolster workers' self-esteem.

4. DON'T TAKE IN UNFAIR REJECTIONS.

Give Due Recognition: Inspire yourself when you've been depressed by events outside of your control. Tape change permissions onto your daily calendar. Listen to motivational tapes. Read biographies of people who have struggled and made the grade.

To Achieve Success: Do anything that keeps your optimism up after it has been shot down.

5. SEEK APPROVAL LESS AND BE YOURSELF MORE.

Give Due Recognition: Be growth and change conscious. Find the seed of opportunity in every crisis and tough transition period. Seek to think clearly.

To Achieve Success: Take pride in who you are, be yourself and stop feeling like you must be someone else in order to be acceptable.

6. TAKE PRIDE IN BEING A THINKER.

Give Due Recognition: Be creative. Don't be afraid of being different when it means freeing up your abilities to perceive a new solution to an old problem. Learn rapidly from getting burned. Find out what you don't know, but need to know.

To Achieve Success: Turn over the best parts of your personality to problem-solving and brainstorming.

7. LISTEN/LISTEN/LISTEN AND LISTEN SOME MORE.

Give Due Recognition: Listen carefully and caringly. Ask for feedback and be a human sponge. Stay unbiased to get to know the perspectives of others. Be receptive to innovative ways of doing things. Use good advice.

To Achieve Success: Know a few areas of your work extremely well. Don't be afraid to learn something new today that you should have known about a long time ago.

8. BE CHANGE-OPEN.

Give Due Recognition: Learn to love change instead of hating what it does to you and your world. Study whether you resist, react or act responsively both to unwelcome and welcome changes. Identify your weaknesses and ameliorate them.

To Achieve Success: Make a bridge to the changing world

instead of disconnecting from it. Value change in all its splendid forms.

9. ACCEPT FAILURE AS A VALUABLE LEARNING EXPERIENCE.

Give Due Recognition: Don't pressure yourself to be successful the first time you try something new. Trial and error is required for learning. Feel free to make mistakes and learn from them to become the best you can be. Don't let the fear of failure turn you into a procrastinator.

To Achieve Success: Feel free to make tons of mistakes without tearing yourself down.

10. DON'T WAIT TO TAKE PAINFULLY NEEDED ACTION.

Give Due Recognition: Drop status barriers to discover problems in the rank-and-file. Speak up and down the authority ladder. "Don't delay, take action today," when a new course of action is indicated.

To Achieve Success: Stumble your way to success by being open to unexpected sources of help. Take uncomfortable risks.

11. SEEK TO PLEASE YOUR FAMILY/CUSTOMERS/BOSS.

Give Due Recognition: Whoever pays for your services deserves your undivided attention. Stay in touch with your customers to find out what they really want. Include yourself, include your peers, include everybody in everything and let false modesty flop.

To Achieve Success: Put pleasing yourself and your family on a par with getting ahead in your career.

This decade will be a renewed time for responsibility, cooperation and emotion-filled connectedness in which all people matter. Whether you wish to be a leader at work or at home, you must take heed of these principles for success.

BUILDING A SPIRIT OF TEAMWORK

Building teamwork at home or on the job is a sure way to boost self-esteem and make team members feel validated and valuable.

Having a good time when team members are stressed out, and cooperating to get the important things done, is not impossible. It just takes fighting the status quo that wickedly encourages you to give less than you are capable of giving.

How can you tell when teamwork is weak or absent? Here are the main symptoms of a weak team or family unit:

Splintering: Complaining becomes commonplace. Members cannot pull together towards a common goal. Repetitive conflicts occur and problems aren't resolved.

Fear: Members don't give independent opinions, and new decisions are met with resentment. Members are afraid they have become victims of the system.

Backbiting: Sending messages via a third-party is an indirect way to express frustration. Anger is also expressed through gossip and withholding important information.

Passivity: The gripe: "Why bother doing something different, nothing is going to change anyway!" is a clear sign that personal investment is low. Passivity makes everyone complacent about changing what can be changed.

How can you reward teamwork? How can each individual help build a spirit of cooperation and esprit de corps? Here are some ways:

1. BE THE FIRST ONE TO BE GIVING.

Reward Teamwork: Keep verbal praise and appropriate physical affection high to gain control of a disintegrating team. Spontaneously praise, and praise some more. Compliment anyone who is giving you what you have asked for. Use negative feedback privately — but forcefully.

Reward Yourself for Success: Be the first to be reassuring during a conflict.

2. KEEP TRYING SOMETHING NEW.

Reward Teamwork: When one avenue doesn't work, try another. Stick with important projects, and don't drop out at a crucial time. Take pride in following through on your promises.

Reward Yourself for Success: Feel happy and successful after you have met a deadline. Be trustworthy.

3. TAKE ON AN EQUAL SHARE OF THE RESPONSIBILITY.

Reward Teamwork: Never dodge your responsibilities or blame your failures on others. Keep your goals and desires out in the open so cohorts know exactly what you are up to.

Reward Yourself for Success: Make your relationships matter more than being right. Let team members know why they are important to you and how they can be the most helpful.

4. DEMAND THE BEST PERFORMANCE FROM YOURSELF.

Reward Teamwork: Expect the most from yourself and demand the best from yourself. Be a role model of competency, and find ways to help people succeed in their jobs. Ask for negative feedback that will help you know what people need from you.

Reward Yourself for Success: Only make fair demands. Reward hard work and loyalty.

5. GIVE SPECIFIC FEEDBACK.

Reward Teamwork: Allow people to be imperfect and take the initiative to help them correct their mistakes. Expect tasks to be done when you request them. Give plenty of concise instructions to accomplish tasks.

Reward Yourself for Success: Catch someone in the act of doing something right — and don't ever let them forget it!

6. BE MORE ACCEPTING — BUT DON'T BE A WIMP.

Reward Teamwork: Help people feel valuable and important without letting yourself be walked on or taken advantage of. Set high and sane performance standards. Make a job well done something to take pride in.

Reward Yourself for Success: Accentuate unique skills. Be understanding, firm and encouraging when a goof-up occurs.

7. ALWAYS DELIVER ON TIME.

Reward Teamwork: Refuse to procrastinate. Be an efficient time manager. Be realistic about your physical energy and learn to say "No." Balance your needs for success with needs for self-care and happiness.

Reward Yourself for Success: Prioritize family, children, career and spiritual needs.

8. HAVE FUN EVEN WHEN YOU ARE STRESSED OUT.

Reward Teamwork: Laughter is the best way to relieve stress. Take time to tell a silly joke, share a foible of human nature or chuckle at your own stupendous errors. Take care of yourself before you become burned out.

Reward Yourself for Success: Revel in hearing about others' wins. Spread positive rumors all over the place.

9. GRIND DOWN GRUDGES.

Reward Teamwork: Get any hidden agendas that are causing bruised feelings out into the open. Clearly explain why you are angry or upset without resorting to blame.

Reward Yourself for Success: Consider making new choices that remove avoidable resentments in order to add to your self-respect.

10. LISTEN CAREFULLY TO EVERYONE.

Reward Teamwork: Listen more than you speak and never

preach! Ask for opinions about new or better ways of doing things. Give credit for good ideas. Stay in close contact with every person.

Reward Yourself for Success: Start freeing up your need to have control over what other people think and feel, or how they choose to perform.

11. BE MORE EMOTIONAL, BUT NOT MOODY.

Reward Teamwork: Show your enthusiasm and disappointment. Analyze the compatibility between who you are and what you do. Tackle your shortcomings. Stop rationalizing. Be willing to feel whatever you feel, and learn to express your feelings assertively.

Reward Yourself for Success: Refuse to be a victim of a bad mood. Act competently even when you are under the influence of negative feelings.

12. ALWAYS BE HONEST EVEN WHEN IT HURTS.

Reward Teamwork: Be brave enough to be honest, and do the right thing. Give accurate information that helps everyone.

Reward Yourself for Success: Develop an identity that is based upon using your strengths and developing your unused potentials, instead of resorting to game playing.

You need to feel important. Make your life matter!

Use teamwork to energize yourself instead of feeling depleted. Validate your strengths instead of diminishing them. Accentuate the best in every person you come into contact with.

Maintaining a romantic loving relationship is of huge concern to high self-esteemers. Why? Fine relationships feed high self-esteem.

KEEPING ROMANCE ALIVE

You know just how easy it can be to drift away from a lover. The magnetic attraction that binds a couple together in romantic love weakens when a partner goes his or her own way for too long.

The romantic spirit is quickly squashed by such foes as unrealistic expectations, unyielding stress, unresolved grudges, time neglect, hurt feelings and the stress of raising children.

You must find realistic ways to enjoy yourself in your romantic relationship in spite of stress. Every self-esteeming couple must take responsibility for keeping negative forces at bay in order for their romance to stay alive and youthful.

Here are some ways to stay attuned to exchanging loads of positive strokes and eliminating negative feelings:

1. STAY SENSITIVE TO FEELINGS.

Enjoy Romance: Know what your partner enjoys and freely give those strokes. To stay free of the neurotic need for relationship perfection, use an "I choose to be vulnerable" attitude.

Give Good Strokes: Talk openly about hurt feelings. Learn to be the first to forgive.

2. ALWAYS DISCUSS WHAT'S MOST IMPORTANT TO YOU.

Enjoy Romance: Keeping too many secrets is asking for trouble. Self-disclosure is a powerful way to create closeness. Talk about anything even remotely connected with creating a healthy and vigorous relationship.

Give Good Strokes: Never keep feelings hidden. Learn the difficult art of careful listening.

3. BEWARE OF BEING OVERACHIEVERS.

Enjoy Romance: Success can be seductive. But substitute strokes can never replace real romance. Stay current with one another's work, and try to spend some time in cross-ventures.

Give Good Strokes: Stop being afraid of healthy conflict, and confront over or underachievement schemes. Deal with the universal fear of intimacy by putting more value in affection and less stock in status or income.

4. DON'T PRETEND TIME WILL HEAL ALL TRAUMAS.

Enjoy Romance: Plan time for growth when everything is going along fine. Nothing kills romance faster than a complacent, "Don't fix it if it isn't broke" attitude. Aim to learn new skills to make the business of your relationship run more smoothly.

Give Good Strokes: Brainstorm a Couple Mission Statement that will make both of you happy. Set big goals and evaluate your progress.

5. GLADLY GIVE YOUR MATE SPACE AND FREEDOM.

Enjoy Romance: Trust means being able to appreciate how a lover needs a life separate from you. Nourish your partner's separate friendships, hobbies and interests. Take time away from your partner without feeling guilty.

Give Good Strokes: Stop expecting your partner to meet every one of your needs. Enjoy time apart as a better way to enjoy time together. Be aware of the abandonment fears that may arise when you enjoy separateness.

6. ALWAYS TAKE CARE OF YOURSELF TO FEEL WORTHWHILE.

Enjoy Romance: Pleasing self and others in about equal measure is best. Sacrificing leads to resentment and can become a bad habit. Balance self-comforting along with partner support.

Give Good Strokes: Never punish yourself by withdrawing for too long when you are angry at your mate. Learn to lean into the relationship for a sense of nourishment. Trade-off caregiving tips.

7. DON'T COLLECT DEBTS OF RESENTMENT.

Enjoy Romance: Unresolved resentments restrict choice. Losing control of our choices always leads to power plays, rude awakenings and ruined intimacy. Be straight about what you dislike.

Give Good Strokes: Convene weekly family grudge meetings to air complaints. Use creative solutions to iron out pesky disputes. Learn to negotiate and value compromise.

8. DO WHATEVER IT TAKES TO SOLVE PROBLEMS.

Enjoy Romance: It's always easier to run from problems than hit them head on. Excuse-making or explaining-away feelings will keep you stuck in blaming cycles. Get to the bottom of problems to keep them from reoccurring.

Give Good Strokes: Brainstorm solutions to a problem. What will it take for the two of you to resolve this problem once and for all? Every problem has a solution. Don't delay, move forward today.

9. DON'T SETTLE FOR SECOND BEST.

Enjoy Romance: Don't sacrifice what you want for the larger picture. Undue sacrificing causes unhelpful anger to surface. Avoid acting out the martyr role with your partner, and shy away from laying on the guilt trips.

Give Good Strokes: Challenge irrational thinking that makes you believe you must please in order to be loved. Let your partner please you more to be more satisfied. Be active in sprucing up your self-esteem on a daily basis.

10. STAY SEXUAL.

Enjoy Romance: Try to keep arguments outside of the bedroom, and make love instead of staying mad. Stop putting off your sexuality "UNTIL _____." For example, "Until you are less tired," "Until the kids are asleep," or "Until all the chores are done." Let yourself get in the spirit of making love even when you may not feel up to it.

Give Good Strokes: Stay charged-up sexually by letting yourself be turned on by life. Don't buy the myth that happy couples don't require frequent sex, or that unhappy couples don't deserve it.

Make a special effort to weave strong bonds of love. Beware of drifting so far apart from your lover that you no longer care whether or not you remain together. Don't wait a second longer to put the spark back into your romance.

PERMIT YOURSELF TO ACCEPT POSITIVE STROKES

Keep stroking your strengths to succeed. Here are the six rational stroke rules that will lead you down the road of success and happiness.

- ✔ **REFUSE TO TAKE IN HURTFUL NEGATIVE STROKES.**
- ✔ **GIVE YOURSELF GOOD STROKES.**
- ✔ **VOLUNTEER HELPFUL NEGATIVE STROKES.**
- ✔ **ASK FOR POSITIVE STROKES.**
- ✔ **GIVE POSITIVE STROKES.**
- ✔ **ACCEPT POSITIVE STROKES.**

Keep stroking your strengths to stay successful!

The chapter counterpoint tells you how to avoid getting stuck up from strokes.

Caring people don't want to become egotistical and fat-headed from a diet too rich in positive strokes.

COUNTERPOINT:

"DON'T PEOPLE GET STUCK UP FROM STROKES?"

Actually, just the reverse is true. Selfishness, greed and envy stem from a lack of strokes. Here's why:

★ *God values unconditional positive strokes.* The old-time Puritan ethic has made everyone feel afraid of giving too much praise, but God is a model of unconditional positive strokes.

★ *The fear of success makes you paranoid about accepting compliments.* Do you expect something bad to follow the good? Waiting for the other shoe to drop is a sure way to reduce the impact of positive strokes.

★ *Subordinates need to admire your strengths.* Subordinates need to develop their own daring by studying your strengths. They will become angry if you do not allow them to admire you.

★ *Feeling like a failure results in self-absorption.* Loads of negative strokes or receiving no strokes at all lead to being stuck up. Losers hoard away strokes for fear of losing out.

★ *The fear of commitment makes you back off from a lifestyle of positive strokes.* Making a commitment to feeling good is a tough decision. Being happy is even harder.

★ *Brushing off positive strokes shows arrogance.* Saying "Yes, BUT.." to every positive stroke is insincere and unappreciative — not humble.

★ *The fear of disapproval makes you prefer negative strokes.* The fear of disapproval encourages you to focus only on the negative. Positive strokes replace trying to control others.

★ *Complaining is a slick way to get strokes.* Complaining is a socially sanctioned way to rip off small positive strokes without getting caught.

★ *Good strokes don't add guilt.* Don't fish for strokes by putting yourself down. Never feel obliged to return compliments or criticisms given to you.

★ *Receiving too few strokes leads to selfishness and negative feelings.* Fear, resentment and depression indicate stroke deprivation.

Keep challenging yourself to accept more and more and more and MORE positive strokes. Stroke your strengths to succeed!

In the next chapter, I'm going explain how pleasing yourself can be the rocket fuel for rapid change.

10

PLEASING YOURSELF FOR A CHANGE

"You know you can't please everyone —
So you've got to please yourself."

Songwriter Rick Nelson.

EQUALLY PLEASING SELF AND OTHERS IS BEST

Have you learned the delicate art of pleasing yourself and pleasing loved ones in about equal amounts of tender loving care? Pleasers who need to be liked too much sacrifice their happiness by giving until their self-esteem hurts.

Everyone has a different opinion about whether or not it is better to give, than to receive. The extremes: pleasers get stuck in a giving mode, while displeasers get stuck in a taking mode. Both camps think their way is the best way to get along in life. Both are wrong.

Why? Pleasers don't insist on the right to be important, while displeasers don't insist on the right to be vulnerable. Neither of them feel free to be who they are.

Displeasers are proud to be different, and are usually labeled as "difficult" people. They are defiant pleasure-seekers who expect people to look after themselves. Disapproval arouses them.

Pleasing others can either be a blessing or a curse. The blessing: being gifted with sensitivity and a willingness to go the extra mile. The curse: naively believing that giving alone will magically resolve difficult problems.

High self-esteemers give to the point of hurting their own self-esteem — and then they say "STOP." Can you be assertive about your needs? Giving more and more when you are already feeling resentful will restrict your self-esteem no matter how noble the cause.

Are you giving too much and getting too little back? If you are then your self-esteem is being drained.

THE PLEASER QUIZ

Are you pleasing others too much, and pleasing yourself too little? Find out about your pleaser habits by taking the following quiz.

TRUE	FALSE	
❏	❏	1. I approve of myself.
❏	❏	2. People close to me know what I really think and feel.
❏	❏	3. I know I should stand up for myself and insist that my needs be met.
❏	❏	4. When my mate or children expect too much from me, I feel resentful.

TRUE	FALSE	
❏	❏	5. Criticism and conflict makes me feel anxious.
❏	❏	6. Receiving approval is very important to me.
❏	❏	7. I enjoy who I am.
❏	❏	8. I will impose on others whenever necessary.
❏	❏	9. Impossible work assignments are put on my shoulders.
❏	❏	10. Heated disagreements protect loving relationships.
❏	❏	11. I catch myself analyzing everything way too much.
❏	❏	12. Hatred is something I fail to understand.

ANSWERS AND DISCUSSION

Incorrect answers mean you are pleasing too much. High self-esteemers give these answers:

1. *True.* Self-approval is valued by high self-esteemers. Pleasers refuse to approve of themselves due to one kind of personal fault or another.

2. *True.* Self-disclosure is valued by high self-esteemers. Pleasers hide their real opinions from intimates in order to obtain love and approval. A pleaser is a chameleon who changes colors to give others what they want.

3. *True.*   Self-protection is valued by high self-esteemers. Pleasers know they should be more assertive, but hurting the feelings of others is considered a crime.

4. *False.*   Self-choice is valued by high self-esteemers. Pleasers don't mind meeting expectations at the time of the giving act. But later when their energy is drained, or their efforts have gone unnoticed, they begin feeling resentful.

5. *False.*   Self-responsibility is valued by high self-esteemers. Pleasers believe they make others feel happy, mad or blue by what they say or do. Pleasers always try hard to remove bad feelings.

6. *False.*   Self-stroking is valued by high self-esteemers. Pleasers are panicked by the withholding of positive strokes or outright disapproval.

7. *True.*   Self-enjoyment is valued by high self-esteemers. Pleasers wrongly believe they aren't quite good enough just as they are. Taking pleasure in the self is rare.

8. *True.*   Self-respect is valued by high self-esteemers. Pleasers don't want to make waves. They won't ask for help or insist their needs be met if anyone is inconvenienced.

9. *False.*   Self-determination is valued by high self-esteemers. Pleasers are known as the workhorses in the company who will quietly accomplish what other co-workers wouldn't dream of doing without complaining.

10. *True.*   Self-assertion is valued by high self-esteemers. Pleasers consider verbal confrontations to be scary, uncontrollable and destructive. Pleasers forgive too quickly and don't stay mad long enough.

11. *False.*   Self-reflection is valued by high self-esteemers. Pleasers think obsessively about problems with difficult people, but they don't take effective action to resolve the problems.

12. *False.*   Self-acceptance is valued by high self-esteemers. Pleasers are kindhearted souls who are prone to being used because they fail to understand the dark side of life. They are naive about the thrills of revenge paybacks.

YOUR SCORE?

How did you fare? Tally up the number of correct items you marked. The higher your score the better. It means you are pleasing yourself in about equal amounts to pleasing others.

10-12 Correct: EQUAL. You value pleasing yourself and others about equally. You work hard to improve your self-esteem, and your efforts are paying off. You stop pleasing when you feel resentful, and please yourself without feeling guilty.

5-9 Correct: UNEQUAL. You typically please others more than you please yourself. Resentments are being collected since you don't pay sufficient attention to your own self-esteem needs. You try too hard to please others, and feel guilty when you please yourself.

0-4 Correct: **UNFAIR.** You please others almost exclusively and neglect yourself. Your self-esteem is suffering from your martyrdom. You keep pleasing others even after you feel resentful. Pleasing yourself causes you great guilt.

Ending the pleasing game will mean you are freer to be who you are, and enjoy who you are more fully. Be sure to please yourself for a change.

As a pleaser you pay a stiff price for being so nice. That's no surprise. The resentments you collect will lower your self-esteem and eventually come out in angry behaviors.

Make certain your self-esteem is in good shape. Learning to please yourself and please others in about equal measures of tender loving care is an interpersonal skill you can master.

THE HIGH COST OF NEEDING TO BE LIKED TOO MUCH

Everyone wants to be liked, but a compulsive need to win every popularity contest keeps you from learning who you are and living a happy, fulfilled life.

If you are busy trying to please others, you no longer are living your own life. But being yourself is more important. It is important to feel entitled to express a strong sense of your selfhood and identity.

Pleasers are geared for winning others' acceptance, instead of concentrating on their own hidden talents. Pleasers value fitting in more than they value breaking the mold or breaking from the herd. Pleasers please because they feel they have to, not because they want to.

Pleasers want to make people happy, even when it means their self-esteem will sink lower. Pleasers are genuinely confused about how to meet their needs without hurting anybody. Pleasers are basically caring souls who value giving above receiving.

Pleasers are willing to sacrifice much of their happiness for the sake of others. They go with the flow, give when it would be better to take and usually don't make much of a muss or fuss.

Pleasers pay a heavy price for being so nice; they give up their right to express their full identity in all of their relationships — particularly in their romantic relationships. Instead of advertising their strengths, they compromise and give up rather than toughly negotiate during conflict-filled debates. They do this all in the name of being liked.

But why?

Most pleasers have had it tough from the start. Their parents expected them to be superpleasers to help keep the family intact. These children got the message that they were somehow bad and wrong — unacceptable as they were. The hurt child then decided that pleasing people was necessary in order to be seen as good, valuable and worth keeping around.

Pleasers must learn they are special, important and liked even when their loved ones are angry at them. We all need to know that somebody who truly loves us won't go away from us forever. Only then can a pleaser turn into a real person — somebody who is delightful, simply as they are.

PLEASERS VS. DISPLEASERS

How can you determine when you are pleasing too much? How do you know when you are in a pleasing versus a displeasing mode of behavior?

High self-esteemers have learned that anyone can act in the role of a pleaser or displeaser. We know that both extremes exist along a continuum inside every person. One mode isn't better than the other, and either mode may be needed at times to increase self-esteem.

There are plenty of times to say, for example, "I don't care what you think, stop hurting me." Or, "I'm unwilling to give you that right now." Or, "I dislike _____." Pleasers shutter to utter such displeasing words.

Pleasers tend to attract their opposites — displeasers. Displeasers are not bad people, they just love to feel in control. Pleasers give them plenty of opportunity to feel that way.

The world is half-filled with displeasers who take pride in being difficult. Displeasers seek to control others and enjoy doing so. Displeasers are the right shoe, pleasers the left, and together they form a pair.

DEFINING THE PLEASING MODE

In the pleasing mode you fear being who you are as if having a strong identity were an act of treason.

You line up behind others goals' and go in directions you do not desire. Blindly, you believe that being approved of makes you a more valuable person.

YOU ARE PLEASING TOO MUCH WHEN

As a pleaser you need to learn to behave in more demanding, displeasing and intolerant ways to achieve balance when:

1. **You try to get disapproving people to like you.**
2. **Self-care takes a backseat to caring for others.**
3. **You agree to do what you really don't want to do.**
4. **You feel resentful after doing good deeds.**
5. **Romance suffers due to unresolved grudges.**
6. **Your decisions are dictated by others' expectations.**
7. **You fail to understand why hatred exists.**
8. **YOU DON'T MAKE A COMMITMENT TO BE HAPPY.**

INTER PLAY:

Pleasers have a hard time taking responsibility for their own happiness. They err by thinking one person's happiness is the other person's misery.

The Anti-Happiness Rule by Which Pleasers Live and Die: Pleasers try to adhere to this neurotic rule: "Please others first, and yourself second." Pleasers wrongly believe that love means giving up their needs.

Pleasers Run Themselves into the Ground for Acceptance: Pleasers receive too few positive strokes — especially from themselves. They hustle to receive conditional strokes from grudging givers.

Typical Attitude of Placation: Pleasers adopt an "I'll do anything to receive your approval" attitude. Giving in is experienced as a gain of self-control.

Typical Impact on Self-Esteem: Taking responsibility for self-happiness is shunned. Low self-esteem and unassertiveness results.

Pleasers dislike anger and other negative emotions for fear of disapproval. By not standing up for themselves though, inappropriate anger is directed their way and accumulated by them.

DEFINING THE DISPLEASING MODE

In the displeasing mode you fear feeling vulnerable as if being insecure were an act of treason.

To stop feeling vulnerable you put your needs first and go after what you want even when you will be disapproved of. Sadness or pain is equated with losing control.

YOU ARE DISPLEASING TOO MUCH WHEN

As a displeaser you must learn how to behave in a sympathetic fashion to achieve balance when:

1. **You don't really care what other people think.**
2. **You try to help others by criticizing them.**
3. **People feel intimidated by you.**
4. **You thrive in situations where you have control.**
5. **Revenge paybacks are rationalized.**
6. **Sadness or disappointment is avoided.**
7. **Disapproval arouses you.**
8. **YOU DON'T MAKE A COMMITMENT TO BE VULNERABLE.**

Displeasers aren't bad people. They struggle with the same issues as pleasers do.

INTER PLAY:

Displeasers have a hard time listening to negative feedback about how their behavior has hurt loved ones. Displeasers erroneously conclude that if they are happy, everyone else ought to be happy too.

The Anti-Sadness Rule by Which Displeasers Live and Die: Displeasers try to adhere to this neurotic rule: "Please yourself first, and others second." Displeasers wrongly believe that love is a one-way street.

Displeasers Run Themselves into the Ground to Be Strong: Displeasers push people away to have separate time, and they prefer to give themselves positive strokes. Since self-strokes aren't enough, displeasers fall apart when a lover leaves.

Typical Attitude of Defiance: Displeasers adamantly contend: "You can't make me do what I don't want to do." Giving in is experienced as a loss of self-control.

Typical Impact on Self-Esteem: Taking responsibility for the happiness of others is shunned. Inflated self-esteem and aggressiveness results.

Displeasers win the battle for control, but lose the war of being loved for who they are.

WHEN PLEASING HURTS MORE THAN IT HELPS

Displeasers are impervious to signs of outright disdain and are able to smile on the rainiest of criticism days. These people do not mind being disliked. In fact, they seem to take pride in it. Pleasers tend to envy displeasers' tough hides.

Pleasers need to adopt some of the traits of displeasers to get along better in the world. Pleasers should feel free to be tough, hardheaded and even obnoxious at times to get their way. Pleasers who are anti-anger though, have trouble making life difficult for others.

Pleasers don't wish to hurt anyone. Pleasers idealistically believe life should be free of pain. If someone must be hurt, pleasers will volunteer for the duty. By not taking care of themselves though, pleasers will do a great deal of unsuspected damage to their relationships in the long run.

High self-esteem means making good choices that are good for oneself, while also being considerate of others' needs. Low self-esteem means self-pleasuring choices are forfeited for fear of causing conflict.

Pleasing hurts more than it helps when your choices are controlled by the fear of disapproval. Good choices bring a mixture of approval and disapproval. Good decisions require making tough choices in spite of the fear of disapproval.

Of course, pleasing isn't always bad. But knowing the difference between when it is a good time to please, and when it is absolutely necessary to be displeasing is crucial for a strong identity, intimacy and communication.

BEGIN PLEASING YOURSELF FOR A CHANGE

Pleasing yourself and others about equally takes time, determination and practice to accomplish. Feel the fire in your veins though, and know that pleasing yourself is not a sin, but a saintly virtue.

Pleasing yourself leads to high self-esteem because you *feel free to:*

- ✔ **Express your individuality.**
- ✔ **Think about angry feelings to control them.**
- ✔ **Feel important just as you are.**
- ✔ **Take positive action in spite of fear.**
- ✔ **Take your own good advice.**
- ✔ **Give your best talents back to the world.**

Fight falling into the pleaser mode of giving until you hurt. You must learn to stick within kindness limits, and express your anger assertively when you are being taken advantage of.

GIVE LESS TO BE YOURSELF MORE

Even though I recommend going the extra giving mile, there are plenty of times you must dig in your heels and refuse to be giving.

When should you stop yourself from giving more-more-more?

RULE #1.

WHEN PLEASING OTHERS IS DONE AT YOUR OWN EXPENSE, FORCE YOURSELF TO STOP GIVING.

RULE #2.

WHEN YOUR GIFTS AREN'T APPRECIATED, STOP GIVING TO AVOID FEELING RESENTFUL.

RULE #3.

WHEN YOU ARE COLLECTING RESENTMENTS, FORCE YOURSELF TO MAKE NEW CHOICES TO CHANGE.

RULE #4.

WHEN THE TEMPTATION ARISES TO GIVE REVENGE PAYBACKS, FORCE YOURSELF TO DO WITHOUT.

Pleasing yourself isn't a crime. In fact, being happy with yourself makes you more capable of, and better able to balance, giving with receiving.

Pleasers deserve to be both happy and successful. Self-esteem requires you courageously express who you are by revealing your unique identity in the world.

The antidote to pleasing others too much is JOY! It is to this very topic I must now turn your attention.

USING JOY TO OVERCOME THE FEAR OF DISAPPROVAL

As a pleaser you don't give yourself the many breaks life has to offer you. Deep in your heart you know this to be the truth. And you hate it.

Breaking free from the compulsive need to be liked is never easy, but it is made easier if you start finding ways to bring more joy into your life.

No, it's never as easy as doing one-two-three cookbook step things to bolster your self-esteem. Knowing in your heart what is good for you to do — and going ahead and doing it — is the secret of high self-esteem. Go forward and do what you know in your heart is good for you to do.

By building the following pleasures into your life, you will irretrievably give up the need to be super-pleasing:

1. IT IS A JOY OF LIFE TO FEEL YOU ARE IN CONTROL.

The Challenge: You have felt forced to cater to the whims of others in order to feel valuable. Some giving is useful, but giving too much undermines your self-worth.

For Feeling Good: Feeling good means enjoying being in control of your emotions, goals and having self-pride. You weren't born to be a convenient whipping post. How can you put more desirable experiences into your life?

Please Yourself for a Change: It is okay to say "Yes" to what makes you feel at your best!

2. IT IS A JOY TO EXPRESS YOUR UNIQUE IDENTITY AND NEEDS.

The Challenge: You have felt forced to go along with opinions that don't reflect your own. Be sure to see things from alternative viewpoints, but don't discourage yourself from speaking up about your own insights.

For Feeling Good: Feeling good means enjoying getting to know yourself more and more as you mature. How can you express your own identity more forcefully?

Please Yourself for a Change: It is okay to be one of a kind!

3. IT IS A JOY TO SAY "NO" WITHOUT FEELING GUILTY.

The Challenge: You have agreed to compromises that your better judgment or intuition told you to avoid. It may be wise to do things you don't want to, but not if you feel resentful about it later on.

For Feeling Good: Feeling good means enjoying setting clear limits that protect your self-worth. How can you say "No" more often to feel better?

Please Yourself for a Change: It is okay to say "No" without feeling guilty!

4. IT IS A JOY TO COMMUNICATE POWERFULLY.

The Challenge: You have felt forced to hide your true opinions, and to pretend you are in agreement when you aren't. Holding back your dissatisfactions is wise sometimes, but most times stuffing dissenting opinions makes life worse.

For Feeling Good: Feeling good means your ideas are fifty percent of what makes a good relationship really work well. How can you express your opinions more openly and more often?

Please Yourself for a Change: It is okay to speak your mind!

5. IT IS A JOY TO RELATE OPENLY AND HONESTLY.

The Challenge: You have felt forced to stop thinking about painful problems, or stay quiet about something uncomfortable. Sometimes it is best to bury problems, but denial is more often harmful.

For Feeling Good: Feeling good means you open yourself up to being hurt by disclosing who you truly are. How can you take risks to be more transparent with trustworthy people?

Please Yourself for a Change: It is okay to be open and honest!

6. IT IS A JOY TO FEEL LIKE A GOOD MAN OR A GOOD WOMAN.

The Challenge: You have felt forced to adopt a role to be liked, instead of being the real person you are inside. Value the gender you are, and never put your self-esteem up for sale.

For Feeling Good: Feeling good means deciding what type of men and women are best for you to be with. How can you rely less on what you "should" do, and rely more on what you "want" to do?

Please Yourself for a Change: It is okay to enjoy the sex you are!

7. IT IS A JOY TO FEEL GOOD ABOUT YOUR BODY.

The Challenge: You have felt forced to change things about yourself that are better left alone. Don't siphon fat off from thighs, straighten crooked teeth or say things you don't believe in to make controllers happy.

For Feeling Good: Feeling good means enjoying your body. How can you take care of your body in ways that make you tingle and feel full of life?

Please Yourself for a Change: It is okay to enjoy your body free of guilt!

8. IT IS A JOY TO FEEL CREATIVE.

The Challenge: You have felt forced to let your best and brightest ideas of a better life go to waste. Sometimes you do need to postpone taking risks, but most times you don't.

For Feeling Good: Feeling good means taking speedy action on your own great ideas. How can you set aside time to brainstorm? Will you do whatever it takes to reach your goals?

Please Yourself for a Change: It is okay to express your creative ideas in concrete ways!

9. IT IS A JOY TO EMBRACE GROWTH AND WELL-BEING.

The Challenge: You have felt forced to let society determine what is best for you to do. Sometimes you should slow your changes down, but more often you resist growth for fear of being criticized or rejected.

For Feeling Good: Feeling good means changing when you aren't required to. How can you express your innate interests and secret strengths more?

Please Yourself for a Change: It is okay to take care of your growth needs even when others don't!

Depression results from pleasing too much. Joy results when you have the courage to please yourself and other people about equally.

Work hard at adding new joy to your life so you will be less tempted to stunt your own self-esteem by pleasing too much.

MINDPLAY:

PLEASING YOURSELF MORE WITHOUT FEELING GUILTY

Now that you know the hazards of pleasing too much, you must take time to pleasure yourself to create a sense of balance in your life.

Free up your mind to consider what you would do each week if you were permitted to give yourself pleasure. Begin to consider self-pleasure as an avenue to feeling closer to yourself, the people you love and to God.

Feel entitled to please yourself. Give yourself the pleasures that will make you feel most pleased!

- ❑ Having a sensual massage
- ❑ Taking an interesting class
- ❑ Going on a dream vacation
- ❑ Dating someone who really interests me
- ❑ Getting a promotion
- ❑ Learning a new skill
- ❑ Going past my limits
- ❑ Taking myself out to dinner
- ❑ Going to a midnight movie
- ❑ Lounging in a bubble bath
- ❑ Having a glass of fine wine
- ❑ Playing with my kids
- ❑ Sunbathing
- ❑ Investing money
- ❑ Pursuing an old hobby
- ❑ Trying a new recipe

- ❑ Attending a support group
- ❑ Spending time with people who like me
- ❑ Risking rejection
- ❑ Buying a new outfit or suit
- ❑ Talking to an interesting person
- ❑ Laughing
- ❑ Laughing louder than usual
- ❑ Enjoying alone time
- ❑ Enjoying time with my mate
- ❑ Listening to music
- ❑ Feeling turned on
- ❑ Thrilling my creative feelings
- ❑ Telling jokes
- ❑ Remembering compliments
- ❑ Disclosing my feelings
- ❑ Walking in nature
- ❑ Attending a counseling session
- ❑ Being "Queen/King For A Day"
- ❑ Telling people how good I feel
- ❑ Going on a retreat
- ❑ Volunteering
- ❑ Exercising
- ❑ Telling people what I really like
- ❑ Enjoying lousy weather
- ❑ Being self-reflective
- ❑ Being myself
- ❑ Being important
- ❑ Being who I am
- ❑ Being...
- ❑ (Make up your own activities)
- ❑ (Be sure to please yourself...)
- ❑ (To feel good...)
- ❑ (Fulfill your needs!)

Start to practice pleasing yourself by doing activities that you have previously considered strictly off-limits.

Pleasing Yourself Reveals Negative Beliefs: Pleasing yourself will make you isolate any negative beliefs that are making you sacrifice your identity in exchange for being accepted.

Feeling Joyful Isn't a Sin: Don't shun joy. Joy is the way to free up your self-esteem and make you stop compromising your best strengths.

Why, when somebody shows off positive strengths, do so many of us look the other way? Answer: The person is delighting in self-pleasuring.

Expressing your strengths is a real turn on. Although some observers will want to draw close, jealousy will force others who don't allow themselves to express their strengths to look the other way.

Express your personal strengths. Being your best is the most pleasing action you will ever undertake.

Time now to tell you a rich fable that focuses on the difference between pleasers and displeasers — and how hatred makes pleasers vulnerable.

MAKING FRIENDS WITH ANGER

Not only are pleasers too nice, but they are naive to boot. Pleasers cannot fathom why people use anger in cruel ways, when acts of kindness are easier to endure and are much more noble to perform.

Being afraid of anger makes a pleaser vulnerable. It leaves you open to being manipulated when signs of strong disapproval are shown. Sometimes though, you must look after your own needs and painfully part ways with displeasers.

The fable of the Scorpion and the White Horse has been passed down through the generations to help you and I clarify the difference between love and hatred.

THE FABLE OF THE SCORPION AND THE WHITE HORSE

Once upon a time there was a tremendous life-threatening fire in the forest. All the animals were frightened and panicked.

The animals frantically ran toward the big river that bordered the forest to reach safety. Most of the animals were able to cross the wide river with the help of a rush of potent adrenaline.

All reached safety except for the Scorpion, who because of his small size was unable to cross alone. Without help, the Scorpion would die in the fire. He knew what he must do.

A marvelous White Horse came galloping up right then. The other animals in the forest greatly admired the White Horse for his good deeds, strength and kind spirit. The Scorpion was no different from the other creatures in this regard.

The Scorpion called out in a tiny voice: "Oh, help me, White Horse, help me get across the river." At once the White Horse answered: "I can't do that. I can't help you. You are a Scorpion; you will bite me if I give you a ride on my back across the river."

"I wish you would trust me," replied the Scorpion. "Biting you would jeopardize my life and would be a foolish thing to do. Wouldn't you agree?" On a sorrowful note the Scorpion pleaded: "Only you can help me White Horse. Please don't leave me behind to be burned alive in this terrible fire."

Reluctantly, the White Horse agreed. Going against his better judgment he said: "Okay, hop on. But you better be careful. Remember, both of us will drown if you pull anything funny."

The Scorpion thanked the White Horse, and with a dark red

glimmer in his eyes, hopped on quickly. The White Horse, swollen with pride and muscles rippling, swam mightily out into the river.

About half way across, the White Horse suddenly felt a horrendous sting. Poison filled his veins.

The White Horse screamed: "You fool! What have you done now?" You'll kill the both of us. We're doomed to drown. How could you do such a stupid thing? Why on God's earth did you do this?"

And the Scorpion calmly replied: "Because my dear White Horse, I'm a Scorpion."

Read the fable carefully and you will find that the Scorpion never promised he wouldn't bite the beautiful White Horse. He simply asked to be trusted, and the White Horse agreed to help against his better judgment.

The moral of the story? Pleasers must face the fact that there will always be cruelty in this world. We must learn to accept that every creature has a role to play in life. No amount of extra giving can — or should — make someone different.

Pleasers really have difficulty imagining that people can be wicked, heartless, cruel and insensitive to others' feelings. This is a phenomenon that pleasers need to remain aware of or they will get stung every time!

Hatred, selfishness and greed need to be accepted for what they are — chaotic feelings that every human being must learn to accept and control.

Make anger a good friend so that you don't have to deny it in yourself or others.

ENDING THE SEARCH FOR APPROVAL

Ending the search for approval isn't easy. But self-acceptance is worth the struggle.

Self-esteem means you must unconditionally approve of yourself by approving of what you think, approving of what you feel and approving of what you choose to do. High self-esteem means you prefer to be accepted, but you can withstand being rejected.

Pleasing others is a sly attempt to buy love. The cost will always be too high. If you sell out your identity to be liked, you will end up hating yourself for agreeing to such a cheap deal. Feeling free to please yourself and risk rejection is a braver call to individualization.

The fear of disapproval plays on your mind and plots against your potential. The desire to win approval makes you adopt facades; those masks that you assume will be better accepted than your genuine self. Tragically, men and women often end up trying to act out artificial roles that ruin their chances for really getting to know each other.

How can you begin approving of your inner self?

- ✔ Make a decision to be yourself.
- ✔ Stake out your claim to be happy in spite of rejection.
- ✔ Stop worrying about what others think.
- ✔ Start worrying about what you think of yourself for a change.

I'm going to teach you now how to remain a nice person while pleasing yourself more. Use these antidotes to dilute the poison of pleasing others too much.

ANTIDOTES TO BEING A PLEASER

Learn to love yourself no matter how poorly you are treated by others. Here are some ways to like yourself more:

1. DON'T WAIT ANY LONGER TO ASSERT YOUR NEEDS.

Be Assertive: Assert your needs on a daily basis. Why delay?

Please Yourself: Allow other people to please you. Be forthright about asking for things that will make life easier for you.

Be Who You Are: Encourage loved ones to give you positive paybacks for all that you have given to them.

2. ATTACK YOUR INSECURITIES.

Be Secure: Don't stay on friendly terms with your real enemy — insecurity. Why delay?

Please Yourself: Fight every negative belief that says, "You're not important." Stop being mentally lazy when glaring errors in your thinking occur. Shed the depressing feeling that your insecurities are the only reality in life.

Be Who You Are: You may be surprised to find out how farfetched your self-criticisms are.

3. LET LOVED ONES STRUGGLE SOMETIMES.

Be Forgiving: Don't help everybody all the time. Instead, let loved ones learn from pain. Why delay?

Please Yourself: Your time and energy is a precious commodity. Learn to restrain yourself from giving to the point of burnout. Help yourself to heaping handfuls of good strokes.

Be Who You Are: You may be surprised to learn how strong people are when you say "No."

4. NEVER PLAY DUMB ABOUT YOUR SECRET NEEDS.

Be Real: Meeting your needs is important. It always will be. Why delay?

To Please Yourself: Pleasers have a way of hiding their needs, even from themselves. You deserve to have happiness in your life. Use your strengths and intelligence to meet your needs.

Be Who You Are: You may be surprised to find out what your needs and strengths really are.

5. STOP WAITING AROUND TO GET YOUR PARENTS' APPROVAL.

Be a Powerful Adult: You must make your own adult choices even when your parents disapprove of your lifestyle. Why delay?

Please Yourself: Pleasers fear they will be rejected when they act independently and successfully. Who you are is not only adequate and acceptable — but preferable. Live your life according to your own standards.

Be Who You Are: You may be surprised when your parents treat you with more respect.

6. LET YOURSELF GO FOR A LITTLE "WILD."

Be Fun-Loving: Get loose. Let yourself go for a little "wild" without downing yourself. Why delay?

Please Yourself: Pleasers put off their own needs for healthy fun to meet their obligations. Don't hold yourself back from enjoying new experiences that bring out your carefree side.

Be Who You Are: You may be surprised when your humorous side is applauded.

7. ASK STRAIGHT QUESTIONS ABOUT THE WAYS YOU ARE LIKED.

Be Thought-Full: Put your insecurities to an experimental test and abide by the scientific findings. Why delay?

Please Yourself: When you think that nobody really loves you for who you are ask them, "What do you value most about me?" "Would you be willing to tell me why you stay with me?" or, "Does it make you angry to see me so unhappy?"

Be Who You Are: You may be surprised how fast blunt questioning can get you out of the super-pleasing mode.

8. ACCEPT MORE REASSURANCES FROM YOURSELF.

Be Truthful: You are responsible for what you think and you must believe in yourself no matter what lies have been told about you. Why delay?

Please Yourself: When no one seems to be in your corner, try being on your own side by saying: "I approve of myself. I approve of who I am, what I do and where I am headed." And make your behaviors match these beliefs.

Be Who You Are: You may be surprised to find that your identity grows stronger from self-stroking.

9. DON'T HOARD DISSATISFACTIONS.

Be Genuine: Don't suppress gripes about your marriage or children to maintain the image of being a super-person who has few needs. Why delay?

Please Yourself: Talking about your annoyances is better than being consumed by thinking angry thoughts. Try unloading dissatisfactions in a calm and caring manner.

Be Who You Are: You may be surprised how quickly people side with you and apologize.

10. DISALLOW PERSONAL PAYBACKS TO CORRECT HURTS.

Be Tough: Set assertive limits and know that revenge paybacks never erase hurt. Why delay?

Please Yourself: Spreading pain around, or passing it back and forth, never resolves anything. Spread around your unique talents and happiness instead.

Be Who You Are: You may be surprised to find out just how tough and disciplined you can be when you're angry.

11. REMEMBER THE GOOD TIMES.

Be Wise: Review the times your advisors, partner or friends came through for you when you felt like the lone failure. Why delay?

Please Yourself: Pleasers have a tendency to become cynical, depressed or pessimistic when their ideals flop. Use positive memories to create trust, hope and faith.

Be Who You Are: You may be surprised at how comforted and optimistic you feel.

End the search for approval before it's too late. Choose to associate with people who like and approve of you just as you are.

Self-acceptance can never be given — it must be learned and earned. Learning to approve of yourself is an invaluable act that takes loads of courage and lots of mundane practice.

The psychological paradox: When you have the courage to give up the need for approval, you will be approved of all the more.

THE NEUROTIC PREFERENCE FOR PLEASING BETWEEN THE SEXES

Our adult romantic relationships — and the expectations we carry into them — are frequently unrealistic. This is because men and women magically hope to receive answers to their problems from the opposite gender.

Pleasers of both sexes feel they must lure the other gender into loving them by being super-giving. In exchange, pleasers expect the opposite sex to restore their lost self-esteem. Any change from this agenda becomes a source of friction and resentment.

The romantic phase of loving relationships, where sleep is lost and feelings eclipse logic, frequently pleases men and women about equally. But then comes the power play phase where raw differences need to be worked out. Pleasers have great difficulty standing up for themselves at this crucial developmental point.

Real loving relationships are bound to bring out intense anger. Pleasers will panic when normal anger and dissatisfaction impacts their relationships. They even stop thinking about their anger, which makes the possibility of inappropriate angry behaviors more likely.

Pleasers fear conflict. Ironically, the fear of conflict makes us please and thus be rejected too much, while learning to resolve conflicts puts an end to the pleasing mode between men and women. The tragic comedy: no one has taught us how to use conflict constructively.

The real shame in any relationship is when we don't take the time to be honest enough to get to know one another. When we are too busy pleasing and trying to psych out what the other wants, intimacy is all but impossible.

All kinds of games are played between the sexes.

Pleasing isn't the way to land the person of your dreams like you would hook a fish. Being yourself, and approving of who you are, is the only way to find an interesting partner. Sadly, I've heard the constant complaint from both sexes that there are no caring people left in this world. Balderdash!

Being able to change is the single best way to obtain and maintain a loving relationship. We men and women must relate to one another as equals. There is no other way to be loved for who we are. And we must please each other about equally for our loving relationships to thrive.

WHAT PLEASING ROMANTIC RELATIONSHIPS REQUIRE

A romantic relationship must be equally pleasing to both partners to foster intimacy. What are some indications that a mutually pleasing relationship is underway?

1. **Anger is thought about not acted out.**
2. **Each partner can effectively confront the other.**
3. **Assertiveness strengthens the bonds of love.**
4. **Pleasing is a two-way street.**
5. **Each partner feels free to do what the other can do.**

6. **Mutually appealing romantic goals are set.**

7. **Change isn't perceived as a threat.**

8. **Conflicts are welcomed not avoided.**

9. **Fair-fight rules are strictly adhered to.**

10. **Tough problems are solved not disavowed.**

11. **Anything can be talked about without censorship.**

12. **Respect is present.**

13. **Sex is thoroughly enjoyed free of guilt.**

Are you able to work with your partner to equally please one another? If so, you are able to find aliveness, humor and laughter with your mate.

Remember, the ability to resolve tough conflicts spurs you and your partner on to change all the more.

MINDPLAY:

WHAT DO I EXPECT FROM A LOVING RELATIONSHIP?

Have you taken the time to define what pleases you romantically? Are you clear about what you want from your partner?

Why wait any longer for something good to come along. Think greedily about your goals and needs. Answer these crucial questions:

➤ My goals for our relationship are:

➤ My goals for pleasing myself are:

➤ How I could feel less threatened by conflict would be:

➤ How I hold my partner or children responsible for my life is:

➤ If I didn't blame the opposite sex for my problems, I would:

➤ If I stopped being afraid of rejection, I would pursue:

➤ What I expect from men/women when I'm displeased is:

INTER PLAY:

Should romantic partners always be pleased with one another? Of course not. But you do need to receive more pleasure than pain in romance.

Pleasers Do Hurt Others: Pleasing isn't a selfless act that incurs zero consequences. Grudges come from pleasing others too much, and resentment restricts intimacy. Grudges hurt the very people you are trying to please.

Pleasers Must Set Important Goals: Pleasing yourself means setting goals and focusing intently on them. Resentment occurs when you forget to promote what is most important to you.

The Real Enemy Isn't Conflict — But the Fear of Conflict: Constructive conflict builds intimacy. Make anger and healthy conflict your best friends to build high self-esteem.

Is it possible for you to end the search for approval? You bet. Let's find out how you can dare to be more successful and more self-approving at the same time.

DARE TO BE SELF-APPROVING

Dare to be self-approving. Let your partner, co-workers and friends find out who and what you really stand for. Face each and every conflict and learn to grow from it.

Why not dare to be self-approving? You know there's nothing to lose. Approve of these rights:

> APPROVE OF YOUR PLEASURE.
> APPROVE OF WHO YOU ARE.
> APPROVE OF YOUR TALENTS.
> APPROVE OF YOUR LIFE.
> APPROVE OF YOUR NEEDS.
> APPROVE OF YOUR ANGER.
> APPROVE OF YOUR GOALS.
> APPROVE OF YOUR ASSERTIVENESS.
> APPROVE OF YOUR AMBITIONS.
> APPROVE OF YOUR MIND.
> APPROVE OF YOUR WORK.
> APPROVE OF YOUR BODY.
> APPROVE OF YOUR GENDER.
> APPROVE OF YOUR CHOICES.
> APPROVE OF YOUR SPIRITUALITY.

Let yourself approve of who you really are! Keep approving of yourself no matter who disapproves of you. You deserve to succeed by being yourself.

Being successful means being free to risk rejection to change, learn and grow. Set you destination for success!

DESTINATION SUCCESS

Success isn't magical. Success occurs when you choose to take positive actions in spite of negative emotions.

Do you want to have a successful marriage, career, spiritual and parenting life? Great! To succeed in any endeavor you must adhere to eight basic-but-tough rules no matter how life treats you.

Choose to be successful by pleasing yourself for a change. Learn to practice what others only preach. Follow these stringent rules in order to be at your best:

1. FIND A WAY TO HAVE ALMOST TOTAL CONTROL.

Conquer Negative Feelings: Lack of control leads to frustration. Being stressed indicates your life is in the hands of controllers too much. Find ways to take back control of your own life. Take pride in controlling your moods, thoughts, habits and body.

Destine Yourself for Success: The more control you can exert the happier you will feel.

2. FIRE PEOPLE WHO BETRAY YOU.

Conquer Negative Feelings: Loyalty is the most valuable trait any human being can aspire to. Be a role model of high integrity. Do not tolerate stupidity, disloyalty or disrespect from anyone — especially from yourself. Respect yourself for who you are and what you stand for.

Destine Yourself for Success: Rid yourself of people who choose to act in ways that undermine your self-esteem.

3. FOCUS ON ONE IDEA AT A TIME.

Conquer Negative Feelings: You probably aren't a genius who can focus on five lofty goals at once and win every single time.

To stay on track, keep everything as simple as possible. Instead, be a single-minded person who wins by focusing on one idea at a time.

Destine Yourself for Success: Huge successes are derived from one small idea after another.

4. PUT A SUCCESS PLAN IN WRITING.

Conquer Negative Feelings: Burn your basic mission in your skin like you would a tattoo to make a total commitment to your success. Put your plan down in writing using specific terms. Force your subconscious mind to agree to make sure your wishes come true.

Destine Yourself for Success: Always go back and review your success plan when difficult people or unexpected setbacks are causing you frustration.

5. ALWAYS INSIST ON HIGH QUALITY.

Conquer Negative Feelings: Don't cut corners or take the easy road when the quality of your relationships, life or product will be sacrificed. Personally strive to be at your best in every transaction without pressuring yourself to be perfect.

Destine Yourself for Success: Stick to your own good ideas like glue and keep doing what works.

6. TAKE TIME TO WORK OUT THE KINKS.

Conquer Negative Feelings: Greed and impatience can make you stop thinking about what needs to be worked out to smoothly move your idea to the next developmental level of success. Take time after you are up and running to work out unpredictable problems that could sabotage later successes.

Destine Yourself for Success: Learn to tolerate the up-and-down process of change and excel in patience.

7. REWARD HARD WORK.

Conquer Negative Feelings: Never forget to reward good followers with praise, affection, excitement or money. Remember, good followers are harder to find and keep on board than good leaders. Be sure to take time to praise yourself when you're working hard.

Destine Yourself for Success: Fight negative feelings by taking out your frustrations in hard work.

8. TRY TO EXIT ON A HIGH.

Conquer Negative Feelings: Try to end all of your transactions on a good note. Whether you are retiring, selling a business or bringing a meeting to a close, seek to end on an upbeat note.

Destine Yourself for Success: By saying good-bye you will free yourself up to say hello to the next opportunity.

Choose to be yourself by destining yourself for success.

Stay true to these eight rules long after you have fastened down and secured your success. Determine your own destiny by choosing success — and feel happier and more in control of your life as a result.

Don't allow your self-esteem to be run over by difficult people or disappointing situations. Fight back. Instead of allowing rejection to run your life, please yourself for a change!

PERMIT YOURSELF TO OVERCOME THE FEAR OF REJECTION

The fear of rejection will stop you from taking appropriate risks. Here are some permissions to insulate your self-esteem against painful rejections:

✔ **REJECT THE IDEA THAT YOU ARE UNWORTHY.**

✔ **BE ONE OF A KIND.**

✔ **ENJOY THE PERSON YOU ARE.**

✔ **TAKE CARE OF YOUR GROWTH NEEDS WHEN OTHERS DON'T.**

✔ **EXPRESS YOUR CREATIVE IDEAS IN CONCRETE WAYS.**

✔ **PRACTICE SAYING "NO" WITHOUT FEELING GUILTY.**

✔ **CHOOSE TO DEFINE YOURSELF AND SPEAK YOUR MIND.**

✔ **NEVER REJECT YOURSELF AFTER YOU HAVE BEEN REJECTED.**

✔ **ACCEPT THAT EVERY HUMAN BEING THINKS DIFFERENTLY.**

✔ **VALUE YOUR HEALTH AND SELF-ESTEEM FREE OF GUILT.**

Trying too hard to receive approval means you never really get a chance to know yourself or anyone else. What a shame and what irony.

COUNTERPOINT:

"BUT HOW CAN I BE MORE ASSERTIVE WHEN I'M AFRAID OF BEING REJECTED?"

Being assertive about your needs may provoke disapproval. Keep these assertive attitudes in mind to be a winner when you are feeling like a loser.

★ *Stand up for pleasing yourself not for displeasing someone who has hurt you.* Please yourself to attain self-esteem, not to obtain revenge.

★ *Doing the right thing does displease others.* Doing the right thing often involves pain. The smart or easy way, and doing what is right, are two very different paths. Remember, you have the most to offer when you take good care of yourself.

★ *Create fair-fight rules and stick to them.* Every relationship between equals requires fair-fight rules. Develop your own set of rules. Stick to these rules when your trust is low, but anger is running on high.

★ *Fight your fear of the unknown.* If you are fighting too much with someone, chances are that conflict has become a way for the two of you to cling together to avoid facing the unknown. Refuse to fight to achieve a warped sense of security.

★ *Never put your happiness on a protagonist's plate.* Your satisfaction is your own responsibility. Force yourself to make your happiness a top priority.

★ *Being an individual may mean going against the grain.* Go ahead and go against the social grain when your values are at stake. Be caring and express yourself by stating differences of opinion.

★ *Don't allow grudges to grind you down.* Don't ask for trouble by agreeing to do what you really don't want to do. There is no excuse for betraying yourself. Refuse to do what you know will make you fighting mad afterwards.

★ *Some people won't ever be pleased.* How sad but true — some people will never agree to change. If the antagonist is a die hard non-changer, you may be better off quitting than fighting.

★ *Reassure an antagonist of your commitment.* Unproductive anger slows down changing. Opposing parties should feel free to change. Never threaten to walk away if an antagonist won't change his or her ways unless you fully intend to leave.

★ *Do anything to heal your hurt.* The purpose of being assertive is to keep hurt to a minimum. Beware of crying when you are angry, or coming across in angry ways when you are hurt. Always seek to share your feelings in deeper ways.

★ *Your partner may need time to adjust to your changes.* The non-changing party may require time to assimilate the new you. Air gripes but stop blaming when you are absorbed in your changes. Have confidence in the other person's ability to adapt.

In the next chapter I will tell you how to neutralize the five change fears that always spring up to sabotage your change chances. And I will be encouraging you to please yourself in spite of them!

11

FREEING UP FROM CHANGE FEARS

"...On you will go though the Hakken-Kraks howl.
Onward up many a frightening creek,
though your arms may get sore and
your sneakers may leak."

From Dr. Seuss' change-affirming book
Oh, The Places You'll Go!

TAKING POSITIVE ACTION IN SPITE OF FEAR

Human beings hate change with a passion.

What you fear you hate. You hate change because it makes you afraid — afraid of failure, afraid of losing control, afraid of the unknown, afraid of rejection and afraid that you will stay in the same place when others are moving ahead of you.

Since the fear of change is universal and is learned, you can also learn to be open to change. To free yourself up to change, stop labeling yourself as a bad or weak person for being afraid. Instead, start accepting yourself for who you really are.

Can you accept being loved for who you are? The more your life is controlled by fear the less open you will be to being loved. Why? Fear smashes your self-esteem and causes you to behave in unloving ways toward yourself and others.

You CAN learn to conquer your fears one fear at a time. Standing up to fear is a tall order, but you are up to the challenge. Make a vow to take positive action in spite of fear to achieve high self-esteem!

THE LOVE QUIZ

Find out how open your attitude is to being loved by answering the following quiz questions.

TRUE	FALSE	
❑	❑	1. Intimacy means being appreciated as a separate person with unique interests.
❑	❑	2. The most successful couples set comprehensive yearly goals.
❑	❑	3. Dependency is unhealthy.
❑	❑	4. Accumulated resentment is the major threat to the survival of every loving relationship.
❑	❑	5. Passion results from building new changes and growth into tired relationships.
❑	❑	6. The best way to receive affection is to ask your partner to meet your needs.

TRUE	FALSE	
❏	❏	7. Sexual intercourse is less important than physical nurturing in strengthening bonds of love.
❏	❏	8. Most people are happy in their current relationships.
❏	❏	9. Anger can be a constructive emotion in love.
❏	❏	10. Pleasing your partner should be a priority.
❏	❏	11. Men think differently about communication and sexuality than women do.
❏	❏	12. Power plays are a normal way to resolve differences.

ANSWERS AND DISCUSSION

Correct answers indicate that you are reducing fear by risking open communication with your partner.

1. *True.* Intimacy occurs when two strong identities interact cooperatively in one relationship.

2. *True.* The most common mistake that couples make is to forget that relationships grow and change successfully when they're aimed at a common goal.

3. *False.* There is such a thing as healthy dependency. It means trusting your partner to meet your needs and is one hallmark of confident relationships.

4. *True.*   Accumulated resentment is the emotion most responsible for destroying intimacy and sexuality.

5. *True.*   The most negative message for couples who want to foster a passionate relationship is "Don't grow or change."

6. *False.*   Ironically, asking directly for needs to be met can come across to a partner as a coercive power play. A better way to get your needs met is to focus first on meeting the other partner's needs. When both partners do this, there is cooperation.

7. *True.*   Physical nurturing, non-sexual touching and holding are some of the best avenues to express unconditional love.

8. *False.*   Research indicates that more than half of us are dissatisfied about the quality of our current relationship and don't know what to do about it.

9. *True.*   Healthy anger can motivate needed changes. Unhealthy anger — characterized by such behavior as name-calling, stonewalling and withdrawing — is unproductive and hurtful.

10. *True.*   Pleasing your partner is both a selfless and a selfish act because he or she will want to please you back.

11. *True.*   Men tend to think sex will solve problems, and women tend to think communication will. But there is a need for both in a healthy relationship, and each partner should be free to initiate both

sex and communication. Men who initiate communication and women who initiate sex are more balanced in their roles.

12. *False.*   Repetitive arguments that don't result in concrete changes are bad habits.

Love means being able to create a relationship that is satisfying to both you and your partner. A self-esteeming relationship requires you to become a more loving, genuine and non-judgmental person.

You deserve to be who you are — happy, and respected as a changing person. Don't settle for less. You can win in all of your relationship quests.

Winners go ahead and take action in spite of their fears and persist in the face of loss. Losers use rationalizations to avoid taking action and give up at the first signs of failure or victory.

Remember, the fear of change is the omnipresent fear from which all other fears sprout.

Take a vow to stop running away from fear. Start taking charge of your fears today to achieve high self-esteem.

REPLACING FEAR WITH AN EQUAL AMOUNT OF SELF-ESTEEM

Self-esteem isn't some magical process reserved strictly for the princesses and princes who are the fairest in the kingdom. Nor is change simply some laundry list of quick-fix tips, a fancy set of written goals or loud proclamations that blare out to others that you should be loved.

Your changes need to have heart and stamina — more soul than "shoulds." They need to be honest and real and not faked.

They need to have your very own personal imprint on them. After all, your changes mean you are standing taller as a result of waging a victorious battle against fear.

But how is such a feat accomplished?

Genuine change demands you face down your worst fears and conquer them head on. Wryly, you may be wondering, "Is that all there is to it?" No, not quite. You must also take positive actions in spite of negative emotions that tell you to stay put because you are comfortable with who and where you are. Not too much to bite off is it?

No one can do the hard work of conquering your personal fears but you. That's the way it should be. After all, your sojourn into the unknown will develop irreplaceable courage, honor and dignity. Mastering negative emotions is an exciting journey in becoming more human.

The change principle: By changing you will replace your anxieties and fears with an equal amount of high self-esteem. Confronting your fears transforms them into solid self-worth every single time. Happiness comes from facing your fears bravely, instead of allowing them to control you.

Some of my clients become frustrated when they change and feel both more successful and more afraid. This happens often. Anticipate the fear of success when you change. Stay focused on success by reminding yourself of the principle that as fear is reduced an equal amount of self-esteem will be given to you.

As fear is mastered, joy is expanded. As you risk positive action when you are afraid, your happiness bursts forth to reward you. Fear then is a special friend you are wise to get to know well. Fear is the doorway to heightened self-esteem.

Beware too of substituting frustration for fear. This is a common communication error. Why? Feeling frustrated or depressed is far less threatening emotionally than feeling raw fear. Let fear be fear.

Do you want to have greater self-worth, confidence and happiness? Do you want to feel more successful and more alive?

Learn to tap into a pipeline of self-love. Changing in spite of your fears will give you these gifts and more.

TAKING CHARGE OF THE FEAR OF CHANGE

You too can master any number of fears one at a time. Lasting change means you must change your learned fear of change. Assertive people who choose change don't let fear stop them from being happy and successful.

What are the specific symptoms that accompany all fears of change?

SYMPTOMS OF THE FEAR OF CHANGE

1. **Expecting perfection.**
2. **Being unable to let go of past rejections.**
3. **Refusing to experiment with the new.**
4. **Self-blaming, faultfinding and blemishing.**
5. **Remaining embroiled in angry relationship struggles.**
6. **Being close-minded and rigid.**
7. **Seeking security compulsively.**
8. **Being bored and experiencing a numbing of senses.**
9. **Feeling resentful.**
10. **Low self-esteem.**

Changing adds a chord of vulnerability to your life song. Don't be afraid of being imperfect. Explore what you can do about the five change fears in order to guarantee your success.

The fear of change is normal. However, living with these symptoms forever is just plain ridiculous. Fear is a part of life never to be catered to nor worshipped.

Might fear be running your life more than you care to think? Find out in the next mindplay.

MINDPLAY:

THE MANY SOURCES OF THE FEAR OF CHANGE

Following is a list of typical worries and fears. Which of these fears have been impacting your life lately?

Check the fears that apply to you:

- ❑ Fear of losing control
- ❑ Fear of not belonging
- ❑ Fear of looking foolish
- ❑ Fear of being weak
- ❑ Fear of losing my mind
- ❑ Fear of going broke
- ❑ Fear of the opposite sex
- ❑ Fear of my own gender
- ❑ Fear of losing a job
- ❑ Fear of public speaking
- ❑ Fear of a tax audit
- ❑ Fear of dating
- ❑ Fear of disapproval
- ❑ Fear of criticism
- ❑ Fear of addiction
- ❑ Fear of success
- ❑ Fear of getting married
- ❑ Fear of the "empty nest"
- ❑ Fear of a major catastrophe
- ❑ Fear of being honest
- ❑ Fear of risking anything new
- ❑ Fear of old age
- ❑ Fear of rejection
- ❑ Fear of happiness

❑ Fear of pain
❑ Fear of setting goals
❑ Fear of asking for what I want
❑ Fear of being wrong
❑ Fear of crowded places
❑ Fear of my own feelings
❑ Fear of living alone
❑ Fear of AIDS
❑ Fear of authority figures
❑ Fear of doctors
❑ Fear of angry people
❑ Fear of darkness
❑ Fear of going back to school
❑ Fear of politics
❑ Fear of going to jail
❑ Fear of parenthood
❑ Fear of ill-health
❑ Fear of retirement
❑ Fear of making the wrong decision
❑ Fear of emotional commitment
❑ Fear of hurting others
❑ Fear of death
❑ Fear of war
❑ Fear of sex
❑ Fear of fear
❑ Fear of love
❑ (Create your own fears)
❑ (It's very easy to do...)

INTER PLAY:

Fear of change is the overriding fear from which all other fears stem.

Fear Is a Powerful, Normal Experience: Fear is a necessary companion in every major life transition you pass through. Befriend your fears to avoid becoming consumed by them.

Fear Can Be Neurotic if You Don't Watch Out: Focusing too much on fear ferments it. Anxiety can become a warped lifestyle that stops you from making positive choices and pursuing the successes you yearn for.

Negative Emotions Are Anti-Change: The more afraid you feel, the higher number of self-criticisms you will use. Plus, the more you self-criticize the less likely you are to take productive steps to change. What a Catch-22.

The "Why Don't You Try Again..." Growth Principle: You can gradually expose yourself to fearful situations without falling apart. Don't expect yourself to feel comfortable the first ten times you try something new.

Don't Let Failure Keep You Down: You may need many trial runs before you can become more relaxed, but you will eventually feel better. Expecting yourself to do it right the first time will defeat you every time.

The Positive Purpose of Fear Is to Teach You to Trust: The positive purpose of fear is to invite you to take bold new action. It forces you to accept yourself, and to reach out and trust others in order to gain self-esteem.

The Negative Purpose of Fear Is to Make You Feel Alone: Experiencing fear can make you feel crazy — but you aren't! Take the risk to relate to others even when you might be rejected.

Remember: Above All Else You Are Not Alone: Being an imperfect human being involves struggle and being afraid. When you deny fear, fear is able to exert undue control over your life. Whether your fears are few or many, you are not alone.

Don't let your fears go unchecked. There are many positive actions you can take to wipe out your fears.

Fight back. Don't avoid the struggle. To achieve high self-esteem, take positive action in spite of fear.

No-Fault Practice To Face Down Your Fears

Negative feelings were never meant to be in control of your destiny. Practice controlling your fears. Make a decision to keep taking constructive steps toward your goals when you feel like a failure. The ability to take risks guarantees you will never fail for long. Here are eight ways that I recommend to fight fear:

1. EXPERIMENT WITH FEW EXPECTATIONS OF SUCCESS.

Take Positive Action: Allow yourself sufficient, no-fault, trial-and-error learning experiments. Set your goal to try something new, instead of setting your goal to be successful at something new.

In Spite of Fear: You shouldn't expect to be good at something you try for the first time. Right?

To Achieve High Self-Esteem: Say, "I choose to feel good when I try something new no matter how well I do."

2. TREAT FEAR AS YOU WOULD A RESPECTED TEACHER.

Take Positive Action: Fear is not an enemy, but a friend who has something valuable to teach you. Good teachers expose students to controversial experiences in order to broaden their understanding.

In Spite of Fear: Even bad habits are good friends that must be let go of. Right?

To Achieve High Self-Esteem: Say, "I can conquer my fears one fear at a time."

3. TAKE YOUR OWN SWEET TIME — BUT TAKE ACTION SOME TIME.

Take Positive Action: New ways of thinking require adequate study and research time. Many times, though, you must take action without being sufficiently prepared. Take plenty of time to decide — but get going once you do.

In Spite of Fear: Don't let fear make you feel either too hurried or too slowed down for your own good. Your pace is the best pace. Wouldn't you agree?

To Achieve High Self-Esteem: Say, "I can take action before I'm totally ready."

4. REMEMBER TO REINFORCE YOURSELF NOW – AND LATER.

Take Positive Action: Many people forget to pat themselves on the back following big wins and significant breakthroughs. If you refuse to stroke yourself for taking bold new actions, you are undermining an important opportunity for building momentum.

In Spite of Fear: Be sure to feel good about yourself when you succeed. Why shouldn't you?

To Achieve High Self-Esteem: Say, "What I just did took guts. All right! Way to go!"

5. CHALLENGE EXCESSIVE SELF-CRITICISMS.

Take Positive Action: Challenge yourself to severely limit all self-critical chatter and judgmental attitudes. You are not bad, especially when you are feeling bad. Stop taking self-criticisms lying down.

In Spite of Fear: Self-punishment does not drive away the demons of guilt. Stop punishing yourself. Bad feelings don't make you a better person. Fear brings on more of what you most fear. Agreed?

To Achieve High Self-Esteem: Say, "I can take positive action even when I'm feeling afraid."

6. BRAINSTORM FOR A CHANGE.

Take Positive Action: Let your mind get fired up. Create your own treatment techniques for curing your most tenacious fears. What good ideas do you have to get over them? Begin and end your day by brainstorming.

In Spite of Fear: Give a fair trial run to your own innovative solutions before you kill your change chances with negative "Yes, but..." thinking. Why not?

To Achieve High Self-Esteem: Say, "I can think clearly even when I'm afraid."

7. ABSORB ADMIRATION AND POSITIVE STROKES.

Take Positive Action: Listen closely to what traits others admire in you. Can you swallow their undaunted admiration with a healthy sense of pride? Praise has never been known to hurt anyone even though self-acceptance is best.

In Spite of Fear: Don't fail to stroke yourself. Soak up the positive strokes. Got it?

To Achieve High Self-Esteem: Say, "I learn about my strengths by listening to positive strokes."

8. AVOID AS MANY NEGATIVE INFLUENCES AS YOU CAN.

Take Action: Don't let doom and gloom forecasts of failure reinforce your programmed fears of change. Feel good about yourself even when others might feel envious or disapproving of you.

In Spite of Fear: Stop accepting guilt-trips about how you hurt others by meeting your needs or by changing. Pleasing yourself makes you a better and happier person. Okay?

To Achieve High Self-Esteem: Say, "Freedom means living a life free of blame."

Change always means you face down your worst fears and act in spite of them. When you change, you are required to master the fears that haunt you in undetected ways every day.

FREEING UP FROM THE FIVE CHANGE FEARS

The first step in conquering your fears is to be able to identify them. The second step is to decide to stop letting fear run your life. The third step is accepting your new strokes for success. Remember, you should learn from fear and challenge it, not sidestep it.

You must take steps to conquer the fears that are controlling you. You must do more than think about changing. You must go ahead and do what you feel uncomfortable doing in order to succeed.

Fear is cultivated through blame and self-punishment.

Take one small step at a time. Avoid criticizing yourself for not having the wherewithal to succeed on the first try. By taking one small change step at a time, you will run over your fears before they have the chance to run over you.

As you change, you will come across new and unexpected fears. That's a normal stage of change. New shades of feelings seek to add color to your personality and expand your self-esteem.

Always remind yourself: "I CAN GO AHEAD AND TAKE POSITIVE ACTION EVEN WHEN I AM FEELING AFRAID!"

There are five primary fears that you must face:

1. **The Fear of the Unknown**
2. **The Fear of Failure**
3. **The Fear of Commitment**
4. **The Fear of Disapproval**
5. **The Fear of Success**

Naming a fear for what it is can take its power away. I'll be discussing each fear in turn in storybook fashion to help you fight your fears more forcefully.

Beware: Each of these five fears can bear down on your self-esteem with the steady drip-drip of a water torture technique.

The fear I hear about most often from my clients is the fear of the unknown.

FREEING UP FROM THE FEAR OF THE UNKNOWN

THE STORY: Change disturbs the status quo. The fear of the unknown will make you feel uncomfortable since you are unfamiliar with the lay of the land. You must venture into many unknowns to have what you want.

A MAN'S FEAR OF WHAT THE NEIGHBORS WOULD THINK:

A client of mine, Don, was married for twenty-one years. Don had it all: beautiful children, more money than he knew what to do with and loads of social status. But each new year was fraught with more boredom.

Don was a "good Catholic" who believed marriage wasn't supposed to be a bed of roses. He thought of his marriage as a trap with no exit. Don knew that marriage was to be a "forever no matter what" venture. It wasn't supposed to be second-guessed with a bunch of ifs, ands or buts.

Although Don and his wife were very unhappy as a couple, most of their friends thought of them as the ideal pair. When it came to social appearances, Don and his wife put up a united front. They were well-liked and respected.

Don and Diane realized that their relationship was as good as it was ever going to get. They were economically comfortable and planning to travel when they retired. Don was miserable and depressed when he came to see me. He hadn't talked to anyone about his problems.

Don's pain didn't go away. He grew more and more removed, unhappy and pessimistic about his marriage. He knew that many marriages were worse off than his. Don chided himself, saying, "I shouldn't let her get to me like this." But Don did keep thinking about leaving his wife.

Don and Diane rarely fought, but when they did anger poured out. Don would drive to work furious about cruel words spoken to him the night before. Although both Don and Diane threatened to leave on the next scheduled bus, neither could get up the nerve to go.

Over time, resentment and misunderstanding choked out all possibility of love. Both Don and Diane felt more alone when they were together than they ever felt when they were alone.

Their marriage provided a false sense of security. Staying together was better than something unknown. Strangely, the unknown seemed unacceptable. Better to stay on safe turf, even though it was desert-like.

The known was painful, but predictable. Predictability. Don and Diane were paying a high price for the commodity of stability and predictability. Do you pay a ransom for security? Why do you do it?

Don doubted if he could live with himself if he were to hurt his wife by leaving. He worried that his children would blame and hate him for the separation. Like Don, changes put you through tests-by-fire to find out just how strong your inner mettle is.

After much soul-searching, Don decided to leave his wife. He tried to reassure his children as best he could about his love for them. Once the decision was made though, he went forward quickly with his plans and felt relieved.

Don told me he would never forget that wintry day at the breakfast table when he made his announcement. With tears in his eyes, and his voice shaking, he said to his wife: "I can't live with you anymore, Diane. I'm very sorry." Then he broke down.

But Diane surprised him with her calm reply: "If you're so unhappy, what things need to be done to bring this to an end?" Don's mouth dropped open. All the years, all the heartache and the good times brought to an end by a businesslike closing.

Don knew then and there that his decision had been the right one.

BE AWARE:

SECURITY CAN BE SEDUCTIVE.

Case for the Status Quo: Routines remove anxiety by structuring your world into comprehensible segments. Security is necessary, comforting and orienting. Stripped of the familiar you are bound to feel lost, self-critical and disoriented.

Case Against the Status Quo: Every worthwhile change involves jumping into the unknown, and learning to cope with the unexpected difficulties to be found there. Self-esteem is gained by transforming the unknown into the known.

Status Quo Says: "Why upset the apple cart?"

TODAY IS YOUR JUDGMENT DAY: HOW DO YOU WANT TO SPEND THE REST OF YOUR LIFE?

FREEING UP FROM THE FEAR OF FAILURE

THE STORY: The fear of failure will make you quit soon after you start, give up at the first signs of difficulty or keep you down after you've gotten tripped up. To overcome the fear of failure, you must keep going forward when you feel utterly hopeless.

FAILING TO TRY AGAIN DUE TO THE FEAR OF FAILURE:

The major reason for failure is the failure to focus. Can you persist in the face of rejection if your goal is important to you? Rejection is more painful than not having what you want. My doctoral degree comes to mind as an example.

All of my life I've been ambitious, desiring to rise to the top of the heap, an achiever who now and then must reign himself in from being too compulsive about success.

Guess what? I've always feared my ambitious side. But why? Because I was anxious about the consequences of success. Would I lose positive relationships in the process? Would I become egotistical? I thought my strength of ambition was "bad."

We all fear our strengths, as if these desires are sinful. We may fear being too smart, too passionate, too creative, too intense, too successful, too intimate, too confident, too sexy, too capable, too talented, too angry or too much of one wonderful trait or another.

Your special strengths — or gifts as I refer to them — hold within them the seeds of self-esteem. They also are spiritual messages. Indeed, your rarest gifts frighten you because of their prophetic power to command you to change.

Fear of failure perversely diverts attention away from your inner strengths and gifts. Most of us have been raised to deny our best sides. But, let me go back to my goal to obtain a doctoral degree in psychology.

The doctoral program I wanted to be admitted to rejected me. Statistically speaking, the odds were against my getting in. I figured the odds could be beaten. I was wrong.

True to the numbers, I was rejected and felt awful. The numbers didn't matter to me; I should have been able to get in anyway. What was wrong with those eggheads? Steamed, I was mad at just about everybody and everything involved in that rejection.

I was employed as a college counselor at the time. Miffed and hurt by the rejection, I complained to my mentor that he would never again find me applying to such a stupid program. He laughed his eerie laugh that always made my insides crawl as if they were coming alive.

He asked me: "But why would you let a single rejection get in the way of accomplishing your lifelong dreams? If this degree means so much to you, why don't you apply again? Dennis, aren't you up to working and fighting for what you want?"

Great questions, aren't they? I was deathly afraid of failing again.

The fear of being rejected a second time made me give up trying. The fear of rejection became my slave master. It took over all of my decisions. Avoiding loss and pain became my battle cry.

Have you known people who have fought change due to the fear of failure? Do you let the chance of being rejected restrict your choices? Have you decided to avoid taking new risks for fear of being hurt or looking stupid? We all act afraid in these ways. How terribly illogical.

Several weeks later, I scheduled a meeting with the Admissions Dean to find out why I had been rejected. The major condition for my entrance to the program was to give up my cozy university job in a quaint college town, and move to the big city to work for a large mental health center to prove my worth.

Pain. I gave up a good paying job and my secure ego, packed up my belongings and took a less desirable job on the chance that I might be looked upon more favorably the following year. Worse yet, in the new job the stress rate was much higher, and the benefits were much lower.

Second try: In 1980 I was admitted into the second selective class of students who were after the highest awarded degree in the field of psychology. The Dean had been playing it straight with me.

My hands shook when I opened that letter of acceptance that began with the words, "Congratulations, Mr. O'Grady, we are proud to inform you..."

Little did I realize the real challenge had just begun.

BE AWARE:

THE FEAR OF FAILURE CAN LULL YOU INTO A FALSE SENSE OF COMPLACENCY.

Case for Avoiding Failure: Failure can dampen motivation. Sadness from failure can make you feel like you might be swallowed up in it. Negative feelings can hypnotize you into believing that every problem in the world is your fault.

Case for Risking Failure: Change-experts accept that life involves risk, risk involves failure and to those who risk the most go the most rewards. The best way to restart the change process is to become aware of your inner gifts following a rejection.

Failure Says: "It's no skin off my nose."

TODAY IS YOUR JUDGMENT DAY: HOW DO YOU WANT TO LIVE THE REST OF YOUR LIFE?

FREEING UP FROM THE FEAR OF COMMITMENT

THE STORY: Forming healthy attachments gives you more

benefits than you lose. The fear of commitment stops you from intensely focusing your energies on one person, object or goal. Commitments are freeing, fun, rejuvenating; they add faith, give hope and provide intimacy.

DISAPPOINTMENTS CAN BE THE DOORWAY TO SUCCESS:

Often you must try and try again before you can get your changes just right. In fact, many of your disappointments will signal that you have begun to take positive actions — and are therefore being successful — although you're not getting the results you want.

Learning something new rarely happens on the first try. Does it really matter how many times it takes you to get your changes just right? Of course not. Who's counting? Well, of course, we all are.

A health example comes to mind. Most of my adult life I smoked cigarettes off and on — mostly on. Beginning in high school, the habit started, caught on and curled its way permanently into my life. Smoking just happened to happen to me.

Smoking went against my athletic pride, ran counter to the image I tried to portray, but was one way I thought of myself as an independent man. You see, my Dad had caught me smoking in high school and really let me have it with his wrath.

He wasn't going to tell me what to do! I'd smoke if I wanted to, and there was no way he could stop me, or search-and-seize my joy sticks every waking second of every day. Nicotine became laced with the drug of unhealthy rebellion and defiance.

I first tried to quit smoking as a freshman at Michigan State University. Writing a note to myself about the hazards of smoking, I put a brand new pack in my bottom desk drawer to bring about a fast end to our relationship. But I took out the stale pack at midterms, and lit up a bitter tasting smoke.

Since then, smoking has been confused in my mind with being my own man, adulthood and wishing for my father's approval.

But nothing replaces a father's blessing for a son. Nothing.

Just before the quiet man left our home some years ago, he said, "Denny, I'm proud of you." I about fell over. It was a high, and tobacco is no match for a father's blessing.

I was an avid smoker. I was intense about the habit. Enjoyment, the thrill of the forbidden and reinforcing a negative self-concept all came together in the smoking. I quit once for several years. I quit again for several more years. Each time I promised myself that this time I would quit forever.

Why did I want to quit? (Kids). Did I really want to quit? (No way). Could I be successful? (Doubtful). When was a good quit date? (Later alligator).

I'd love to tell you what an honorable, brave and sensible person I've been to give up smoking, but that would be a lie. I wanted to be around for a long time in my wife's life.

But the smoker in me figured I would be around like George Burns who was able to smoke cigars well into his 90s, versus Sigmund Freud whose jaw cancer created a nightmarish decade of pain for him due to his cigar smoking.

Love motivates. I didn't quit for health reasons. I didn't quit to prove something. I didn't want to start new habits. I quit on the spur of the moment. I quit on a lark. I quit for the love of it.

Don't require yourself to get in line with positive changes before you go ahead and change. You don't have to want to change in order to change.

To help me stop, every night before going to sleep I imagined that I was slowly dying in a hospital bed, gasping for breath from emphysema. I pictured my loved ones standing near my bedside while I proudly chain smoked my life away.

Too ghastly? Dramatic images, indeed. Images of loss to be sure. Were these terrible images to feed my mind? I had hoped so. And I hoped my subconscious mind would blame all the misery on those little sticks of cancerous dynamite.

The third try has been a charm.

BE AWARE:

**COMMITMENT IS THE KEY TO RELEASE YOU
FROM A SELF-MADE PRISON CELL.**

Case for Avoiding Commitments: Commitment forces you to answer one tough question: "What do I really want?" Commitment also may not be much fun since other options are taken away. Emotional commitments can make you feel small, vulnerable and dependent.

Case for Making Commitments: Ninety-nine percent of success is due to making commitments and developing loyalties to people, places and causes. And every successful person I know of has made a commitment to accept vulnerability in exchange for happiness.

The Free Spirit Says: "Don't put all your eggs in one basket."

TODAY IS YOUR JUDGMENT DAY: HOW DO YOU WANT TO SPEND THE REST OF YOUR LIFE?

FREEING UP FROM THE FEAR OF DISAPPROVAL

THE STORY: So what's new? You want to be liked, have an easy and pain-free life and you want to avoid conflict. Unrealistic expectations cause many avoidable conflicts since the people involved aren't allowed to be who they really are.

"EXPECTATION CRASHES" HAPPEN IN LOVING RELATIONSHIPS:
We all tend to expect more from ourselves and others than is actually possible for any human being to deliver. "Expectation crashes" cause more hurt feelings than people do. Being realistic about relationships builds high self-esteem.

Idealizing causes pain. In fact, expectation crashes are the leading reason we divorce or give up trying to be optimistic about finding the person or job of our dreams. Rather than give up our ideals, we give up the person who has failed to live up to them.

For example, my clients Bill and his wife Melissa told me they had a terrific relationship during their courtship. Their romantic life seemed magical, filled with wonder and simply sublime; each enjoyed the other with great ease.

Bill had been burned before by women, and Melissa by men. For both, their relationship was everything that they had ever wanted and more. Bill had felt tremendous joy toward Melissa. And she toward him. "Tough life," I joked.

Both felt blessed and extremely fortunate early in their romance. They were deeply in love and brave enough to marry the respective person of their dreams — which causes more vulnerability. And then came the honeymoon. It was tragic. Everything that could have gone wrong did.

Bill and Melissa missed their plane, became physically ill and received a phone call that Melissa's older sister was in the hospital. Tensions ran high, as did their disappointments. And they, "the talkers," were unable to talk about it.

Like a hydrogen-filled balloon, their relationship, which had been flying high, crashed and burned into nothingness. Their intimacy vanished in the short time it took to put a ring on a finger. They were both terrified, and neither of them knew what to do about it.

Bill and Melissa became accusatory, angry and blameful. Bill blamed his misery on Melissa, since he felt he had remained unchanged. Why had she changed? Why couldn't she cope with stress better? Melissa felt that it was Bill who had changed and proven to be the greater disappointment. Neither of them had any clue as to what to do.

Both were in great pain. When as a last resort they came to my office, both Bill and Melissa sounded defeated and depressed. Their comments were full of disapproval for one another. They looked very sad, yet both spoke only of how angry and disappointed they were feeling about each other.

I explained to them that expectation crashes happen in every good relationship. In fact, I told them that because they had been so deeply in love, the romantic crash that had to come sooner or later hurt them far more than a less caring couple. I explained that love can deepen from pain and disappointment.

What did Melissa and Bill learn that saved their relationship? They learned that sadness can be hidden by angry blaming, and pain shouldn't be passed back and forth like a hot potato. They also learned that lasting satisfaction and self-approval emanates from a genuine relationship — not a heavenly one.

Many people aren't as fortunate as Bill and Melissa.

BE AWARE:

SELF-APPROVAL CAN GROW FROM THE ASHES OF EXPECTATION CRASHES.

Case for Avoiding Conflict: Displeasers abuse anger by disapproving of you to try and gain control of your self-esteem. Overcoming negative emotions requires you to engage in constructive conflict to keep resentment at bay — all of which takes a great deal of hard work, high trust and a willingness to grow up.

Case for Conflict: Helpful anger builds strong relationships and clears the way for two competent individuals to negotiate how to be close but independent. Must everyone think like you, see things your way or always be required to agree with you? Of course not. Being different is enjoyable.

Displeasers Say: "All is fair in love and war."

TODAY IS YOUR JUDGMENT DAY: HOW DO YOU WANT TO LIVE THE REST OF YOUR LIFE?

FREEING UP FROM THE FEAR OF SUCCESS

THE STORY: Being successful means you must expand your identity and please yourself more. Being competent requires tedious emotional work, and makes you stand out more as an individual. Successful people celebrate their wins and learn from their losses.

BEING SUCCESSFUL IS A CHALLENGE FOR THE BEST OF US:

Successful people have learned that winning isn't anything. Success doesn't make life perfect, teach a mate to respect you more or make up for not being loved as a kid. Success means your emotions flow freely all over the place.

Success is difficult to accept because it is confused with so many other emotions: happiness, power, revenge, quelling insecurities, winning, overcoming shame or becoming a famous superhuman who can't die.

The word "success" has multiple meanings. What does the word mean to you? How do you wrap up love, money, sex or power in your use of the word? My definition of success is being who you are.

You must be willing to be emotionally open, available and responsible to be successful. Success means having the courage to be a fully feeling human being. You must remove accumulated anger to feel the subtle and tender emotions such as mercy or love.

Before meeting my wife, I began freeing up and dating more. Inwardly shy, I decided to fight my fears by asking out women who appealed to me. The outcome? Women turned me down time and again for dates, or refused to go out with me after a few fun outings.

An underlying sense of frustration nagged me. If success meant understanding the opposite sex, I wasn't doing so hot. Many women who had a good time with me on our dates didn't want to see me again. Was I doing something wrong? I was perplexed.

These same women would complain to me how badly most men treated them, and how there were no good men left. Now I was really baffled. We went to nice places, and had a blast. I bitterly mused: "Must I treat women badly to get them to like or respect me?"

Unbeknownst to me, I was finding out a great deal about what I liked in women, and whether women liked to be close with me. When I was ready to settle down, I was amazed to find how few women seemed interested in getting involved with a successful single man.

While I was vacationing one summer along the beautiful shores of Lake Erie, a good friend asked me almost absentmindedly: "Dennis, why haven't you been able to attract a good woman who simply loves you for who you are? Why does it always seem like the women you choose pull a fast one on you?"

As the waves crashed up against the pier that night, I wasn't sure why attracting one woman who would like to get to know me for who I am was so difficult. Of course, I wasn't perfect, but I wasn't some awful monster either. My friend went back to the cottage, and the moon began rising in full form overhead, as the summer wind brushed lightly against my skin.

Why indeed couldn't I be loved just as I was? Can you? I'd never thought much about it before. Have you?

It was a moment of crystallization. Pattern after pattern danced before my eyes. To think about it honestly, I never really believed that I could find a woman who would be sexy, fun-loving, trustworthy and fully loving of my manhood. I figured women just wanted to be mad at men.

Alone by the waterside, I sat and stared, sending my questions up to God and the full moon. The reply: I felt tremendous aloneness, loneliness and an internal ache that had never before been so painful. I realized that I longed to be loved by someone who enjoyed me — and loved me — as a successful/emotional man.

Resting easier inside my own skin, I vowed to enjoy my success, and reach out to people who liked me. To keep my spirits up, I reminded myself that dating allowed me to compile a list of what I really wanted in one woman.

I returned to work refreshed and hopeful. No excuses, no bad feelings. I stopped looking for love in all the wrong places. I vowed to enjoy life just as it was. I vowed to feel my way through life, instead of trying to be strong by being in control of my emotions.

Two weeks later, I met my wife to be.

When I was ten years old and walking down by the creek behind my childhood home, I imagined meeting a little girl with whom I would share great, romantic adventures and become fast friends.

To me, my wife is that little girl.

BE AWARE:

SUCCESS COMPLICATES LIFE.

Case for Denying Success: You must be able to use anger assertively, overcome negative emotions and be willing to accept any feeling large or small without censorship to be successful. Emotional mastery is complicated.

Case for Accepting Success: Nothing feels more exciting and worthwhile than being successful. When everybody else in the world may reject you, you can still nurture and enjoy your past and present successes.

Self-Defeatism Says: "Don't wear your feelings on your sleeve."

TODAY IS YOUR JUDGMENT DAY: HOW DO YOU WANT TO SPEND THE REST OF YOUR LIFE?

How would you like to spend the rest of your life? Fear robs you of feeling fully alive. When fear growls at you to remain still in your tracks, choose to charge forward with change anyway.

Allowing just one of these fears to rule your life can reduce your chances for change to rubble. Don't falter when you find them getting in your way — pick your feet up higher and keep trudging forward.

I would now like to focus your attention on the major symptoms of the fear of change: blaming, faultfinding and blemishing that results from trying to be perfect.

Blaming is a symptom of fear that must be checked and check-mated.

BLAMING LESS TO CHANGE MORE

Some psychotherapy clients fail to reach their goals despite loads of good intentions and lots of elbow grease applied by all parties concerned. Why, I wondered?

To answer the riddle, I asked myself this probing question: "If neither my client, nor myself, are to blame for this apparent lack of change then what exactly is holding back change from taking place?"

My discovery: The propensity to stick a label of blame on anyone stalls out wanted changes. Blame must be let go of and given up for change to occur. The worse type of blame is to label oneself as a "bad," or defective person.

All forms of blame impede effective change. I'm encouraging you to blame less — to change more!

The following mindplay will tell you why.

MINDPLAY:
THE LESS I BLAME THE MORE I CHANGE?

Who or what do you hold responsible for your lack of change? How much blame do you put on your own shoulders? How much blame do you place on others' shoulders?

Put a check by the blame-games you might be perpetrating on yourself:

- Making my fears bad
- Making my depression bad
- Making failure bad
- Making my aspirations bad
- Making my bad habits bad
- Making lust bad
- Making my weaknesses bad
- Making a feeling bad
- Making a religion bad
- Making aging bad
- Making my children bad

- ❏ Making men bad
- ❏ Making women bad
- ❏ Making my past bad
- ❏ Making my intelligence bad
- ❏ Making my lack of changing bad
- ❏ Making great sex bad
- ❏ Making my fantasies bad
- ❏ Making honesty bad
- ❏ Making my personality bad
- ❏ Making the government bad
- ❏ Making my mate bad
- ❏ Making death and dying bad
- ❏ Making another race bad
- ❏ Making my willpower bad
- ❏ Making conflict bad
- ❏ Making my parents bad
- ❏ Making trust bad
- ❏ Making money bad
- ❏ Making self-disclosure bad
- ❏ Making strangeness bad
- ❏ Making the truth bad
- ❏ Making hard work bad
- ❏ Making jealousy bad
- ❏ Making different opinions bad
- ❏ Making reality bad
- ❏ Making anger bad
- ❏ Making thinking bad
- ❏ Making failure bad
- ❏ Making mistakes bad
- ❏ Making feeling bad into something bad
- ❏ (Fears have a way of spawning...)
- ❏ (...more fears)

INTER PLAY:

All blame impedes change. The more you label yourself or others as "bad," the more often your changes are stalled out.

Emotional Indifference Kills the Spirit: When you label yourself "bad," you become numb and feel powerless to change. You quit trying to better your life.

Game-Playing Proves Nothing: The badness label causes people to play games to try and prove who is worse off, the persecutor or the victim. Whoops. All parties end up feeling bad by the end of the game.

Self-Criticism Stinks to High Heaven: Celebrating your good traits, while being aware of your weaknesses, is a good way to determine how self-accepting you are. Self-criticism is a setup because it crucifies you for twitching independently.

What IF Torrid Criticisms Spoken About You Are True? Doesn't it prove something if the criticisms said about you are true? Nope. Any type of criticism will keep you stuck in the negative glue of non-change. The fact that the criticism is true is incidental.

Changing Is Far Better Than Magic Any Day: Change is a no-nonsense and practical process that is far better than magic. You can't pull real people out of a hat.

Learn to accept yourself when you are feeling afraid. Being "bad" is a state of mind.

FREEING UP LOVING RELATIONSHIPS
TO CHOOSE CHANGE

Practice shaking up the stodgy beliefs that you hold near and dear that claim fear has control over you. Fear is not your lover. In fact, fear interferes with your love life.

Fear makes you feel like quitting. Don't you stop! Get up and get going again when you feel rejected. Choose to be close with your inner self and intimate with others.

Choose to be an excellent man or woman, friend and partner in spite of rejection. Allow yourself to charge forward. Choose change!

I know, it's easy for me to say, "Keep up your spirits!" But how can you keep striding forward with positive changes when fear is breathing down your neck?

Ten key change permissions can keep you choosing loving changes.

Use any one of these *Action Beliefs* in your loving relationships to put fear in its place:

1. **Being an imperfect human being is best.**

2. **My choices are my own to make.**

3. **It's important to be disliked at times.**

4. **I can feel angry at someone and do nothing about it.**

5. **I don't have to do it right the very first time.**

6. **I can take care of my own pain.**

7. **I can excel just to make myself happy.**

8. **I have the right to be selfish.**

9. **I can take pride in my own good advice.**

10. **I trust myself to learn and grow.**

When you are frustrated, drop back and think about your goals, choices and abilities to charge forward with change.

I want to explain each of these change-permitting attitudes more fully.

1. BEING AN IMPERFECT HUMAN BEING IS BEST.

Permit Yourself: Trying hard to be perfect can make you procrastinate, be apathetic or slip back into any of a variety of other self-defeating behaviors. This permission encourages you to meet your inner needs better without harming others.

To Charge Forward: Allow yourself to be imperfect!

2. YOUR CHOICES ARE YOUR OWN TO MAKE.

Permit Yourself: When a partner pressures you to make choices for their sake, you resent them for being controlling. This permission encourages you to realize that your choices have the greatest impact on your own life.

To Be Loved: Allow yourself to make your own choices!

3. IT'S IMPORTANT TO BE DISLIKED AT TIMES.

Permit Yourself: The pressure to be accepted by a companion makes you back off from the struggle for self-acceptance. This permission encourages you to stick with important decisions and take any heat that comes from them.

To Charge Forward: Allow yourself to be disliked!

4. YOU CAN FEEL ANGRY AT SOMEONE AND DO NOTHING ABOUT IT.

Permit Yourself: Suppressing angry thoughts or feelings can build up your frustrations to the bursting point. This permission encourages you to behave well despite your angry feelings, and to find constructive outlets for your anger.

To Be Loved: Allow yourself to get angry and act sanely!

5. YOU DON'T HAVE TO DO IT RIGHT THE VERY FIRST TIME.

Permit Yourself: The fear of failure can make you quit new relationships or success projects prematurely when you hit a snag. This permission encourages you to view change as a "try, try again" process.

To Charge Forward: Allow yourself to be wrong!

6. YOU CAN TAKE CARE OF YOUR OWN PAIN.

Permit Yourself: The pressure to absorb others' pain can distract you from healing your own wounds. This permission encourages you to be sympathetic to another's hurt without becoming a sucker to emotional manipulation.

To Be Loved: Allow yourself to take care of yourself even when others are hurting!

7. YOU CAN EXCEL JUST TO MAKE YOURSELF HAPPY.

Permit Yourself: Outside pressures and expectations to perfectly please others can blind you to your talents and gifts. This permission encourages you to lay claim to your own victories.

To Charge Forward: Allow yourself to win in your own way!

8. YOU HAVE THE RIGHT TO BE SELFISH.

Permit Yourself: The pressure to be unselfish actually increases selfish behavior. This permission allows you to clearly define your needs and feelings separate from the needs and feelings of others.

To Be Loved: Allow yourself to think of your own needs first!

9. YOU CAN TAKE PRIDE IN YOUR OWN GOOD ADVICE.

Permit Yourself: The pressure to rely solely on authorities' advice undermines your own learning abilities and decision-making capacities. This permission encourages you to know yourself.

To Charge Forward: Allow yourself to take your own best advice!

10. TRUST YOURSELF AND YOUR PARTNER TO LEARN AND GROW.

Permit Yourself: Mistrusting the inner self invites you to blame yourself and others for the quality of your own life. This permission encourages you to build planned changes into your life even when life is rosy.

To Be Loved: Allow yourself to be trusted and trusting!

You deserve to enjoy warm and loving relationships. Allow everyone to appreciate you for being who you are.

Keep permitting yourself to charge forward with change!

PERMIT YOURSELF
TO TAKE SMALL STEPS TOWARD SUCCESS

Use these beliefs to make your fears smaller and your self-esteem larger.

- ✔ **TAKE ACTION BEFORE YOU ARE TOTALLY READY.**
- ✔ **KEEP YOUR EYES OPEN TO NEW OPPORTUNITIES.**
- ✔ **REMEMBER YOU CAN THINK CLEARLY WHEN YOU ARE AFRAID.**
- ✔ **DEFINE SUCCESS AS BEING A FULLY FEELING HUMAN BEING.**
- ✔ **CHOOSE TO FEEL SUCCESSFUL WHEN YOU TRY SOMETHING NEW.**
- ✔ **PAT YOURSELF ON THE BACK FOR JUST TRYING.**
- ✔ **USE YOUR HUMOR TO FIGHT THE FEAR OF REJECTION.**
- ✔ **USE FRUSTRATION TO MOVE FORWARD WITH YOUR GOALS.**
- ✔ **BE IMPERFECT AND STILL BE SELF-APPROVING.**
- ✔ **NEVER SHY AWAY FROM BEING WHO YOU ARE.**

Conquer your fears one step at a time. Take positive action when you're feeling afraid.

COUNTERPOINT:

"CAN'T CHANGE EVER BE BAD?"

It's true. Change isn't always good, and fear may be a signal telling you to stop and think.

Here are some ways to tell if you are changing to avoid coming to grips with fear:

✻ *When you abruptly live a life counter to your typical one.*
The Bad News: Anxiety may be running your life.

✻ *When you are addicted to rapid change to avoid coming to terms with an issue.*
The Bad News: To be happy and successful you must resolve problems.

✻ *When you are running away from working things out in a relationship.*
The Bad News: The same problems will crop up again later on down the road.

✻ *When you have an affair because you are lonely.*
The Bad News: Problems with your mate will never be addressed when your energies are siphoned off in other directions.

✻ *When you are successful and figure you deserve to slack off.*
The Bad News: When you stop doing what makes you successful, your self-esteem and effectiveness drops off precipitously.

✻ *When you really can't afford a purchase, but you buy it anyway.*
The Bad News: Money is only a temporary band-aid for depression.

✻ *When you are trying hard to be loved by someone who won't love you unless you change.*
The Bad News: You can't relax and be who you are when your every move is judged.

★ *When you are trying to get even with someone.*
The Bad News: Vengeful changes rarely last for very long and taste bittersweet.

As your fears decline, your self-esteem will pick up steam. Enjoy both your struggles and your successes.

In Chapter 12, I am going to turn your attention to the exciting topic of how to manage high self-esteem.

12

MANAGING HIGH SELF-ESTEEM

"If there is any such thing as a universal evil or sin, it is the words: 'I can't change.'"

Dr. Nathaniel Branden, pioneer in self-esteem

SELF-ESTEEM IS LOVING TO LEARN AND LEARNING TO LOVE

Adopting a positive attitude toward change means you fall in love with learning new things instead of bemoaning the fact that you don't know everything. Self-esteem is falling in love with learning and learning to be more loving toward yourself.

You can't love life if you are busy resisting this changing world. Nor can you learn to love new aspects of your personality if you put your strengths into a tightly sealed little box. Changing means you feel free to open yourself up to being loved for who you are.

Don't be fooled though. Developing high self-esteem is hard work. Facing yourself in a mirror of self-reflection is the toughest work you will ever be called upon to do. But you're up to the challenge. Learn to look long and hard at yourself in the revealing mirror of self-esteem to be happy.

Self-esteem is earned "day-by-day-by-day" in loads of little ways. It means taking great advice and running with it. Self-esteem means squeezing positive strokes out of every stone thrown in your way. High self-esteem means refusing to remain down for very long following a failure.

How's your self-esteem been lately? Self-esteem is your feeling of belonging to the world, including the essential right for good things to happen in your life.

THE SELF-ESTEEM QUIZ

Take the following quiz to determine the level of your self-esteem.

TRUE	FALSE	
☐	☐	1. When people are successful, they become less stressed.
☐	☐	2. People enjoy being happy and satisfied.
☐	☐	3. People who brag are really insecure.
☐	☐	4. Parents are to blame for low self-esteem in their children.
☐	☐	5. Women feel as successful as men these days.
☐	☐	6. Men depend less on women to build their self-esteem than the reverse.

TRUE	FALSE	
❑	❑	7. Good friendships are secondary for high self-esteem.
❑	❑	8. Tactful criticism usually motivates people.
❑	❑	9. People with high self-esteem are more outgoing and extroverted.
❑	❑	10. Studies show that 65 percent of Americans are completely satisfied with their self-esteem.

ANSWERS AND DISCUSSION

1. *False.* Success adds many new life stressors to cope with, and stress weakens self-esteem.

2. *False.* Although many people enjoy being happy, anxiety may lead you to think, "Oh, this is just too good to be true," or, "This is never going to last."

3. *False.* Being honest about your strengths and your weaknesses is an assertive declaration of independence.

4. *False.* Many forces shape the child, and to blame low self-esteem on parents reduces parental pride.

5. *False.* Studies show that women are more apt to ascribe their work success to luck, while men view their work success as a result of hard work or talent.

6.   *False.*   Men typically receive comfort only from their
                  wives, while women receive reassurance from
                  several other sources besides their husbands.

7.   *False.*   Good friendships are now considered on equal
                  par to a good marriage in helping you feel
                  worthwhile and whole.

8.   *False.*   Many of us experience criticism as outright ego-
                  deflating, non-motivating and as an unneeded
                  roadblock to positive change.

9.   *False.*   People with high self-esteem report a greater
                  need for privacy, reflection and solitude.

10. *False.*   Studies show the reverse. Sixty-five percent of
                  Americans are dissatisfied with their current level
                  of self-esteem and wish they could feel better.

Use this quiz at the dinner table as a family discussion tool to
raise self-esteem.

Ask your children what goals they have set to increase their
self-confidence. Ask your spouse what types of strokes make him
or her feel good. And encourage your own talents to come out
and shine in the world.

Self-esteem is a learned skill that you must work for daily.
Effort spent improving your self-esteem today will pay handsome
dividends tomorrow to increase your sense of well-being.

ASSUME LOW SELF-ESTEEM IS ALTERABLE

Low self-esteem can be mastered.

Difficult relationships are the leading reason you aren't able to
focus on needed changes. No, all problems can't be blamed on

difficult people. But unhelpful anger in the guise of rejection, resentment and revenge quickly diverts your attention away from being able to focus on your goals, choices and competencies.

Think of negative people as anti-change. Keep your energy high by conquering negative emotions that reinforce low self-esteem. Don't let the fear of change add more frustration to your life. The solution to negativity? When you do get uptight, focus your thinking inward to find your growth answers.

And try out each and every good idea that comes your way to raise your self-esteem to new heights.

LOOKING AT—NOT OUT FOR—NUMBER ONE

What must you know about mastering the fears and frustrations that accompany self-change? And what must you know to keep going forward instead of quitting?

As a change-expert you have learned that your answers lie within the self, like mounds of gold that are hidden under the belly of a sleeping dragon. And somehow you must find your way into, and back out of, the lair of negative emotions without being eaten alive.

There is no other way to grow.

The positive purpose of every negative emotion is to force you to think clearly about changing even when you might not want to. Take a good look at yourself when you feel frustrated. Developing adequate self-esteem requires you to "LOOK AT #1" in order to conquer fears that block success.

Self-worth is diminished with these three words: "I CAN'T change." Dr. Nathaniel Branden, who has studied and written about self-esteem for over forty years, contends that those three words are pockmarked and wormholed with evil. Strong words, indeed, from a rational scientist.

Only the mastery of forbidden emotions can release you from "CAN'TISM." You must fear no feeling. Rather, you must make even anger into a friend in order to master the tasks and risks of happiness, sexual intimacy and love. Negative emotions are meant to be a bleak and rough reminder that YOU CAN TOO CHANGE!

Guess what? You have met the anger family throughout this work: shouldism, self-criticism, blame games, lack of goals, complaining, negative strokes, rejecting advice, the five fears and so on are a few members of the anger family that you have already learned to accept more comfortably.

I've told you that unprocessed anger erases your secret strengths. I explained how suppressed anger predictably lowers your self-esteem. I've told you that you must own up to your strengths and anger or risk being controlled by them. So? Choose high self-esteem by learning equally from love and frustration.

Managing high self-esteem in loving relationships means learning something new from every failure, hurt and rejection instead of being alarmed and disarmed by these negative emotions. Men and women must learn to communicate better to stop reinforcing the fear that the opposite sex cannot be trusted to volunteer for change.

Masters of change keep traveling through lonely, dark places even when they are filled with fear. All feelings are made equal: fear/trust, resentment/intimacy, jealousy/pride, pain/happiness, revenge/success, anger/self-esteem, rejection/confidence and so on. No feeling is too strong or petty to ignore.

Your change-challenge: the more you can master negative emotions, the more likely you are to change at your own healing speed and build high self-esteem. Remember, low self-esteem can be mastered!

Self-worth is diminished when frustration dominates your life. But underneath the belly of futility lies the chance to reclaim your ability to change. High self-esteem means challenging the fear of change by getting to know the inner self.

Change-experts have learned how to master the exciting art of looking down deep into the self-interior to gaze at the genuine self to find curative answers. Such answers heal the spirit and call for positive actions and attitudes.

MASTERING NEGATIVE EMOTIONS

Absolute happiness should not be your goal.

Many of my clients idealistically believe that hurt goes away when high self-esteem is reached. But to my way of thinking, blissful, pain-free living is not a positive nor realistic goal.

Change-experts don't split off from any emotion. Never put value on being a psychologically perfect human being who only wishes to experience positive emotions. Your goal should be to feel all of your feelings instead of denying or being controlled by any one of them.

You can learn to alter any negative emotion. Begin by assuming that answers can be found to resolve problems when you keep an "I CAN TOO CHANGE!" open mind. And believe that the purpose of negative emotions is to educate yourself.

High self-esteemers do feel badly. Trying to be strong, and pulling yourself up by the emotional bootstraps, just won't work for very long and isn't worth the effort. To overcome difficult feelings, keep an open attitude and learn from negative feelings.

Be a change-expert. Use painful emotions to grow!

CONCRETE WAYS TO CONQUER NEGATIVE EMOTIONS

Don't believe all those complainers who say change is impossible. Keep one change rule in mind: Any frustration is alterable!

Learn to conquer any negative emotion or person by keeping these change pointers in mind:

1. ASSUME THAT LOW SELF-ESTEEM IS ALTERABLE.

The Change Rule Is: Low self-esteem is not a permanent state.

Just Be Yourself: Work on your self-esteem daily. Set boundaries around your self-esteem to avoid being drained by displeasers. Learn to take your own good advice.

To Conquer Negative Emotions: Force yourself to think clearly when you are upset. Use brainstorming methods to keep an open attitude.

2. USE RESPONSIBLE ANGER FOR MOTIVATION.

The Change Rule Is: Change yourself first and others never.

Keep an Open Attitude: Make your anger a friend and not an enemy. Stop pounding yourself down when you mess up. Anger wants to support you in taking positive actions to raise your self-worth.

To Conquer Negative Emotions: Use assertiveness skills. Be giving to a preset point and then stop.

3. EMBRACE NEGATIVE EMOTIONS TO LEARN FROM THEM.

The Change Rule Is: Change what you complain most about.

Change More Than You Complain: You are stronger than any negative emotion that tries to weaken you. Put your mood back under your own direct control.

To Conquer Negative Emotions: Use self-reflection. Don't let complainers dump their negative emotions on you.

4. LAUGH AT YOURSELF IN HEALTHY WAYS.

The Change Rule Is: Challenge self-criticism to fight the universal fear of change.

Love the Child Inside of You: Be serious about change, but take time to laugh along the way. Unload your burdens through laughter.

To Conquer Negative Emotions: Use humor to reduce stress. Use permissions to challenge and replace criticisms.

5. LEARN AS QUICKLY AS YOU CAN FROM YOUR MISTAKES.

The Change Rule Is: Your choices are your own to make.

Accept Positive Strokes but Never Accept Failure: Remember, if you aren't failing at least daily than you aren't really succeeding. Change is inevitably a stair-step, up-and-down phenomenon.

To Conquer Negative Emotions: Use trial-and-error learning.

6. FORESTALL COLLECTING RESENTMENTS.

The Change Rule Is: Make some new independent choices to reduce resentment.

Please Yourself Free of Guilt: Make new choices that are pleasing to your self-esteem. To remove resentments, figure out what game difficult people are playing. Solve problems instead of taking them on or passing them along.

To Conquer Negative Emotions: Use goals in every area of your life. Review your goals when you feel unhappy.

7. INDULGE RARELY IN SPITEFUL ACTIONS.

The Change Rule Is: The fastest route to a destination of success is to stop giving revenge paybacks.

Focus On Success by Using Goals: Use positive strokes but don't be a sucker. Stand up for yourself instead of expending so much energy trying to get even. Take a more forceful stand after much thought and only when alternative strategies have failed.

To Conquer Negative Emotions: Use positive paybacks.

8. ADDRESS CHILDHOOD WOUNDS THAT STILL CRIPPLE YOU.

The Change Rule Is: You can choose to act differently today than you have in the past.

Utilize Good Advice: God has stacked the deck in your favor. Old ideas about how worthless or bad you are can be repealed. You are allowed to make new choices at any time across the board.

To Conquer Negative Emotions: Replace negative beliefs with positive behaviors.

9. GO AFTER WHAT YOU WANT WITHOUT EXCUSE OR DELAY.

The Change Rule Is: You can take positive action in spite of fear.

Fear the Status Quo: Put an end to waiting. Don't delay — do it today! You can take positive action on your own behalf in spite of feeling negative. Change means you don't wait to feel good to take practical action.

To Conquer Negative Emotions: Use self-change, goal setting, time saving and leadership strategies to conquer the fear of change.

10. DON'T BLAME THE OPPOSITE SEX FOR YOUR PROBLEMS.

The Change Rule Is: Every form of blame impedes change.

Learn to Respect Differences: Psychological problems are about the same between the sexes. The major reason changes fail to take is due to blame. Stop using the opposite sex as a whipping post.

To Conquer Negative Emotions: Use good listening skills.

11. BE WILLING TO ENGAGE IN CONSTRUCTIVE CONFLICT.

The Change Rule Is: Healthy conflict and disagreement protect prized relationships.

Abide by Fair-Fight Rules: Change means antagonists talk out problems to fill in loneliness with love. Constructive conflict is the best way to keep all of your relationships strong, growing and interesting.

To Conquer Negative Emotions: Use fair-fighting techniques.

12. NURTURE YOUR STRENGTHS AND RELATIONSHIPS.

The Change Rule Is: You must own up to your unique talents and secret strengths or risk being controlled by them.

Give Thanks for Strengths: Can you care for yourself when you have been unfairly rejected? Accept yourself. Give yourself more positive strokes than you know what to do with, and give good strokes to people who truly care for you.

To Conquer Negative Emotions: Use positive stroking rules.

13. LET GO OF PEOPLE WHO AREN'T INVESTED IN YOU.

The Change Rule Is: Only you can grant yourself the freedom to be who you are.

Dare to Be Self-Approving: Negative people will keep you so confused that you won't be able to stay on the right track. Don't spend your life trying to change people who claim they don't have a problem. Change means saying "good-bye" to people who mess up your life and saying "hello" to new opportunities.

To Conquer Negative Emotions: Value achievement and intimacy equally.

14. KEEP LOOKING FOR ANSWERS AND REMAIN HOPEFUL.

The Change Rule Is: Keep stroking your strengths to succeed.

Just Be Yourself: Even when there isn't any hope, get up and keep going. Choose to admire who you are right now, even though you are incomplete and vulnerable. You may not be able to change negative people, but you can control your attitude when you have to be around them.

To Conquer Negative Emotions: Use anything that works!

If you are hesitant to develop skills in any of these areas, chances are that negative emotions are more in control of your life than is good for you.

POSITIVE RULES FOR DEALING WITH NEGATIVE FEELINGS

Difficult people are difficult because they fear change. Negative emotions result from the fear of change.

What rules of emotional conduct must you consciously use as

a change-expert to master negative emotions? Use these new rules of emotional order to contradict programming that leaves you filled up with negative emotions.

RULE #1:

EVERY FEELING
HAS SOMETHING WORTHWHILE TO TEACH YOU.

Be Feeling: Our society is obsessed with feeling good and being positive all the time.

Be Vulnerable: This rule attempts to reverse anti-feeling programming.

Be Who You Really Are: Stop trying to get rid of painful emotions.

RULE #2:

YOUR CHANGES WILL ALWAYS AFFECT YOU THE MOST.

Be Thought-Full: Our society is obsessed with making changes to please others.

Be Vulnerable: This rule attempts to reverse anti-individuality programming.

Be Who You Really Are: Stop thinking good changes hurt others more than they help you.

RULE #3:

RISKS MUST BE UNDERTAKEN TO GROW AND CHANGE.

Be Open to Change: Our society is obsessed with maintaining security and avoiding failure.

Be Vulnerable: This rule attempts to reverse anti-change programming.

Be Who You Really Are: Stop believing that thinking alone is sufficient to solve a problem.

RULE #4:

TRYING TO CONTROL EVERY EVENT IN LIFE CAUSES UNNECESSARY ANGER.

Be Self-Controlled: Our society is obsessed with trying to control our thoughts and feelings, and trying to influence our decisions.

Be Vulnerable: This rule attempts to reverse anti-vulnerability programming.

Be Who You Really Are: Stop being responsible for everything.

RULE #5:

RESPONSIBLE ANGER IS HEALING NOT HURTFUL.

Be One of a Kind: Our society is obsessed with fitting in and not causing a fuss.

Be Vulnerable: This rule attempts to reverse anti-intimacy programming.

Be Who You Really Are: Stop making anger the bad guy.

RULE #6:

BEING AN IMPERFECT HUMAN BEING IS GOOD ENOUGH.

Be at Your Imperfect Best: Our society is obsessed with physical, psychological and now spiritual perfection.

Be Vulnerable: This rule attempts to reverse anti-learning programming.

Be Who You Really Are: Stop tearing yourself up for being flawed.

RULE #7:

YOUR CHOICES ALWAYS REMAIN YOUR OWN TO MAKE.

Be Feeling: Our society is obsessed with making right decisions.

Be Vulnerable: This rule attempts to reverse anti-decision programming.

Be Who You Really Are: Stop living with decisions that decrease your self-esteem.

You are constantly being exposed to programming that pressures you to dismiss your feelings instead of experience them. Learn from your emotions and entrust your feelings to loved ones.

Be free to feel okay even when you are feeling down. Don't let your self-worth be affected by negative emotions. Boost your self-esteem when your charge is low.

PRACTICAL WAYS TO RAISE UP LOW SELF-ESTEEM

Self-esteem permits you to interact in a world that basically welcomes the best of your ambitions and talents. In such a world, you can become a positive actor on the stage of life, instead of a passive member of the audience.

When your self-esteem comes under attack, refuse to think negatively, or act irrationally against your own best interests. Accept that you are adequate and deserving of love and success.

Negative feelings often disguise the fact that you are changing successfully. Learn to reinforce small positive changes.

Do you panic when you are running dangerously low on self-esteem fuel? Or do you take a deep breath, review your goals and keep on changing? Low self-esteem is not a permanent state.

Recall, being a winner means staying in a learning mode. Beware of pleasing others too much, beating yourself up with self-criticisms or getting caught in power plays that use up your best energies.

Stay in the driver's seat. Challenge any beliefs that say you aren't allowed to change and feel happy. Don't delay a second longer.

MINDPLAY:
THE THREE TYPES OF SELF-ESTEEM

Which mindset do you find yourself in most of the time? Do

you have Excessive Self-Esteem (ESE), High Self-Esteem (HSE) or Low Self-Esteem (LSE)?

Put a mark next to the descriptors that fit you right now. The category with the greatest number of check marks will tell you a great deal about your current level of self-esteem.

Have some fun, and don't be too serious about analyzing yourself. The same trait is used in numbered sequence across types so you can see how people change their personalities when self-esteem is added or subtracted.

EXCESSIVE SELF-ESTEEM (ESE)

- ❑ Aggressive (1)
- ❑ Hedonistic goals (2)
- ❑ Arrogant (3)
- ❑ Takes daring risks (4)
- ❑ Intolerant (5)
- ❑ Blaming (6)
- ❑ "I don't care what you think." (7)
- ❑ Verbally abusive (8)
- ❑ Too focused (9)
- ❑ Feel superior (10)
- ❑ Cocky (11)
- ❑ Worth more (12)
- ❑ Brutally blunt (13)
- ❑ Physical attractiveness is priority (14)
- ❑ High energy (15)

HIGH SELF-ESTEEM (HSE)

- ❑ Assertive (1)
- ❑ Goal-seeking (2)
- ❑ Confident (3)
- ❑ Takes reasonable risks (4)
- ❑ Tolerant to a point (5)

❑   Self-encouraging (6)
❑   "What do you really think?" (7)
❑   Verbally affirming (8)
❑   Focuses and unfocuses when needs to (9)
❑   Feel adequate (10)
❑   Courageous (11)
❑   Worthwhile (12)
❑   Direct and honest (13)
❑   Inner attractiveness is priority (14)
❑   Positive energy (15)

LOW SELF-ESTEEM (LSE)

❑   Passive victim (1)
❑   Goalless (2)
❑   Self-doubting (3)
❑   Afraid to risk (4)
❑   Too tolerant (5)
❑   Self-critical (6)
❑   "Nobody cares what I think." (7)
❑   Verbally demeaning (8)
❑   Unfocused and scattered (9)
❑   Feel inferior (10)
❑   Ashamed (11)
❑   Absolutely convinced of worthlessness (12)
❑   Indirect and evasive (13)
❑   Judges self as unattractive (14)
❑   Low energy level (15)

INTER PLAY:

Yes, self-esteem can be excessively high or excessively low.
Both ends of the self-esteem spectrum are exaggerations of high
self-esteem.

Unmanaged Strengths Can Be Weaknesses: Different words have been used to describe the same trait across the three types of self-esteem. For example, (1) aggressive (ESE), assertive (HSE) and passive victim (LSE) are each part of the self-esteem spectrum. Refuse to let your strengths become a weakness.

Displeasers Have Excessive Self-Esteem (ESE): As one ESE was fond of telling me: "It's tough to soar like an eagle when you are surrounded by sparrows." Intolerance, blaming and despising weakness makes these people quite intimidating.

Pleasers Have Low Self-Esteem (LSE): Pleasers are trying to receive high self-esteem as if by magic. What they get instead is lowered self-esteem, and more-of-the-same frustrations.

Pleasing Yourself Leads to High Self-Esteem (HSE): Pleasing yourself forces you to raise your low self-esteem. High self-esteem reduces the need to please.

Self-esteem matches your inner beliefs to a tee. Learn to think of any belief as changeable. Changing self-critical beliefs always adds to the level of your self-esteem.

Due to the devilry of negative thinking, who you think you are isn't necessarily who you really are. My clients hang on to their negative self-opinions with the power of a death grip. Learn to let go of your negative self-ideas more easily.

CAN EXCESSIVE SELF-ESTEEMERS BE HELPED TO CHANGE?

Excessively confident people can tone down their act.

Don't envy or be angry at those suffering from ESE. Fear and sadness have been out of their control for some time. ESE's must learn they don't have to deny tender feelings or be a pillar of strength for everybody.

Changing excessive self-esteem into high self-esteem is harder to do than raising up low self-esteem. So don't feel awful when your self-esteem is in the pits — the alternative is even worse.

ESE's can grow and change. Here are some ways:

1. DON'T WAIT UNTIL YOU LOSE OUT BIG TO CHANGE.

To Be Successful: Chances are you don't know what people really think. You may not know someone as much as you think you do. Take interest in opinions other than your own.

Ask for Negative Feedback: Begin to care how people think and feel.

2. MAKE SURE TO LISTEN TO NEGATIVE FEEDBACK.

To Be Successful: Find out what grudges people are carrying toward you. Listen to even small gripes. Don't isolate yourself from negative feedback through intimidation.

Take Pride in Being Wrong: Care to know what people expect from you.

3. LEARN TO EMBRACE YOUR OWN WEAKNESSES.

To Be Successful: Stop defending your weaknesses. Your strengths have less to teach you than your weaknesses do.

Make Your Relationships Really Matter: Weaknesses do not make a human being bad.

4. STOP LIVING IN A BUBBLE.

To Be Successful: Stop protecting yourself with money, power or status. Nurturing who you are is more important.

Expose Yourself to Opinions Different from Your Own: Let yourself be stroked for your genuine self not your status.

5. STOP PUSHING PEOPLE AWAY TO PROVE A POINT.

To Be Successful: Is being right more important than being loved? Never. Pull people toward you.

Be Vulnerable: Winning isn't anything compared to warm attachments.

6. FACE YOUR FEARS OF INTIMACY.

To Be Successful: Intimacy means receiving a part of another human being, and gifting that person in turn with a part of yourself. Face your fears of being hurt by intimacy.

Be Interdependent: Stop being so high and mighty, and start trusting and depending upon others.

7. LET YOUR SENSITIVITY AND CARING SHOW THROUGH.

To Be Successful: Sure you're tough. But softness will get you where you want to go. Balancing the two is best and will provide you with insight and intuition.

Be Emotionally Balanced: Begin to express your sad feelings in small ways during the day.

8. FACE YOUR UNDERLYING DEPRESSION.

To Be Successful: Stop being a fanatic about work, fun or success — lead a more balanced life. You are strong enough to stand up to depressive feelings.

Be a Genuine Human Being: Focus on allowing yourself to experience a full range of feelings instead of just the good feelings.

9. JOIN A GROUP WHERE YOUR STATUS IS UNKNOWN.

To Be Successful: Attend events where you are unknown and don't say what you do for a living. Be a small fish in a big pond.

Be Grateful: Enjoy finding out how you come across as a person.

10. STOP MISSING THE GLORY OF YOUR PAST SUCCESSES.

To Be Successful: Learn to be self-accepting when you aren't a big star. Help support the successes of others more.

Be a Team Player: Humility is superior to greatness.

11. GET THERAPY EVEN WHEN YOU DON'T NEED TO.

To Be Successful: Hire a therapist who is not intimated by you. Unblock yourself and become a caring human being.

Be a Good Listener: Praise people. Take your future back into your own hands.

Being a superior human being means being intellectually and emotionally open. Learn to be genuine and vulnerable.

FIGHTING NEGATIVE BELIEFS
THAT CREATE LOW SELF-ESTEEM

Low self-esteem is a powerful state of mind. It can influence your mood and your willingness to take risks.

Low self-esteem is corrected by challenging the negative beliefs that create victim thinking. When you remove the self-criticisms that keep pounding down your self-esteem, your self-esteem will be permitted to grow proportionately.

Here are ways to know when you are in a easy-to-manipulate, low self-esteem state. Take time to drop these attitudes and try out some new ideas to raise your self-confidence.

1. YOU TREAT SUCCESSES AND WINS LIKE FUTURE FAILURES.

LSE Beliefs: Success doesn't last so why try.

Result in Self-Criticism: "I'm going to be expected to perform at my best every single time now." Or, "I bet the other shoe is going to drop soon."

New Idea: Set down your own expectations for success in writing. Even though you can't predict the future with a crystal ball, you can still become a consistent winner. Learn something new no matter how well or poorly you have done in the past.

Be Successful by Being Your Best: Believe, "I can make my successes last."

2. YOU KEEP YOUR STRENGTHS, SPECIAL ABILITIES AND ACCOMPLISHMENTS HIDDEN FROM SOCIAL VIEW.

LSE Beliefs: Internal strengths aren't legitimate or important.

Result in Self-Criticism: "It's best to keep my accomplishments to myself. My ego doesn't require a booster shot."

New Idea: You must own up to your own special abilities or risk being controlled by them. Pride in your accomplishments can be balanced with humility.

Be Successful by Being Your Best: Believe, "I can learn to use my strengths."

3. YOUR SELF-CRITICISMS DOMINATE YOUR MIND AND CROWD OUT SUCCESS PERMISSIONS.

LSE Beliefs: Self-criticism is motivating.

Result in Self-Criticism: "I can't change because I keep doing the same stupid things. When I do succeed, it's only a matter of time until I blow it."

New Idea: Self-criticisms are repetitious lies constructed by you to explain why you feel bad. Speak self-steadying permissions that contradict the criticisms. Use positive strokes to balance negatives.

Be Successful by Being Your Best: Believe, "I can become a better self-encourager."

4. YOU JUDGE NEW PERFORMANCES BY STANDARDS THAT ARE TOO SEVERE.

LSE Beliefs: Positive strokes should be given only for perfection.

Result in Self-Criticism: "I could have done better. My nervousness and inadequacy showed."

New Idea: Give yourself time to practice and perfect a skill by shooting to be in the upper ten percent. Seek feedback from a trusted evaluator who will judge you fairly. Allow positive feedback to replace old stale messages.

Be Successful by Being Your Best: Believe, "My mistakes don't make or break me."

5. YOU ERRONEOUSLY ASSUME LIFE SHOULDN'T BE DIFFICULT.

LSE Beliefs: Pain should be avoided at all costs.

Result in Self-Criticism: "I can't always expect to get what I want." Or, "You can bet your bottom dollar that bad things follow good things in time."

New Idea: Set up assertive fences to protect your self-esteem and solve problems in your life. Don't expect life to be pain-free, but don't be continually upset either. Manage the anxiety that comes on the heels of happiness and success to make life easier.

Be Successful by Being Your Best: Believe, "Crisis is another opportunity to change."

6. YOU FEAR CONFLICT AND AVOID IT.

LSE Beliefs: Conflict is destructive.

Result in Self-Criticism: "I don't want to hurt my partner." Or, "Every time I try to talk with my co-worker the conversation goes nowhere."

New Idea: Force yourself to begin valuing constructive conflict. Speak up assertively to avoid collecting resentments. Become more comfortable with conflict by using fair fighting techniques.

Be Successful by Being Your Best: Believe, "I can use my anger in caring ways."

7. YOUR POSITIVE STROKES ARE LIMITED IN SCOPE.

LSE Beliefs: Approval is required for survival.

Result in Self-Criticism: "If people really knew me, they wouldn't like me," or "Since I can't take being rejected, I rarely disagree."

New Idea: Allow yourself the luxury of having goals related to: the inner self, a chosen calling, a life partner, the children, sexuality, money, time, your God and life. Bundling all your goals into one is bound to stifle your self-esteem.

Be Successful by Being Your Best: Believe, "It's okay to feel worthwhile."

8. YOUR SECURITY TAKES PRIORITY OVER ALL OTHER NEEDS.

LSE Beliefs: Happiness is an illusion.

Result in Self-Criticism: "I really hate my job, but good jobs are hard to come by these days," or "I can't leave my mate because I wouldn't know how to survive financially."

New Idea: Debunk the myth that the predictable pain of the status quo is preferable to the unexpected pain which might await you in the unknown. Don't delude yourself by thinking that the status quo can keep you safe from failure.

Be Successful by Being Your Best: Believe, "I take risks even when I'm afraid."

9. YOU DON'T LISTEN TO SELF-WISDOM CAREFULLY ENOUGH.

LSE Beliefs: My own advice is unimportant.

Result in Self-Criticism: "I should know what to do but I don't. What do you think I should do?"

New Idea: Treat yourself as the leading expert on you. Take your own advice to heart. Trust you inner wisdom more to resolve problems.

Be Successful by Being Your Best: Believe, "I take my own good advice."

10. YOU VALUE SELF-REFLECTION MORE THAN TAKING ACTION.

LSE Beliefs: Thinking is the same as doing.

Result in Self-Criticism: "I suffer from analysis paralysis. I rehash my problems, but don't do anything about them."

New Idea: Life is to be celebrated, not calibrated. Explore yourself as a person by taking risks and doing something different. Take action to discover the unique tastes, interests, causes and abilities that enliven you.

Be Successful by Being Your Best: Believe, "To be a lovable and competent adult I must take action."

11. YOUR SENSE OF FITTING IN OR BELONGING IS ABSENT.

LSE Beliefs: Being different leads to rejection.

Result in Self-Criticism: "Everyone else is so normal compared to me. I always feel like a stranger on the outside of life looking in."

New Idea: Stop trying so hard to fit in. Take pride in being different. Use that energy to come to terms with your strengths. Vow to make a distinctive contribution to life because of your differentness.

Be Successful by Being Your Best: Believe, "I enjoy being different."

12. YOU HAVE PARANOIA ABOUT SELF-CONFIDENCE.

LSE Beliefs: Good feelings don't last.

Result in Self-Criticism: "If I let myself feel too good, I'll be disappointed later on. I shouldn't get a big head over this. It's just a matter of time until the bottom falls out."

New Idea: Exude quiet confidence. Go ahead and feel good. Of course your good moods won't last forever. But don't mess up a good mood with neurotic worrying. Try to be in good spirits even during difficult times.

Be Successful by Being Your Best: Believe, "I enjoy my confidence."

13. YOU EXPECT REJECTION FOR SPEAKING THE TRUTH.

LSE Beliefs: No one wants to know how you feel.

Result in Self-Criticism: "I can't truthfully tell her how I really feel," or "When I tell him what I need, he says, 'You shouldn't be so needy.'"

New Idea: Be honest and tell the truth even when you know that you may lose something important to you by doing so. Don't let the guilt of hurting another be in charge of your life. People need to know where you stand.

Be Successful by Being Your Best: Believe, "I can cope with my feelings better than I give myself credit for."

14. YOU PERCEIVE GOD AS AN ALMIGHTY PERSECUTOR.

LSE Beliefs: Being mad at God results in punishment.

Result in Self-Criticism: "God doesn't know what He's doing. The bad people get ahead, while the good people fall behind."

New Idea: Let yourself be angry at God in order to start talking to Him. Demand a response, and ask for guidance. Releasing angry thoughts will help you learn to live in a spirit of thankfulness and appreciation.

Be Successful by Being Your Best: Believe, "I trust God to take care of me."

15. YOU BELIEVE LONELINESS AND ISOLATIONISM IS COMMONPLACE.

LSE Beliefs: I must be strong and not complain.

Result in Self-Criticism: "No one wants to hear about my problems. They just want me to do my duty as a father/mother, husband/wife, boss/employee, son/daughter... etc."

New Idea: Roles are separate from people. Don't play a role that causes you suffering and pain. Find ways to be around people who enjoy you, and allow others to openly admire you.

Be Successful by Being Your Best: Believe, "I can choose to feel valuable and wanted."

16. YOU SEE TIME AS AN ENEMY.

LSE Beliefs: There's not enough time.

Result in Self-Criticism: "I can't control my time. Time has a way of slipping away from me." Or, "Why bother now? My time has run out and it's too late for me."

New Idea: Stop using time as an excuse for not changing. Live in the present, and take small steps to achieve larger successes. Predicting a dire future, or drowning in dreary memories of a bad past are ways to avoid feeling good today.

Be Successful by Being Your Best: Believe, "My past doesn't have to repeat itself in my present life."

17. YOU ACCEPT RESPONSIBILITY FOR EVENTS BEYOND YOUR CONTROL.

LSE Beliefs: Painful events are all my fault.

Result in Self-Criticism: "If I had been more/less _____, this would never have happened." Or, "I've brought this all on myself."

New Idea: Sensitive people take on more responsibility than they should to avoid feelings of anger. Don't let people put their responsibilities in your lap like a hot potato. You can't control the choices of others — just your own.

Be Successful by Being Your Best: Believe, "I learn to take responsibility for myself."

18. YOU SEE SETBACKS AS PERMANENT OBSTACLES.

LSE Beliefs: Failure is a sign you should give up.

Result in Self-Criticism: "Everything was going so smoothly and I was making such terrific headway UNTIL _____." Or, "This setback means I won't ever be able to reach my goal."

New Idea: Setbacks are temporary diversions. A learning curve, the up-and-down time required to perfect a new skill, must be navigated by everyone.

Be Successful by Being Your Best: Believe, "Success means getting up again."

Beware these secret enemies of high self-esteem. Negative attitudes like these can lead to your mood being controlled by depression. Unchallenged, failure beliefs can keep you from starting to walk up those feeling-good peaks.

How fragile is your self-esteem? Is it like a scared school kid, anxious and uncertain, or is it like a self-sufficient adult, trusting and strong?

How immobilized is your self-esteem? Do you pass on your pain of low self-esteem to others, or do you confront problems head on?

If you pretend low self-esteem does not exist, or that it is an unalterable state that you have no control over, then you will become immobile, crippled in your career and distant in your closest relationships.

Low self-esteem is not the path to changing.

12 SELF-ESTEEM RIGHTS TO LIVE BY

High self-esteem does not come naturally to most of us. It is a learned process, a habit practiced day after day.

High self-esteem begins with a declaration that you deserve to change your defeatist thinking into self-control, self-competence and self-acceptance.

High self-esteem is a gift only you can give yourself. It is learning to appreciate who you are, and where your special talents belong. It is learning to put those talents to good use, and then giving yourself credit for the accomplishment.

There are certain fundamental rights that go along with self-esteem. The building blocks of high self-esteem can be summed up in twelve rights that each and every human being has in common.

Go back to these rights when you are dealing with difficult people or impossible situations. Use them to overcome negative emotions, and help you design new ways to protect your self-esteem.

ESTEEM RIGHT #1:

"I CLAIM THE RIGHT TO NURTURE MY STRENGTHS AND UNIQUE TALENTS."

ESTEEM RIGHT #2:

"I CLAIM THE RIGHT TO REINFORCE MYSELF FOR SMALL POSITIVE CHANGES."

ESTEEM RIGHT #3:

"I CLAIM THE RIGHT TO LOVE MYSELF EVEN WHEN OTHERS REACT IN DISAPPROVING WAYS."

ESTEEM RIGHT #4:

"I CLAIM THE RIGHT TO MAKE NEW CHOICES WHICH ARE GOOD FOR ME."

ESTEEM RIGHT #5:

"I CLAIM THE RIGHT TO IMPROVE MY SELF-WORTH BY SETTING GOALS."

ESTEEM RIGHT #6:

"I CLAIM THE RIGHT TO USE GOOD ADVICE TO GROW."

ESTEEM RIGHT #7:

"I CLAIM THE RIGHT TO LIVE MY OWN LIFE FREE OF RESENTMENT."

ESTEEM RIGHT #8:

"I CLAIM THE RIGHT TO CHANGE MYSELF WHEN EVERYTHING IS GOING WELL."

ESTEEM RIGHT #9:

"I CLAIM THE RIGHT TO START PLEASING MYSELF MORE."

ESTEEM RIGHT #10:

"I CLAIM THE RIGHT TO TAKE POSITIVE ACTION IN SPITE OF FEARS THAT MAKE ME FEEL UNDESIRABLE."

ESTEEM RIGHT #11:

"I CLAIM THE RIGHT TO USE ALL OF MY FEELINGS CONSTRUCTIVELY INCLUDING ANGER."

ESTEEM RIGHT #12:

"I CLAIM THE RIGHT TO HAVE MY CHANGES NOTICED AND STROKED BY LOVED ONES."

Claim your right to self-worth by making a commitment to your inner self. What others think of you is less important than what you think of yourself.

Add to your self-esteem by making your positive thoughts count.

THE SEVEN SELF-ESTEEM MYTHS

Seven self-esteem myths keep you from stroking yourself when you are changing and acting in successful ways. Don't wait to approve of your changes, no matter how small they are.

Ever look at the other person and wish you had as much confidence? She seems to always know what she's doing. He seems to always be in control. And here you are struggling just to get through the day.

Look again. Are those people you admire really high self-esteemers, or are they counterfeit? Here are seven myths about self-esteem. Maybe in dispelling the myths you will feel more free to fight negative thinking.

Start stroking your strengths with the ferocity that you hold yourself accountable for your weaknesses. After all, self-criticism only proves that you can bathe your mind in negative strokes when positives are hard to find.

MYTH #1:

SELF-ESTEEM MEANS FEELING HAPPY ALL THE TIME.

To Achieve High Self-Esteem: Only fake happiness can last forever, and it is used by charlatans who promise a magical cure-all to the pains of being a human being.

Challenge Idealism: HSEs experience all feelings free of judgment. And even though their hurts may seem too heavy to carry, they refuse to close up tight like a clam. HSEs value caring, intimacy and unconditional love.

Make Reality Work for You: HSEs deal with pain honestly, instead of denying or displacing it on innocent bystanders. HSEs contend that feelings of inadequacy shouldn't be allowed to control their destiny.

To Feel Happy: Don't cop out on becoming a better person due to bad feelings.

MYTH #2:

HIGH SELF-ESTEEM MEANS NEVER FEELING AFRAID.

To Achieve High Self-Esteem: HSEs doggedly try to turn fears into opportunities to test their competencies. The promise of increased self-esteem gives them the extra push to learn something new from every frustration.

Challenge Idealism: HSEs refuse to let subconscious fears rule their life. HSEs use anti-doomsday thinking: "I can change." "It's okay to excel." "I am lovable and capable." "It's normal to feel frustrated the first few times I try something new."

Make Reality Work for You: Challenge slick failure beliefs to an empirical test: "If it doesn't come easy, it wasn't meant to be." "My worth is based on what you think of me." "Nobody cares whether or not I do better." "Everything will be taken care of some day." "Nice guys and gals finish last."

To Feel Happy: Lasting success means learning to overcome self-limiting beliefs.

MYTH #3:

HIGH SELF-ESTEEM MEANS NEVER FEELING FRUSTRATED.

To Achieve High Self-Esteem: HSEs often feel frustrated but learn to let frustrations go. They realize that some difficult people and situations will never change. HSEs value learning how to control their own feelings.

Challenge Idealism: HSEs make their anger a good friend and not some shamefaced enemy.

Make Reality Work for You: Displeasers use angry behaviors to try and make high self-esteemers tow their line of dependency by implying: "I won't approve of you if you don't do it my way." HSEs don't turn over their self-image to any persecutor who gives positive strokes in exchange for control.

To Feel Happy: Feel free to change whatever frustrates you.

MYTH #4:

PEOPLE WITH HIGH SELF-ESTEEM ARE PERFECT.

To Achieve High Self-Esteem: HSEs work hard to control their own behaviors, thoughts and feelings, and refuse to exert control over the choices or moods of others. The imperfect is considered praiseworthy.

Challenge Idealism: HSEs won't allow any fear to stop them from being who they are, or from correcting a wrong. HSEs get mad, but they refuse to get even.

Make Reality Work for You: When mistakes are made and frustrations mount, HSEs are able to soften their attitudes and change their perceptions to plot new flight paths. They have the flexibility to view reality from many different angles.

To Feel Happy: Refuse to reject either your strengths or your weaknesses.

MYTH #5:

PEOPLE WITH HIGH SELF-ESTEEM NEED FEWER STROKES.

To Achieve High Self-Esteem: HSEs need a wider variety of strokes than most people do. They believe that "adulthood" never means being so strong that no strokes are needed.

Challenge Idealism: HSEs give to the point of collecting resentments and then stop. Sexuality, romance, spirituality, career goals and friendships are all used to provide positive strokes.

Make Reality Work for You: HSEs love to make love, love to raise children and love to contribute their very best in a career. HSEs strive to accept all forms of pleasure without feeling guilty.

To Feel Happy: Love yourself with all your heart.

MYTH #6:

SELF-ESTEEM CAN NEVER BE CHANGED AFTER CHILDHOOD.

To Achieve High Self-Esteem: Low self-esteemers are unconfident people who are mild-tempered, success-phobic, careful listeners whose self-criticisms are counterfeit. They underestimate their skills and abilities to change.

Challenge Idealism: Insist on the right to have a good life even when you are feeling bad.

Make Reality Work for You: HSEs live a moderate mental life. They subscribe to the fundamental importance of high quality and equal responsibility relationships.

To Feel Happy: Use good advice to fuel high self-esteem.

MYTH #7:

PEOPLE HIGH ON SELF-ESTEEM ARE ALWAYS ALTRUISTIC.

To Achieve High Self-Esteem: HSEs do hold back gifts of energy when someone is taking them for a ride. They know that being a rescuer always precedes feeling like a victim. HSEs go back to their basic goals when frustrated.

Challenge Idealism: HSEs put up fences and selfishly guard against having their positive energy drained. Their bottom line is to be realistic in a world that worships "make believe."

Make Reality Work for You: Receiving positive strokes is crucial for sustaining high levels of self-esteem. The most powerful strokes are for being who you are, while strokes for doing good deeds are next in line.

To Feel Happy: Reject unfair negative strokes.

HSEs believe that there are enough positive strokes to go around for everyone. They value being a fully feeling human being.

Can you keep up with love? To do so you must neutralize myths of love that are self-defeating.

KEEPING LOVING RELATIONSHIPS

Self-esteem is directly impacted by the quality of your romantic relationships. The success rule: The higher your self-esteem, the higher the quality of your romantic relationships.

Divorce statistics, gender grudges and difficulties of the single person finding a suitable mate attest to the high hopes — and hard feelings — that irrational romantic expectations have wrought.

Delusions of romance are promoted using potent images of limitless love, undying understanding and total devotion. What a rude awakening for every man and woman who strives to live up to the movie version of a perfect romance.

Their high hopes have only one place to go — crashing downward.

Delusional romance occurs when you use rigid expectations about needing absolute caretaking or about living in perfect harmony with your partner.

For example, mates may get into power plays when normal differences in desires arise. Turned backs in bed after a fight about what type of sex is best is a failure to compromise and a form of control.

All controlling strategies result from the inner fear (or fury) that your partner isn't going to meet your most urgent needs.

Confident couples refuse to play the game of delusional romance. They seek honest answers to questions based in reality. For example:

1. **"How are we going to maintain our individual identities while building our identity as a couple?"**
2. **"What feelings threaten us?"**
3. **"What are we planning to achieve in the future?"**
4. **"How can we handle boredom and frustration better?"**
5. **"What needs do we have for fun and nurturing?"**

Under the illusion of romance, normal disappointments are fused with intense anger, which can result in the shutdown of communication between mates. Resentments then begin to replace romance.

Too many good lovers quit when they hit this disillusionment stage.

So how can you protect your prized relationships? By recognizing that false beliefs of true love are just that — false. Here are the top ten false beliefs.

MYTH #1:

WE MUST GET ALONG PERFECTLY AT ALL TIMES.

Expect High Self-Esteem: Do you believe that something is wrong if you aren't always in sync? Compulsive arguments, or smoothing differences over without discussion, are symptoms of the drive for relationship perfection.

First from Yourself: Normal fluctuations of emotional closeness and separateness occur in every good relationship. Let your partner go away from you without giving paybacks.

MYTH #2:

YOU MUST BE MY EVERYTHING.

Expect High Self-Esteem: Are you afraid that your world would end if you lost your mate? Guilt, resentment and closeness phobias result from the pressure on any person to be the sole protector.

First from Yourself: Separate friends, creative work and hobbies serve to enrich a partnership and take the heat off a mate as the sole source of support.

MYTH #3:

YOU BETTER PLEASE ME WHEN WE DISAGREE.

Expect High Self-Esteem: Do you feel you must be a placating approval-seeker to receive love? Swallowing anger, withholding true opinions and defiant rebellion develop when a couple can have only one private opinion.

First from Yourself: Equal power means equal voice is given to every idea. Speak up even when you are in doubt of your position.

MYTH #4:

YOU MUST NEVER BE MAD AT ME.

Expect High Self-Esteem: Do you believe assertive anger and creative conflict are destructive? Suppressing sexuality, unpredictable blowups or abrupt walkouts occur when positive anger isn't given enough space in your home.

First from Yourself: Healthy anger protects every good relationship. Learn to harness its vital growth energy. Fight fair.

MYTH #5:

YOU MUST STAY THE SAME.

Expect High Self-Esteem: Do you believe that positive change in your partner is a threat to you or causes couple instability?

Boredom, complaining and infrequent lovemaking come from trying to fight against the winds of change.

First from Yourself: Lasting relationships take charge of change by encouraging it. Relationships that change are invigorating not boring.

MYTH #6:

YOU MUST ALWAYS BE READY FOR SEX.

Expect High Self-Esteem: Do you believe physical intimacy grows tired over time when you or your mate aren't turned on at the drop of a hat? The fear of intimacy results in repressing your needs, crushing sensual exploration and avoiding the sexual act.

First from Yourself: The two of you deserve to create a satisfying sexual relationship that is uniquely your own. Have fun establishing sexual goals.

MYTH #7:

YOU'RE THE ONE AT FAULT WHEN THINGS GO WRONG.

Expect High Self-Esteem: Do you believe that partners should be punished for subconscious problems they bring to a relationship? Alibis, procrastination and revenge occur when you don't accept your own or your partner's weaknesses.

First from Yourself: It takes a strong person to apologize and admit when he or she is being controlled by inner pain. You are responsible for healing your own pain.

MYTH #8:

YOU MUST GIVE ME WHAT I WANT.

Expect High Self-Esteem: Do you believe that your partner should be a mind reader? Power plays, affairs and feeling under-nurtured occur when you fail to take responsibility for meeting your own needs.

First from Yourself: Refuse to pout if you can't get your partner's undivided attention. Use positive strokes freely.

Cooperate and compromise to best meet everyone's needs.

MYTH #9:

YOU MUST HEAL ME OF OLD WOUNDS.

Expect High Self-Esteem: Do you believe that your partner is your soul mate? Subconsciously, every partner is chosen as a therapist to heal childhood traumas, to help you own up to your own strengths and to gain the valuable talents of the beloved.

First from Yourself: Many of your problems as a couple are painful childhood memories that are being accidentally reactivated. Beware of projecting individual problems on your current relationship.

MYTH #10:

YOU MUST NOT DEPEND ON ME TOO MUCH.

Expect High Self-Esteem: Do you believe that your mate should be superstrong and do everything on his or her own? The fear of commitment, unfair male and female stereotypes and lack of trust come when a lover doesn't know what you want most.

First from Yourself: Disobey the parental rule that you should be seen, but not heard. Acquire each other's hidden strengths. Have fun giving and receiving good things.

You must protect your relationships by replacing old hurts with new realities.

Falling in love is easy with the aid of romantic feelings, but staying in love takes a lot more hard work than most of us care to admit.

PERMIT YOURSELF HIGH SELF-ESTEEM

Sometimes, you may think difficult people have control over your life. Think again by claiming these ten change freedoms as your own.

✔ **VENTURE INTO THE UNKNOWN.**

✔ **BE A TOTALLY FEELING AND IMPERFECT HUMAN BEING.**

✔ **RISK REJECTION TO RECEIVE WHAT YOU WANT.**

✔ **REFUSE TO GIVE UP BEING WHO YOU ARE TO BE LIKED.**

✔ **LEARN FROM FRUSTRATION BY USING YOUR ANGER ASSERTIVELY.**

✔ **TAKE FIRM STEPS IN THE DIRECTION OF YOUR GOALS.**

✔ **APPROVE OF YOURSELF WHEN OTHERS REFUSE TO.**

✔ **SAY "YES" TO WHAT MAKES YOU FEEL AT YOUR BEST.**

✔ **GIVE CARING NEGATIVE AND POSITIVE FEEDBACK.**

✔ **LISTEN TO YOUR OWN SAGE ADVICE.**

As a change-expert, be sure to permit yourself to enjoy your well-deserved successes.

Create the kind of life you want!

COUNTERPOINT:
"WHEN IS IT WISE TO REFUSE TO CHANGE?"

Do change-experts purposefully refuse to change? You bet! The wisdom to know when to change and when to stay the same takes some practice.

When do you need to lay claim to your own choices and steadfastly refuse to compromise them? Here are some good times to stay the same and refuse to change:

★ *Experts refuse to change in order to pretend to be the perfect person, parent or partner.*

Use This Change Freedom: Your unique personality is your own.

✴ *Experts refuse to change when it will mean denying helpful anger.*

Use This Change Freedom: Your helpful anger is your own.

✴ *Experts refuse to change in response to unfair criticisms lodged against them.*

Use This Change Freedom: Your goals are your own.

✴ *Experts refuse to change just to please someone.*

Use This Change Freedom: Your ability to focus is your own.

✴ *Experts refuse to sacrifice their lives in order to make others happy.*

Use This Change Freedom: Your happiness is your own.

✴ *Experts refuse to underplay their successes so loved ones won't feel threatened.*

Use This Change Freedom: Your successes are your own.

✴ *Experts refuse to block out great advice just to frustrate authority figures.*

Use This Change Freedom: Your wisdom is your own.

✴ *Experts refuse to change a behavior as a condition for being loved.*

Use This Change Freedom: Your self-esteem is your own.

✴ *Experts refuse to keep changing their minds after a good decision has been made.*

Use This Change Freedom: Your good decisions are your own.

✴ *Experts refuse to change attitudes that have helped to conquer old fears.*

Use This Change Freedom: Your desire to learn new things is your own.

Don't let anything stand in the way of your changing. You deserve to have high self-esteem.

To conclude our journey together, I want you to be thankful for what you have, and be thankful for what you are going to receive.

But more importantly, I will be asking you to keep on changing after you have achieved success and happiness.

CONCLUSION:

KEEP ON CHANGING!

"Reality is a major source of stress."

A smart-aleck coffee-cup motto

KEEP ON CHANGING WHEN YOU ARE SUCCESSFUL

You too can keep on changing! And you must keep on changing to remain successful, especially when you are successful. Happiness means never putting the aliveness of your life on freeze-frame.

Change means life. In reverse, fighting change means predictable failure and stagnation.

WHY ONE RADIO STATION FAILED

A friend of mine spun records for a living. Eventually, he worked his way up to being a radio station manager. A few years back he had a tremendous opportunity.

A wealthy owner of twelve southern radio stations was

frustrated when his hometown station began losing money hand over fist. In short order, his prize station was about to go under. The owner couldn't figure out why his favorite station was performing so poorly.

In the mood to try anything new to save the station, he brought my friend on board. Evan's instructions were clear: "Make sure this station is profitable within two years. I'm too busy to look over your shoulder, so you have my blessing to try anything new."

My friend was ecstatic. He had been waiting a long time for an opportunity like this one to come his way. Evan's fear of failure was overcome by the opportunity for total creative control. He agreed to take on the challenge.

Evan brought a fresh perspective to the station. He asked the listeners what music they most wanted to hear coming over the airwaves. He fired staff who had been freeloading. And he hired creative, not controlling types, who weren't afraid to voice novel or different ideas.

The new staff loved the unknown of it all. They weren't looking for approval, afraid of looking foolish should they fail and were willing to take calculated risks to be successful. The "mavericks of music" began to try anything and everything under the sun to improve ratings.

They worked as a team, and had great fun. What worked to improve ratings they continued to use, and what didn't work they threw away. The "mavericks" knew they were on the right track when their programming and advertising techniques were mocked by the other stations. "Never will work here... It's already been done before..." were just a few of the slams.

But soon new listeners began to tune in to hear the mavericks' antics. Staff really began getting fired up by the warm response. Their zany gimmicks continued to keep everyone in stitches and people talking.

In fact, the staff was so busy being creative and working hard that they hardly noticed when the advertising dollars went from a trickle to a flood!

What a change. Feeling successful was very pleasing to all parties involved. The ratings continued to climb. Staff took a great deal of pride in their accomplishments. Their self-esteem went up with the ratings. Evan was proud of his team and personally ecstatic.

The miracle was that within one short year the station took over the number one ratings honors in the city. Creative change had become the norm and positive strokes the status quo. And the exuberant hometown station owner flew into town to congratulate everyone.

As a change-expert, you've probably already guessed what took place. The staff were wined and dined that festive night at a posh restaurant to celebrate the successes. Feelings of pride were running as high as the tab for the expensive meal.

My friend passed out congratulations in his speech to all involved, and made a toast to a brighter future. Then the owner strode to the podium, and said: "All of you have done a tremendous job. Now, whatever you do, don't change a thing! Keep on doing what you've been doing."

What sad advice.

New ideas and changes were stifled in this one brief announcement. What had made this team successful — feeling free to change — now became forbidden. But there was no arguing with the boss. He claimed to know what was best for business.

Ratings began to slide downwards, and morale took a steady nose dive. Complaining quickly replaced creativity. It didn't take long after that for the staff to become glum and demoralized.

Evan became disillusioned and disappointed. I listened to his anger and pain over a few weeks of late night calls. Then my good friend decided to move on. He felt confused and irritated that what was working so well was not allowed to flourish.

Later, in their final meeting together, the owner said to my friend: "What went wrong? Everything was going so well. I just can't figure out what happened."

Evan couldn't believe his ears.

The moral of the story? Success derives from the momentum of creative change. Rest on your laurels for awhile to celebrate your victories, but then get right back up and keep on changing to remain successful. Embrace change when you aren't required to.

Make this one of your change mottoes: "Why not fix it when it ain't broke?" Keep thinking about your life and how to better yourself. Change, being paradoxical by nature, must be allowed to run free or your self-esteem will get trampled in the stampede.

The one and only guarantee for sustained happiness? You must keep growing and changing — now and forever! Misery comes from resisting needed changes. Be certain to keep on changing even when you are successful.

LOVING CHANGE AS AN ADULT

By changing you feel less controlled by difficult people, and more in control of your own self-esteem. You stop struggling to prove your worth and start enjoying your own worthwhileness.

Self-control means that you give up trying to change others in favor of changing yourself. You stop waiting around for others to change, and get started changing someone you have control over — you.

Open your mind to learning about change like a child would. Know that change really means the freedom to be who you are.

Being who you are means many powerful things. It means feeling unpressured about growing and changing instead of getting in your own way. Being who you are means thinking that your life has just begun.

You have sacrificed many of your best traits to pretend you are part of the grown-up world. You need to "grow down" again into the wellsprings of your deeper being. You must claim your desire to change for the fun of it.

Does change mean giving up being who you really are?

Absolutely not! Just the reverse is true. Change is such a difficult developmental process because it requires you become more attuned to who you are.

Being a "real" adult was meant to mean:

1. **Enjoying the benefits of a positive attitude.**
2. **Bringing what you most want into your life.**
3. **Feeling free to choose your own changes.**
4. **Learning from frustrations.**
5. **Enjoying success, prosperity and sexuality.**
6. **Growing from romantic relationships.**
7. **Being hopeful instead of helpless.**
8. **Having fun and laughing loudly.**
9. **Letting pain be pain.**
10. **Trying to control only what you can control.**
11. **Feeling worthwhile.**
12. **Being happy much of the time.**

Unfortunately, being an "adult" has come to mean you forget to have fun and grow in favor of performing your obligations. Stop sacrificing what you really want in exchange for approval.

You must have access to the openness, silliness and spirit of a child to facilitate growth. Attaining adulthood is not an end in itself. It never was. Being a successful adult was never meant to be an event that signals you no longer need to keep changing. Keep growing and changing throughout life.

Adulthood wasn't meant to be the bittersweet experience of pleasing others until it hurts. Do you settle for less than you know you deserve? Are you confusing misery with maturity? I hope not.

Being successful is your birthright. Suffering does not make you a more responsible "adult." Being unhappy or bored means just the reverse.

Keep on welcoming change to remain successful! Live a heroic life instead of a mediocre one.

ARE YOU A HERO?

The spirited inner child is being championed from coast to coast and in bestselling books and there's nothing wrong with that. In fact, our children — and the child in all of us — sadly and too often come last during a hectic day.

The inner child feels, sees and hears the truth. Take time to make the connection and listen. Although your unique talents are God-given gifts, they are only accessible in the inner child. I believe that you must keep stroking your strengths to succeed.

Why is it so hard to love and approve of yourself? Ironically, I find myself balking at loving my baby daughter, and freezing up when it comes to loving myself. My conclusion? How anti-feeling and numbed to change I've learned to become as a "grown-up."

You need to be loved and cared for. How can you love and enjoy yourself, your children, colleagues and loved ones more? How can you tone down all of those unfair expectations you place on all of your relationships?

I encourage you to write a letter to your inner self to find out what you are expecting from yourself. Stay in touch with yourself on your journey of change, and never forget to think clearly about what you need to feel good.

Here is my personal letter to my spirited inner self related to the writing of this book:

> *Dear "Little" Dennis:*
> Did you know that you are my hero?
> I've taken every weekend for the past year and one half to write our first book. I am so sad about how I've treated you. I don't quite understand how you have endured the pace.

You've been ignored. I've exhausted you and made you wait your turn. I've expected you to support me while getting little in return.

I've expected you to be patient and understanding. I've expected you not to make a fuss. I've expected you to keep smiling, and to keep your pain to yourself.

I've expected you to stay calm about the delivery of our first child. I've expected you to help me keep going strong in our career, even when you have felt totally vulnerable and spent.

I've expected you to be creative and caring. I've expected you to be stoic and superstrong. I've expected you to be behind my dreams. I've expected you to share your humor with our clients.

I've expected you to praise God, and to fight demons. I've expected you to be giving, even when you have nothing left to give. I've expected you to be refreshed after a string of fourteen-hour work days.

I've expected you to play by yourself, and not to bother me. I've expected you to change, grow and learn to be more forgiving. I've expected you to work quietly alongside me without griping.

I've expected you to respect, and play spontaneously with our wife. I've expected you to be filled with faith, and to act courageous when failure was lurking everywhere. I've expected you to tell the truth, when you would be hurt by doing so.

I've expected you to put others needs before your own. I've expected you to tell a good joke, and make people laugh. I've expected you to do things you don't like to do, with little or no encouragement from me.

I've expected you to need fewer strokes than most living people do. I've expected you to perform NOW and rest and pray later. I've expected you to forgive nasty people who have hurt your feelings.

I've expected you to be satisfied with less sleep. I've expected you to do without time for friendship. I've expected you to be bright and articulate. I've expected you to take care of yourself.

I've expected you to be super-independent, and not to need others too much. I've expected you to keep your feelings to yourself. I've expected you to feel safe even when you don't.

I've expected you to be caring when you aren't. I've expected you to be loving when you're mad. I've expected you to be some other person you weren't ever meant to be.

How great my expectations are for you. I'm certain you mind my pressuring you to be perfect, and being taken for granted. Please forgive me.

My expectations are like huge boulders that are too heavy for anyone of any age to carry. Forgive me. I am just another run-of-the-mill adult who knows so little about little children.

Did you know? You are my hero.

Be sure to take time to write a letter to your inner self. Learn to be like a child again. Spend time with your feelings, goals and change dreams today.

I guarantee you that your spirited inner self has been expected to be too strong and too infallible for too long and desperately needs your gentle touch and guidance.

WHY WAIT ANY LONGER TO CHANGE?

Where are your footsteps taking you? Are you waiting for a signal that something dramatic is about to change your life? Why wait any longer to change?

The herald: now is the best time to go inside yourself and find out just how important, acceptable and worthwhile you are. Changing is a time of self-renewal for adults who consider the most pressing questions ever: Am I worth it? Am I worthwhile?

Ask yourself the following questions about your self-worth:

Do I feel worthwhile enough to open up my heart to accept love?
      ...If not, *WHY WAIT ANY LONGER?*

Do I open my eyes to opportunities which exist all around me?

...If not, *WHY WAIT ANY LONGER?*

Do I open up my ears to listen to good advice?
...If not, *WHY WAIT ANY LONGER?*

Do I live a deeply meaningful inner life equal to the role I
   fulfill in life?
...If not, *WHY WAIT ANY LONGER?*

Do I feel wise, ultimately important and acceptable as a
   unique human being?
...If not, *WHY WAIT ANY LONGER?*

Do I feel a sense of warm attachment, belonging and find
   ways to fit in just as I am?
...If not, *WHY WAIT ANY LONGER?*

Am I genuine, honest and assertive when I need to be in all of
   my relationships?
...If not, *WHY WAIT ANY LONGER?*

Do I feel self-confident, self-assured and in charge of where I
   am going?
...If not, *WHY WAIT ANY LONGER?*

Do I feel ambitious, excited and focused on challenging goals
   in my career?
...If not, *WHY WAIT ANY LONGER?*

Do I feel kind yet demanding, sensitive yet tough and tender
   yet talkative when reality demands I be that way?
...If not, *WHY WAIT ANY LONGER?*

Do I stroke others' positive strengths?
...If not, *WHY WAIT ANY LONGER?*

Do I encourage loved ones to go for success?
...If not, *WHY WAIT ANY LONGER?*

Do I work on my marriage to make it enjoyable?
..If not, *WHY WAIT ANY LONGER?*

Do I value taking time to listen to my children?
...If not, *WHY WAIT ANY LONGER?*

Do I reward winning performances at work?
...If not, *WHY WAIT ANY LONGER?*

Do I allow others to admire my skills in return?

...If not, *WHY WAIT ANY LONGER?*

Do I feel worthwhile enough to set important goals, express my hidden talents and make dramatic changes in my life?
...If not, *WHY WAIT ANY LONGER?*

Do I feel comfortable being guided by my strengths and letting go of unneeded self-criticism?
...If not, WHY WAIT ANY LONGER?

Do I exert control over bad habits related to time, communication or addictions of any kind?
...If not, *WHY WAIT ANY LONGER?*

... WHY WAIT ANY LONGER TO CHANGE?

Why do you wait? You wait not knowing what else to do when you are faced with the fear of change.

Correct cozy rationalizations that say your unhappiness isn't any big deal, your frustrations will magically vanish or that you don't need anybody else to love you the way you want to be loved.

Depressing thoughts like those are anti-esteem.

Let today be the time your soul seeks answers to old questions of low self-esteem. What if your life doesn't get better tomorrow, or next week or even next month, and you're stuck right back in the same emotional place?

Say it won't be so! End the waiting. Act today to raise up your level of self-esteem. Go ahead and get on with being the very best person you are capable of being.

After all, your one beautiful candle of self-confidence will warm a dreary wintry world of low self-esteem, and guarantee the arrival of a springtime of new hope.

Appreciate all the hard work and struggle that changing outmoded attitudes and habits takes. And enjoy your success!

Whatever you do keep on changing! Even when you are

successful, keep growing and changing as your needs and your world dictates. Remember, you can choose to charge forward into the unknown and face any fear to unleash high self-esteem.

Believe in yourself again. Fight the brave battle of being who you are. Do honor yourself by remembering: "I CAN TOO CHANGE!"

Believe it!

And thank you for honoring me by reading this work and by joining me in these pages.

RESOURCE DIRECTORY

Berne, Eric. 1964. *Games People Play.* New York: Grove Press.

Berne, Eric. 1971. *Sex In Human Loving.* New York: Simon and Schuster, Inc..

Berne, Eric. 1972. *What Do You Say After You Say Hello?* New York: Grove Press.

Branden, Nathaniel. 1971. *The Psychology Of Self-Esteem.* New York: Bantam Books.

Branden, Nathaniel. 1973. *The Disowned Self.* New York: Bantam Books.

Campbell, Susan. 1980. *The Couple's Journey.* San Luis Obispo, California: Impact Publishers.

Clarke, Jean Illsley. 1978. *Self-Esteem: A Family Affair.* Minneapolis, Minnesota: Winston Press.

Ellis, Albert. 1977. *Anger: How To Live With And Without It.* Secaucus, New Jersey: Citadel Press.

Frankl, Victor. 1959. *Man's Search For Meaning.* New York: Simon and Schuster, Inc.

Hill, Napolean. 1967. *Grow Rich With Peace Of Mind.* New York: Ballantine Books.

James, Muriel, and Dorothy Jongeward. 1971. *Born To Win.* Reading, Massachusetts: Addison-Wesley.

Kaufman, Gerschen. 1980. *Shame: The Power Of Caring.* Cambridge, Massachusetts: Schenkman Publishing Company.

Kushner, Harold. 1983. *When Bad Things Happen To Good People.* New York: Avon Books.

Paul, Jordan, and Margaret Paul. 1983. *Do I Have To Give Up Me To Be Loved By You?* Minnesota: CompCare Publishers.

Peck, M. Scott. 1978. *The Road Less Traveled: A New Psychology of Love, Traditional Values and Spiritual Growth.* New York: Simon and Schuster, Inc.

Piper, Watty. 1988. *The Little Engine That Could.* New York: Putnam Publishing Group.

Satir, Virginia. 1976. *Making Contact.* Millbrae, California: Celestial Arts.

Seuss, Dr. 1990. *Oh, the Places You'll Go!* New York: Random House.

Smith, Manuel. 1975. *When I Say No I Feel Guilty.* New York: The Dial Press.

Steiner, Claude. 1974. *Scripts People Live: Transactional Analysis of Life Scripts.* New York: Grove Press.

Tannen, Deborah. 1990. *You Just Don't Understand: Women and Men in Conversation.* New York: Ballantine Books.

Waitley, Dennis. 1987. *Being The Best.* Nashville, Tennessee: Oliver-Nelson Books.